501+

Great Interview Questions for Employers

and the Best Answers for Prospective Employees

REVISED 2ND EDITION

Dianna Podmoroff

501+ Great Interview Questions For Employers and the Best Answers for Prospective Employees Revised 2nd Edition

Copyright © 2016 by Atlantic Publishing Group, Inc.

1405 SW 6th Ave. • Ocala, Florida 34471 • 800-814-1132 • 352-622-1875–Fax

Web site: www.atlantic-pub.com • E-mail: sales@atlantic-pub.com

SAN Number: 268-1250

Library of Congress Cataloging-in-Publication Data

Podmoroff, Dianna.
  501+ great interview questions for employers and the best answers for prospective employees / by Dianna Podmoroff. -- Revised 2nd Edition.
    pages cm
  Revised edition of the author's 501+ great interview questions for employers and the best answers for prospective employees, 2005.
  Includes bibliographical references and index.
  ISBN 978-1-62023-066-4 (alk. paper) -- ISBN 1-62023-066-6 (alk. paper) 1. Employment interviewing. 2. Employee selection. I. Title.
  HF5549.5.I6P63 2015
  650.14'4--dc23
                              2015031534

Printed in the United States
BOOK PRODUCTION DESIGN: T.L. Price • design@tlpricefreelance.com

Reduce. Reuse. RECYCLE.

A decade ago, Atlantic Publishing signed the Green Press Initiative. These guidelines promote environmentally friendly practices, such as using recycled stock and vegetable-based inks, avoiding waste, choosing energy-efficient resources, and promoting a no-pulping policy. We now use 100-percent recycled stock on all our books. The results: in one year, switching to post-consumer recycled stock saved 24 mature trees, 5,000 gallons of water, the equivalent of the total energy used for one home in a year, and the equivalent of the greenhouse gases from one car driven for a year.

Over the years, we have adopted a number of dogs from rescues and shelters. First there was Bear and after he passed, Ginger and Scout. Now, we have Kira, another rescue. They have brought immense joy and love not just into our lives, but into the lives of all who met them.

We want you to know a portion of the profits of this book will be donated in Bear, Ginger and Scout's memory to local animal shelters, parks, conservation organizations, and other individuals and nonprofit organizations in need of assistance.

– Douglas & Sherri Brown,
President & Vice-President of Atlantic Publishing

Table of Contents

Introduction

Interviewing potential employees is one of the most difficult and intimidating tasks a manager or business owner will ever face. The task is made even more daunting by the fact that repercussions of a poor hiring decision can haunt the employees, management and the company for a long time to come, and can potentially cost a great deal of money. Discovering how to decrease the risk and maximize the predictive ability of interviews is key to successful hiring.

We're taught that preparedness is the key to dealing with most challenging and stress-inducing situations. When applying for a bank loan or talking to investors or pitching a big sale, we plan and prepare diligently, and the same should be done before interviewing. The problem is that in an interview situation, the interviewee is at least equally as nervous, and usually even more so, than the interviewer. This lethal combination of nervous tension often negates even the most diligent planning and leaves the interviewer with very little information on which to base a solid recommendation.

It is so easy for an interview to become little more than a conversation. I'm not suggesting you want the interview to come off as an interrogation either, but what you need is for the information gained from the dialogue to be useful for, and relevant to, making a hiring decision. This means going beyond deciding what questions to ask and actually giving thought to what kind of answers you are looking for. What response will indicate that the candidate is a good fit for the position and your company? Are there responses that are totally incompatible with your organization's goals, mission and values? How will you deal with and evaluate completely unexpected (outrageous or brilliant) answers?

If you've done a good job of pre-selecting candidates for the interview stage, then all of the interviewees should be capable of doing a good job. Choosing which one will do the best job for you is not easy. The person who gives all the "right" answers often gets the job, but if there is no consideration given to what the right answers for your organization

are, then a savvy, well-coached interviewee may be chosen over a less polished but more appropriate one. What this book is designed to do is help you determine the best questions to ask and determine the best answers. Not the best answers from a candidate's standpoint (their motivation is simply to get the job), but the best answers for you; satisfying your motivation to hire the person with the best fit, period.

Chapter 1

ASKING THE RIGHT QUESTIONS

A successful interview is one that provides unique insight into the ability and willingness of a candidate to do a good job for your company. That means that the interview has to go beyond assessing the technical competence to do the job and get to the real core of the issue—does the person as a whole suit our company: our culture, our values, our ethics, our personalities? Will the person fit in and become a valuable addition to the workplace by doing excellent work, while at the same time contributing to a healthy work environment?

To uncover the answers to those questions, what you have to assess are the person's core business and professional competencies. By the time a potential employee gets to the interview stage, he or she better have all the technical skills and abilities necessary, otherwise you are wasting your time. The interview is the place to analyze the so-called "soft" skills that are not easily amenable to testing. The absence or presence of these skills is what leads to the diagnosis of such common job maladies as poor interpersonal skills, an attitude problem, a personality conflict, unable to work in a team, poor communication skills, and problem with authority. Some individuals truly are difficult and hard to get along with, but most, if given the right environment, are very able to adapt and fit into a workplace that is right for them.

Note: Companies are notorious for hiring based on skill and ability, and firing based on fit.

Competency and Fit

Companies are notorious for hiring based on skill and ability, and firing based on fit. Many interviewers make the mistake of equating knowledge, skills and ability (KSA) with competency. In fact, competency is more closely related to an individual's suitability to the workplace than their actual education and experience. If you're hiring for a graphic artist, candidates can be easily eliminated based on their education, experience and portfolio of work. These factors are prerequisites for developing competency, but none of them (alone or in combination) can ensure that the candidate will indeed perform the job at the level you deem suitable. The final component in determining competency is the fit factor, and the best way to evaluate a candidate's overall competency is to screen for skill and ability and interview for competency and fit.

In practical terms this means limiting interview questions that are technical in nature and focusing more on questions that reveal a candidate's true character. Challenging questions, ones that make the applicant really self-assess, and even a few strategically placed, unexpected questions that throw the candidate off-guard, are the best types of questions for determining overall competency and fit. The interview should not be

set up to be an intimidating interrogation, but it needs to be different enough that the even best-coached applicant has to stop and think and give an answer that is not anticipated or rehearsed. Remember, once the hiring decision is made, the interview façade is removed and the new employee with all of his or her innate characteristics, reactions and behaviors is unleashed in your workplace: you owe it to yourself and your current employees to figure out who this person is and what makes him tick before adding him to your team.

Key Competencies

The entire list of competencies for any job will, of course, be different according to the job itself and the level of responsibility. A plumber must have expert plumbing skills whereas a computer programmer does not, but they both need to be able to communicate well and handle stress appropriately. The key competencies presented in this book are a compilation of the most common skills required to be successful on the job. Not every job will need all the competencies but most jobs will require most competencies. The specific areas of competence addressed in this book are:

- Communication
- People/Interpersonal skills
- Sociability
- Conflict resolution
- Decision-making
- Team-building

- Organization
- Judgment
- Adaptability
- Motivation
- Initiative
- Compliance
- Stress management
- Leadership
- Analytical ability
- Creativity
- Integrity

It is up to each individual employer to assess the job and decide which competencies related to work habits and personal effectiveness are required for success in the position. Once that list has been established, it is time to turn your attention to developing questions that address each competency. At the same time you must learn how to ask the question and probe for details when required and construct an idea of the answer that is "right" for you, your team and your company. A candidate's fit can then be fairly and adequately assessed, and you should have a clear idea of who can and will do an excellent job for you.

Chapter 2

INTERVIEWING FROM THE BEGINNING

Interviewing is intimidating for all parties. The interviewer wants to present a positive image of the company, and the interviewee wants to present their "best self" in hopes of being offered the job. This nervous tension provides the perfect environment for false impressions and social niceties when what you really need in an interview is a real conversation with a real person. That way both parties can assess whether or not there is a good fit and how likely it is that an employment relationship will be successful.

Interviewing at its best is a structured conversation. The interviewer is in control of how the conversation will flow, and the interviewee determines the actual content of the conversation through his or her responses to questions and probes. An ineffective interview is one that deteriorates into an impromptu conversation. While having a chat with someone is a way to pass the time, it is not going to reveal anything other than what the interviewee wants to reveal: usually a false impression. Basing hiring decisions on a "gut-feel" approach is the most common source of grievous hiring mistakes, and this approach needs to be avoided at all costs.

From the moment the candidate walks in the door to the moment he or she leaves, the interview needs to follow a set, but somewhat flexible, script. From the introductions to the question-and-answer period to the final good-bye, the interviewer must remain in control, and the best way to ensure that is through planning and preparedness. This is not to imply you should deliver interview questions like a robot or read from your piece of paper with hardly a glance at the person; the intention is to make the interview a smooth and objective process, facilitating a natural conversation within predetermined boundaries. This way the interviewer gains the information he or she needs, and the interviewee's responses can be compared to other candidates' responses quite easily.

A well-structured interview follows the same basic format:

- Introductions
- Small talk
- Explanation of the interview process
- Get-to-know-you questions
- Behavioral-based questions—assess competencies
- Interviewee asks questions
- Next steps in the hiring process
- Thank you and good-bye

It is important to begin the interview with some small talk, an explanation of the interview process, and some ice-breaker-type questions. This sets everyone at ease and prepares the candidate for what is to come. Remember, the objective of the interview is not to intimidate the candidate or set up the person for failure; you want to create an environment where the person can demonstrate to you whether or not he or she can do the job. For the interviewee to be able to do this, he or she must be relaxed. Unless you are recruiting for a position that requires nerves of steel, placing a candidate under undue stress and pressure will only elicit pressured responses. If you rely on this type of approach, you run the substantial risk of eliminating the more qualified person simply because of a difference in their ability to tolerate stress.

You're nervous, the candidate's nervous, but you have the ability to break the tension and set the stage for an informative and insightful discussion where the candidate can showcase his or her unique qualifications and you can assess whether or not the profile presented is a good fit for your company.

Organization and planning will get you 90 percent of the way— add some spontaneity and a genuine interest in getting to know the person sitting in front of you, and you have the perfect foundation for a meaningful and effective interview.

Start the Interview Off Right

Your job as the interviewer is to lay the groundwork for an open, honest exchange of information. One of the best techniques for doing this is to start the interview off on a positive note. Set the interviewee at ease and ask questions that they are expecting and for which they will likely have fairly well prepared answers. When a candidate realizes that you are not trying to deliberately fluster them or catch them off-guard, they are more likely to let their guard down and give you answers that reflect their true person rather than the person they want to project in the interview.

Although your ultimate goal is to uncover the real person behind the interview façade, this is best accomplished by establishing rapport with the candidate. In this way you build trust and confidence, and you are in a much better position for discovering the individual's attitudes, beliefs and past patterns of performance. Ask the candidate to list their best qualities or tell you what factors they think are critical for success. The answers you get won't be particularly unique or insightful; they might not even be very truthful, but they will ensure the overall interview is effective and informative.

Remember, the insight value of opening questions is not intended to be high. The intention of these questions is simple: set the candidate at ease. A candidate who is confident with his or her responses at the beginning of the interview will likely remain confident in giving you honest and candid answers even as the questions become more probative and demanding. The end result is that you get progressively more relevant information as the interview progresses. Interviewing is a skill that requires patience, and as I'm sure you've heard, "good things come to those who wait!"

Explanation of the Interview Process

Before beginning it is a good idea to prepare the candidate for what to expect. Make sure you cover the following:

- Small talk
- Who is performing the interview
- Necessary introductions
- Discuss and explain behavioral questions
- Talk about the interview process—who will be asking questions, time, next steps
- Inform the candidate that you will be taking notes
- Answer the candidate's questions   **

At this point you are ready to begin the questions. You, the other interviewers and the candidate are prepared for what is to come. Stay focused, yet friendly, and remember your ultimate purpose is to get the answers you need to make an employment decision.

Get-to-Know-You Questions

1. Tell me about the hobby or activity you have participated in the longest.

2. What are the first three things you do when you get up in the morning?

3. What activities do you do in your spare time?

4. What do you consider to be your greatest accomplishment?

5. If you had to describe your major philosophy in life (without referring to any religion in particular), what would it be?

ANALYSIS: The answers to these questions will give you a glimpse at what the interviewee values, or at least what he thinks you want him to value. For instance, if the candidate is intent on showcasing his or her education, the answers you get will likely emphasize academic performance or activity. The person might describe himself in terms of the degree or diploma he holds, or his greatest accomplishment may be a scholastic achievement. If the candidate focuses more on practical work experience, then he or she likely has more on a work record than on a school transcript. Still, other people may focus more on interpersonal skills and accomplishments.

The conversation will inevitably shift to the person's comfort zone and to the area of development in which he or she feels most confident. Make a note of the impression the candidate wants to give from the start and then make sure to probe fully into questions that deal with the areas not emphasized. The more well-rounded a person, the higher the chances of being able to deal with the changes and interpersonal skills required in most work environments.

Work History

6. Tell me about the job you have right now.

7. What particular skills and abilities do you bring to your current job?

8. Does your current employer know you are actively seeking other work?

9. Can you give me a brief summary of your work history up to this point?

10. What have you accomplished in the past that makes you particularly qualified for this position?

> **11.** Why are you leaving your current position?

ANALYSIS: The main purpose for asking these questions is to get the candidate comfortable talking about their previous positions. You get information that goes beyond the traditional résumé list of responsibilities, giving you insight into the context of prior work. Gaining a better understanding of the person's prior work will help enormously when trying to make sense of the answers given to the behavioral questions ("Tell me about a time when…") that come later.

Why This Job?

> **12.** Why did you apply for this job?

> **13.** How did you hear about this job opening?

> **14.** What have you done to prepare for this interview?

> **15.** What motivated you to be interested in this position?

> **16.** This job is very different from your current position. Tell me more about your choice to change the direction of your career.

ANALYSIS: The answers to these questions are good to have, especially if you are torn between two or three outstanding candidates. Often the person who wants the position more will put in the extra time and energy necessary to be successful in a new position. If the person is venturing into a career change, knowing his or her motivation will help you judge the answer to specific behavioral questions even if the example is not industry relevant.

Scholastic Experience

17. What was your favorite subject in school?

18. What was your best subject in school?

19. Why did you choose to major in _____?

20. What course gave you the most difficulty?

21. I see you attended college out of state. What was that experience like?

22. What courses have you taken that you feel best prepared you for this position?

23. What traits do you possess that made you a good student?

24. What traits do you possess that cause you to perform at a level below your potential?

ANALYSIS: These questions are most suitable for recent graduates looking for their first job. They are also useful to set someone at ease who may not have a great deal of industry- or position-specific work experience.

A person applying for his or her first supervisory job will gain confidence sharing course information that is particularly relevant, as will the person branching into a different career or one who upgraded his or her education.

When dealing with a recent graduate that has little previous work experience, the answers to the behavioral questions will come from educational experiences. It is important to understand his or her educational experience and the context in which he or she learned and performed well, and not so well. Although work is different than school, it still requires most of the same competencies: communication, teamwork, motivation, initiative, organization, etc.

Job Performance

25. What kind of supervision do you think brings out the best in you?

26. Tell me about the supervisor with whom you got along the best.

27. Do you prefer to work alone or as part of a group?

28. What are some job responsibilities you do not like?

29. What aspects of your last job did you really like?

30. What is the most important element you require in a job?

ANALYSIS: These questions set the foundation for future behavioral-based questions that deal with how the person performed on the job rather than just what duties they performed. Use these questions as practice for the more inquisitive and precise behavioral questions that assess a specific competency in depth. These questions simply ask the candidate to self-assess or give an opinion, but it gets him or her in the habit of thinking about a job in particular rather than work in general.

Some of these questions will also help you determine overall fit. There are times when a particular culture or style of supervision is obviously not going to work with a particular candidate. Rather than going through the entire interview, you have the option of cutting the process short if it is a clear mismatch from the beginning. Hopefully the pre-interview process has uncovered any glaring fit issues, but sometimes the rapport built during the early stages of the interview is enough to break through even the most heavily armored shell.

Career Objectives

31. What is your long-term career objective?

32. Why have you decided to leave your past jobs?

33. How does this job fit with your overall career goals?

34. Where do you see this role taking you in the future?

35. What areas do you need to further develop in order to meet your career goals?

36. What specific events or activities in your past have most influenced your current career objectives?

ANALYSIS: Study after study have proved that a satisfied employee is a productive employee, and one of the key elements of job satisfaction is a stimulating work environment. Not everyone who works for you will be promoted, but building a workforce that is enthused about and eager to take on extra assignments and responsibility creates a very dynamic and productive environment. People who have already set goals for their career will be much more amenable to setting goals for on-the-job results, and these are the type of people who will contribute the most to your company. Employee selection is a costly function, and doing it right the first time will save a great deal of time and money in the long run. Hiring employees who are interested in, and capable of, contributing a wide range of skills and talents to your workplace are the ones who have the greatest long-term potential.

PERFORMANCE

☑ **Excellent**

☐ **Very Good**

☐ **Satisfactory**

☐ **Marginal**

☐ **Poor**

Self-Evaluation

37. As an employee, how do you describe yourself?

38. How would your last supervisor describe you?

39. How would your coworkers describe you?

40. In what type of job-related activity are you most confident performing?

41. What has given you the most satisfaction at work?

42. How do you know when you have done a good job?

43. When you assess your performance, what factors do you use for your evaluation?

ANALYSIS: These questions are purely opinion; questions meant to get the candidate used to opening up about their previous work performance. You'll be able to tell what behaviors and characteristics the person feels are critical for success; you won't be able to tell how well the person actually applies those behaviors and characteristics. The primary purpose of self-evaluation questions is to uncover which characteristics a candidate finds the most valuable. Whatever qualities the candidate focuses on are the ones that he or she believes are the most important to the position for which they are applying. Use the answers to gauge fit with the company's values.

Managing Others

44. What is your overall philosophy when managing or supervising others?

45. How do you motivate others to perform their very best?

46. When evaluating the performance of a person who reports to you, what factors do you consider are the most important?

47. What do you do that sets an example for your employees and coworkers?

48. How would you describe your basic leadership style?

49. If I asked your employees to describe you, what would they say?

50. How frequently do you meet with your employees as a group?

ANALYSIS: When interviewing for a management or supervisory position, it is crucial that you consider how well the person will fit with your current employees and what leadership philosophy to which the person ascribes. Different work environments and industries are more suited to some styles of leadership than others. What you need to know is what style the candidate is most comfortable with and what has given him or her the most success in the past. There are some very fair yet dictatorial managers who are considered good leaders by their people. Whether or not your people and your culture will see it that way is another story.

Throughout the getting-to-know-you phase of the interview, be aware of the applicant's poise, style of delivery and communication ability; these are all valuable clues to whether or not the person is suitable for the job and whether he or she will fit into the work environment.

Application: Starting the Interview Off Right

APPLICANT: Charles Davenport

POSITION: Administrative Assistant

INTERVIEWER: "Hello Charles, I'm Dianna. We spoke on the phone. I'm pleased to meet you in person. Were my directions OK?"

INTERVIEWEE: "Oh yes, I found the place with no problem."

INTERVIEWER: "Great. I see you've met Carol our receptionist. I'll introduce you to others as we go. We're ready to get started so if you want to follow me, I'll show you to the boardroom."

INTERVIEWEE: "Sure."

INTERVIEWER: "I know we discussed the fact that two of us will be doing the interview. Don't worry, we're not here to intimidate you; we simply find it's very valuable to get more than one opinion on a person's suitability."

INTERVIEWEE: "I understand, and I've been preparing for the interview."

Enter Boardroom

INTERVIEWER: "Charles, I'd like you to meet Greg. Greg is our Administration Manager and is the direct supervisor of the position for which you are applying. He and I will be conducting the interview together. The types of questions we'll be asking are mostly behavior-based questions. That means we are looking for you to describe a particular situation you have encountered in the past:

what the situation was, what you did, what other people did, and what the outcome was. We're interested in discovering what you have actually done rather than what you think you would do in a given circumstance. Do you have any questions about this type of interview?"

INTERVIEWEE: "What happens if I can't give you an example from my past experience?"

INTERVIEWER: "Well, the questions we ask in the interview process focus mostly on personal traits and characteristics rather than specific skills. If you haven't encountered a work situation that deals with the particular attribute we are discussing, the likelihood is very high that you've encountered it in another area of your life. Remember, Greg and I are not here to trick or confuse you; we need to get to know who you are and how you react in various situations in order for us to evaluate whether this job is a good fit for you and if you are a good fit for our organization.

"We're each going to take turns asking the questions, but please feel free to direct your responses to either of us and ask questions if you are unclear about anything as we progress. Also, silence does not bother us—we want you to give us a really good example of the characteristics we are talking about; if it takes you a moment to think of an example, that's OK. If you need some help, we'll try to rephrase the questions or jog your memory as best we can. Are you ready to get started?"

INTERVIEWEE: "Sure, as ready as I'll ever be."

INTERVIEWER: "Oh, one last thing: In order for us to remember your responses we will be taking notes. Please don't let that distract you."

INTERVIEWEE: "OK."

INTERVIEWER: "OK, let's start by having you telling us a bit more about yourself. Tell me something that I wouldn't know just from reviewing your résumé."

INTERVIEWEE: "Well, I'm sort of an expert at barbecue. I took a course a while back and really enjoyed it so now I experiment with all different kinds of meats, vegetables and techniques, I've created my own marinades, and all my neighbors seem to pop in for a surprise visit just after I've lit the barbecue."

INTERVIEWER: "We'll just highlight your address at the top of your résumé! Thanks for sharing your special talent with us. Now, I see you are currently working in administration; can you tell me why you are applying for this job?"

[The candidate demonstrated a willingness to share personal information so no further probing is needed. This is where you want to set the candidate at ease and develop rapport—his response indicates that the interviewer has done that.]

INTERVIEWEE: "Sure, I've been in my current role for three years and I really enjoy it but the company is small and there is very little room for advancement. I am really looking to establish a long-term career in a company where I can grow and develop my skills."

INTERVIEWER: "So what is the most important element you require in a job?"

INTERVIEWEE: "What I require is the knowledge that my efforts will be rewarded with opportunities for career development. I get pay raises at my current job, but what I really want is the opportunity for more responsibility."

INTERVIEWER: "How do you know when you've done a good job?"

INTERVIEWEE: "I know when I do a good job because I feel like I did everything I could in the situation. I don't need someone else to be constantly telling me what a good job I did, although that's nice every so often. I can tell in myself when I've worked hard at a job and done my best."

INTERVIEWER: [Probe] "Tell me about a time when you knew you did an exceptional job and no one commented specifically on it."

INTERVIEWEE: "Actually, it was just last week. It was our company's year-end and we were so busy. The accounting clerk was just run off her feet so I was slated to process the payroll and I only received my cross-training last month. I am proud to say that I got the payroll completed on time and error-free. I got confused a couple of times but I managed to work it out using the resources from the payroll company and without having to get the accounting clerk to do it for me."

The interview is underway and the candidate seems calm and relaxed. Now is the time to start asking competency-focused questions. These questions are behavioral-based and require specific examples for each answer. By building a comfortable interview environment, you are now in a prime position to get honest, straightforward answers that will help you determine whether or not the person sitting in front of you has the right mix of personal competencies and technical skills.

Building the Interview Questions

The following chapters provide examples of questions designed to assess each of the core competencies recognized by most employers. While a well-rounded person may exhibit competence in most of the core areas, each position typically has four to six competency areas that are absolutely critical. Examine your job description and determine which areas require the greatest amount of attention. Think about what specific attributes will set one technically qualified candidate apart from another equally qualified candidate; by focusing on these distinguishing characteristics, the key competencies for the job will emerge.

Once you've determined which competencies you want to interview for, ask two or three of the questions per category. This will ensure adequate coverage of positive and negative examples that relate to the attribute, and it gives the candidate an opportunity to provide more detail and, often, another example. The answer guidelines are provided to give you an idea of what to look for and will also highlight what types of answers are better suited to particular cultures and work environments in general.

Probes

Follow-up questions are designed to give you, the interviewer, more information about the situation being described. By asking questions, you will be able to get answers that you want and not just answers the candidate is most willing to provide. Often the candidate will stall during their explanation of an event, and probes from you help them stay focused and recall details they might have otherwise missed. Probes are also an excellent way to demonstrate effective listening. You can't "zone out" if you're listening for areas in the explanation that need more clarification or elaboration.

Examples of effective probes include:

WHY?
- Why did you decide to do that? HOW?
- How did you feel?
- How did he or she react?
- How did you handle that?
- How did you resolve that?
- How did you prepare for that?

WHEN?
- When did this happen?

WHERE?

- Where were you when this happened?
- Where was your supervisor/coworker?

TELL ME MORE

- Tell me more about your interaction with that person.

CAN YOU GIVE ME AN EXAMPLE?

LEAD ME THROUGH THE PROCESS.

WHO?

- Who else was involved?
- To whom did you report?

WHAT ?

- What did you do?
- What did you say?
- What was your role?
- What steps did you take?
- What action did you take?
- What happened after that?
- What was your reaction?
- What was the outcome/result?
- Were you happy with that outcome/result?
- What do you wish you had done differently?
- What did you learn from that?
- What was your logic?
- What was your reasoning?
- What time was it?
- What was your role?

- What obstacles did you face?
- What were you thinking at that point?

When probing an applicant to expand on their answer, it is important that you don't lead the person to the "right" answer; good probes are simply a request to "tell me more." Try to avoid judging an answer or leading the candidate to the correct answer. Examples:

QUESTION: "How would your coworkers describe you?"

ANSWER: "I think most of my coworkers would say I'm pleasant and easy to get along with."

JUDGMENT: "So, when you work with teams you're the one everyone still talks to when there is conflict?"

ANSWER: "I suppose, I actually try to stay out of the drama as much as possible."

LEADING PROBE: "Working in a team environment would likely be a good option for you?"

ANSWER: "Oh yes, I love to work with other people."

GOOD PROBE: "Tell me more about the context of your interactions with coworkers."

ANSWER: "Well, I do most of my work alone in the back, but we all go on break together and we get along real well. It is a really great team environment."

Notice that with the first two probes the interviewer assumed that since the candidate reported being friendly and easy to get along with, that he or she was also a good member in a team environment. The answers shed no light on the candidate's actual work performance, only reinforced the erroneous assumption that the candidate worked in a team environment. By asking a direct probe regarding the candidate's interaction with other coworkers, the interviewer is quickly able to determine that the person doesn't actually work in a team environment.

It is very easy to lead a candidate to the correct answer but it is often imperative that you get more information than the candidate originally offered. Don't be afraid to probe if you don't feel the answer gave you sufficient insight. Sometimes the candidate will continue to offer superficial answers, so you have to get used to rephrasing questions and asking for details until you are satisfied with the answer given.

Chapter 3
COMPETENCY QUESTIONS

Communication

We hear so much today about the importance of communication or the ability to communicate with others, both in written and verbal formats. The difficulty in assessing or evaluating communication is that it necessarily involves two people. Effective communication for one person may be deemed ineffective by the other for no other reason than a difference in style. Does that make one of the parties a better or worse communicator? Not necessarily: it depends on the context. For a person employed in a job that involves public speaking, his or her communication style must have broad appeal in order to be considered effective. For the research scientist working in the lab, effective communication will likely involve much less flamboyance, but a direct and to-the-point style is not necessarily ineffective. Effective communication is about sending and receiving messages, so it is important not to have an idea set in stone about what constitutes effective communication before evaluating the purpose of the communication required.

Being able to hear the message being sent is equally important to effective communication as being able to send a message. The second part of effective communication is, then, active listening. Listening for clues to discover the intent behind the communication is vital for deciding how to respond and, thus, completing the communication cycle. An interview is an excellent forum to evaluate both sides of the communication equation—it involves active listening and clear expression, and you should know by the end whether or not the individual sitting before you is an effective communicator.

Effective communication, regardless of the style, requires five skill areas:

Asking questions

In order to fully understand a message being sent, and thus respond appropriately, a person must ask clarifying questions when necessary.

Not asking questions will eventually lead to misunderstandings; the root cause of most communication breakdowns.

Effective listening

For good communication to occur, the message receiver must listen attentively to the speaker and provide the speaker clues that he or she is being listened to. A simple nod of the head or affirmative response conveys to the speaker that their message is being heard and respected.

Detecting inconsistencies

Taking information at face value is a potentially fatal mistake that many people make. The ability to detect and then question inconsistency is essential for effective communication. A message that is untruthful but well heard can cause more harm than plain ignorance of an accurate message.

Paraphrasing/Summarizing

Active listening is the first step toward true understanding, but the best way to guarantee understanding is to summarize the points made by the speaker. The speaker then has the opportunity to make corrections, and both parties are secure in the knowledge that the message is clear.

Maintaining contact

OK, so you've exchanged a message with someone; now it is important to follow up. The discussion of an impending deadline and assigning tasks may be executed very effectively, but the only way to evaluate the final outcome of the communication is to maintain contact and keep current. Needs or circumstances may change, making follow-up critical to an effective communication cycle.

When asking a candidate questions that involve communication skills, it is wise to keep these five skill areas in mind. Evaluate the candidate's answer based on how well they demonstrate the appropriate skills and techniques in order to communicate effectively. Essentially, the entire interview provides clues about a person's ability to communicate. Does the applicant communicate effectively with you? Does he or she ask questions and paraphrase in order to fully understand what you are asking? In an interview situation, the candidate is nervous and, thus, he or she will likely use the same level of communication skills used on the job and in other stressful situations.

Interview Questions for Assessing Written Communication

51.   Tell me about a time in which you had to use your written communication skills in order to get an important point across.

ANALYSIS: Use this question to assess whether or not the candidate understands when it is best to use written communication versus direct oral communication. In this day of e-mail and instant messages, it is extremely important for people to recognize the limitations of written communications and also know when it can be used most effectively.

52. Describe for me the last written communication you had with your boss.

ANALYSIS: This question allows you to determine if the candidate recognizes when written communication is more appropriate than verbal communication. Not everything in the workplace needs to be done in writing, and no one has time to put everything in writing. Knowing in what circumstances a written memo or letter is required is key to working efficiently and communicating effectively.

53. Describe the most significant written document, report or presentation that you worked on.

ANALYSIS: To evaluate the extent of the applicant's written communication experience and expertise. Discovering the reaction to the written material is key to be able to determine level of skill.

> **54.** Tell me about one of the most important written documents you were required to complete. How did you determine when it was finished? What reaction did it receive?

ANALYSIS: Written documents can be edited and revised forever. What this question is designed for is to understand if the candidate knows when a document covers what it needs to.

> **55.** Tell me about the best-written proposal you have created. Why was it the best? How did you know that it was good?

ANALYSIS: Ask this type of question if the ability to prepare and present written communication represents a significant skill for the job. Delve into why the document or presentation or proposal was so important and what the candidate contributed that was equally significant. Pay close attention to the external and internal cues the candidate used in order to evaluate the effectiveness of the communication. Candidates who rely mostly on intrinsic cues and rewards are more likely to produce high-quality work regardless of the circumstances, while those who need extrinsic responses usually need more coaxing to produce superior work.

56. Often the problem with written communication is that we never know if the person receiving the message followed up or took action. Can you give an example of a time when your written request was not acted upon? What did you do about it?

57. When have your verbal communications been important enough to follow up in writing?

ANALYSIS: What you are looking for with this question is whether or not the individual follows up written communication with further contact. It is not enough to fire off memos and letters; the onus is on the person who initiates the communication to make sure his or her message was received. Answers that indicate the person has learned this important component of communication are desirable.

Interview Questions for Assessing Verbal Communication

58. Discuss a time when you had to assert yourself (speak up) in order to get a point across that was important to you.

ANALYSIS: Assertiveness is an important quality. A person may communicate very well when everyone is in agreement, but if he lacks the gumption to speak his mind and fears, creating dissension or conflict, then the person's usefulness as a team member is limited. It's also a fine line between assertion and aggression, and you need to ensure the candidate you choose clearly knows the difference.

> **59.** Have you had to "sell" an idea to your coworkers, classmates or group? How did you do it? Did they "buy" it?

ANALYSIS: In the world of work, the most common use of communication is to persuade someone to do something: buy something, sell something, complete something, do something correctly, etc. Listen carefully to what the person's example is, though; some people are very good at the "art of the sale," but if what they are selling is not useful, then the effort is wasted. Again, it is a fine line between persuasion and coercion, so do some extra probing if you suspect the person has a tendency toward the latter.

> **60.** Give me an example of a time when you were able to successfully communicate with another person, even when that individual may not have personally liked you. How did you handle the situation? What obstacles or difficulties did you face? How did you deal with them?

ANALYSIS: This question involves interpersonal communication, a competency that will be discussed in depth in the next chapter. However, the act of communication is about communicating with other people, and it is the most challenging when you are dealing with someone you don't like. What you are looking for in this answer is an acknowledgment that not all people are likable but that the candidate can reign in his or her personal feelings for the sake of the company.

> **61.** Describe a situation you were involved in that required a multi-dimensional communication strategy.

ANALYSIS: This question is another way to determine if the candidate knows how to use written and verbal communication appropriately, and how well he or she combines the two mediums for maximum effect.

> **62.** Give an example of a difficult or sensitive situation that required extensive communication.

ANALYSIS: Sensitive situations call for highly effective communication skills. Clearly understanding the original message and then clearly articulating a response are imperative for the dialogue to be constructive. Communication at its best is open to so many opportunities for breakdown, so when the subject matter is highly sensitive, the communication must be as close to perfect as possible. Look for the effective use of listening, empathy and maintaining contact.

> **63.** How do you ensure that someone understands what you are saying?

ANALYSIS: The essence of this question is to learn if the candidate recognizes the importance of active listening and actually practices the skill.

64.   Give me an example of a situation where proper communication allowed you to get the task/project done quickly.

65.   Tell me about a time when the ability to communicate effectively was critical to the success of a task or project. How did you handle it?

66.   Give me an example of a time when you had to explain a complicated procedure to someone who was new to the situation. What did you do? What were the results?

67.   Describe a recent situation when miscommunication created a problem on the job.

ANALYSIS: Effective communication builds a foundation for efficiency. Ideally, the candidate will be able to give you an example that demonstrates his or her understanding of this relationship. When communication falters, it can cause significant lags in a project's completion. What you want to uncover is how the candidate handles communication breakdown: what are the signals, what does he or she do about it, how effective is the intervention, etc.

68.   Tell me about a time when you really had to pay attention to what someone else was saying, actively seeking to understand their message.

69. Tell about a time when your active listening skills were critical to the success of a project.

70. Describe for me a situation where you missed some important details that were communicated to you. What was the outcome? How did you resolve the situation?

ANALYSIS: Active listening is so important, and it contributes to effective communication as well as sets the stage for good interpersonal relationships. Many high-energy individuals have a bad habit of not listening carefully. These people get jobs done quickly and show a great deal of initiative and motivation, but they often misplace their energy. What you want to know is whether or not these enthusiastic types have learned from this mistake and recognize the importance of active listening.

71. Describe for me an instance when you jumped into a task or project before you fully understood the entire concept.

72.   Discuss a situation where your failure to listen attentively to a coworker or supervisor caused ill feelings because of their hastiness to get going before you fully understood what they were trying to communicate.

ANALYSIS: Poor listening is one of easiest ways to create communication breakdown. Situation comedy writers rely on miscommunication for their source of humor. Fortunately, on TV, by the end of the 30 minutes the situation gets resolved. In the workplace it takes much longer and can cause a significant amount to damage to productivity and relationships. Ineffective listening happens all the time, so you want employees who understand this fact and have learned how to avoid it. Look for indications that the candidate summarizes and paraphrases by listening to the examples given, as well as the way he or she answers and clarifies questions.

73. Describe a situation you observed or were a part of where you feel communication was handled particularly well by someone else. What did they do? Why do you think it was effective?

74. Tell me about a time when you had difficulty understanding a conversation and the point the person was trying to make. What did you do? What was the final outcome?

75. Give me an example of a time when you were unclear about the directions given to you for a work assignment. What did you do to clarify the directions? What was the final outcome?

ANALYSIS: Good communication skills are often best learned in a practical setting. When a candidate can relay an example of communication that is in fact representative of excellent communication, that is a strong indicator that he or she truly "gets" what good communication is. The reverse is also true: If a candidate knows first-hand how frustrating it is to be the one who does not understand, he or she will likely make a concerted effort to be understood when speaking.

76. Tell me about a time when you worked with someone who was very difficult to understand. Perhaps the person's first language was not English or he had a disability that affected his ability to communicate. Explain how you overcame the situation.

ANALYSIS: Workplaces today are multicultural and inclusive of people with varying degrees of ability. The likelihood that an employee will need to communicate with a customer or coworker who is hard to understand is very high. Use this question to discover what types of strategies the candidate employs in difficult situations. Does he or she mention body language and other non-verbal clues? Does the person recognize the power of paraphrasing, summarizing and asking questions? Probe the candidate about the outcome of the communication. Ask if he or she felt frustrated and how those feelings were handled.

> **77.** Tell me about how you communicate with your current supervisor concerning project process, concerns and suggestions.

> **78.** Your supervisor has given you instructions to complete a project. You are not clear as to some of the details of the instructions. What do you do?

> **79.** Describe for me the last conversation you had with a person in your organization that was senior to you but not a direct supervisor or manager.

ANALYSIS: Communicating with supervisors is slightly different than with coworkers. There is a level of responsibility and authority that needs to be respected, and an astute interviewer uses this question to determine how much the candidate adjusts his or her communication as it goes up the organization chart. This is not to say that you want employees who are intimidated by, or scared of, talking to superiors. What you want are employees who recognize a reporting authority exists and make a concerted effort to keep the supervisor informed and advised as required.

80. Describe a situation when you were able to strengthen a relationship by communicating effectively. What made your communication effective?

81. Describe how your ability to communicate effectively and build relationships with many different types of people has contributed to one of your greatest accomplishments.

ANALYSIS: These are general questions aimed at determining what factors the candidate considers essential to effective communication. There is no clue given as to what the interviewer thinks effective communication should entail, so the candidate must come up with his or her own definition. These are excellent opening questions for the topics of communication and interpersonal skills.

82. Describe some tough or tricky situations in which you had to talk to people to obtain information you needed to make an important decision or recommendation.

83. Walk me through a situation in which you had to obtain information by asking a lot of questions of several people. How did you know what to ask?

ANALYSIS: An element of active listening is the ability to ask enough questions to make sure you understand the message being sent. The key, though, is to ask enough of the right questions. Neither party wants to keep trying to make himself or herself understood, so an effective communicator gets to the point quickly and efficiently and avoids frustration.

Interview Questions for Assessing Presentation Skills

84. Tell me about a time when you had to make a presentation to a large group.

85. Tell me about a time when you had to make a presentation to a small group.

86. What has been your experience with giving presentations to large or small groups?

87. Have you prepared and communicated ideas and information in a formal setting? Please explain.

88. Tell me about a time when you were required to give a presentation and it did not go as planned. What happened? What contributed to the problem? What would you do differently?

ANALYSIS: While some jobs do not have a presentation requirement, it is a skill that is used in a wide variety of positions. While a receptionist or administrator may greet clients/customers, answer questions and present information informally, the position still requires confidence and poise. Similarly, when the safety inspector tours a facility, the production worker may be asked to demonstrate machinery or answer questions, again requiring basic presentation skills. Being able to present information coherently is not a requirement for self-confidence, but it is often co-relational. Confidence is usually exhibited by the most talented people, and those are the people you want working for you.

> **89.** Tell me about a recent speech or presentation you gave that you consider successful. How did you know it was successful? How did you prepare? What obstacles did you face? How did you handle them?

> **90.** What has been your most successful experience in speech making?

> **91.** Think about the last presentation you gave. Describe for me the supplementary materials you prepared and any other aids you used. How were these materials received by the audience?

ANALYSIS: Presenting information well requires a great deal of time and preparation, and this type of question should be used to determine how much energy a candidate puts into the prep work. Some people think that by "winging it" they can present a balanced and professional presentation, but it usually comes across as haphazard and scattered. If formal presentations to various stakeholders are part of the job description, then be sure to probe for the details.

> **92.** Tell me about a time when you had to present complex information.

93. Many jobs require us to give a formal, stand-up presentation. Tell me about the most challenging presentation of this type you ever had to make. What made it so challenging? How did you prepare for it? How did it turn out?

ANALYSIS: Giving presentations is a highly specialized skill. Public speaking is stressful, and when the subject matter is complex or difficult to explain, the task is even more intimidating. This type of question allows the interviewer to determine what the candidate considers challenging and how he or she goes about including the audience in the presentation and facilitate learning or understanding. Probe to find out how the candidate measured the success of the presentation: did he or she give a quiz, provide follow-up, require feedback, etc.?

Application: Communication Skills Questions

APPLICANT: Charles Davenport

POSITION: Administrative Assistant

INTERVIEWER: "In the role as Administrative Assistant you will be required to assist the Sales Manager with presentations. Have you prepared and communicated ideas and information in a formal setting? Please explain."

INTERVIEWEE: "Yes, I have. In my last position I was very involved with helping my manager present new policies or procedures to the employees. One of the main projects I worked on was preparing a new policy and procedure manual, and I was in charge of preparing all the material needed to present the new information to the employees at the staff meeting. My manager gave the overview of the project, the rationale and process used, and I was responsible for the actual dissemination of specifics. What I did was prepare a Power Point presentation that had each of the new policies, and we went through the key changes one by one. Everyone had a chance to ask questions of both of us, and it was very well received."

INTERVIEWER: "Tell me about how you communicate with your current supervisor concerning project processes, concerns and suggestions."

INTERVIEWEE: "Well, I try to keep my boss very well informed. I work as her assistant so she needs to know where I am at with all my projects. We have an arrangement where I can come to her with any questions and concerns and she requires a daily update on my progress with long-term tasks."

INTERVIEWER: "What about suggestions you may have? How do you communicate those ideas?"

INTERVIEWEE: "I try not to spring things on her. I think my ideas through, and then if they truly make sense, I ask for a meeting. That way I have time to prepare my suggestion, and I know she has time to hear what I am saying."

INTERVIEWER: "Communication is often a key stumbling block for a project's success. Give me an example of a situation where proper communication allowed you to get a task/project done quickly."

INTERVIEWEE: "That happened a few months ago. My boss asked me to pull all the training records for the staff. I knew that was a huge undertaking because some of the records were in the employee files, some in the personnel files and some in the computer database. I asked her the purpose for pulling the files and when she said she needed it to determine if all the first-aid certificates were up to date. When she said it, we both realized that we had created a database for that exact purpose last year when the last group attended their re-certification. By asking that one question, I saved a lot of time and got the information to her within the hour."

Notice how the interviewer helps Charles understand the relevance of the question being asked. Rather than just jumping right in with the question, he provides some background information about why the question is being asked. This sets the candidate at ease and it also provides strong contextual clues so the candidate can discuss an example that is both applicable and appropriate. The key with providing these lead-ins is to make sure you don't lead the candidate toward the "right" answer. You shouldn't have to use these explanations with every behavioral question, but it is a technique that often saves time.

Charles did not appear to need many explanations, and his answers to the communication questions were quite good. Certainly no red flags were raised, and the interviewer probed for more specific information regarding how the applicant actually used good communication to work efficiently.

{ Use explanatory lead-ins to supplement your behavioral questions, making them relevant to your company and the position. }

Chapter 4

INTERPERSONAL SKILLS AND CONFLICT RESOLUTION

Interpersonal skills are the broad range of skills that allow people to communicate effectively, build rapport and relate well to all kinds of people. Listen for self-awareness, understanding and an ability to communicate effectively with others regardless of differences. Be sure to probe for as many details and specifics as possible, such as names, dates and other verifiable information. Skilled interviewers will also ask candidates for their thoughts or feelings about a situation to gain further insight.

Interview Questions for Assessing Interpersonal Skills

94. Describe the types of people you get along with best and why.

95. How have you developed your interpersonal skills?

96. Describe your relationship with the people you work with.

97. Tell me about your relationship with a coworker whom you work well with.

ANALYSIS: These are good openers for the interpersonal section. Use probes to get the details and ask for specific examples. What you are looking for is an understanding that although a person may not like a coworker, customer, boss, etc., he or she must develop coping mechanisms to ensure communication is clear and the work environment is pleasant. Often a person will get along best with someone who has a similar personality and outlook on life, so the answers to these questions can reveal quite a bit about the candidate's true self.

98. Describe the most difficult working relationship you've had with an individual. What specific actions did you take to improve the relationship? What was the outcome?

99. Describe the types of people you have difficulty getting along with and why.

100. Think about a difficult boss, professor or other person. What made him or her difficult? How did you successfully interact with this person?

101.   Tell me about your relationship with a coworker whom you do not have a good working relationship. What steps have you taken to improve that relationship?

102.   Describe how you handle rude, difficult or impatient people.

103.   Tell me about a time when you had to work with a difficult boss.

104.   Tell me about the most difficult or frustrating individual that you've ever had to work with, and how you managed to work with them.

105.   Describe a situation when you wished you'd acted differently with someone at work. What happened? What did you do about the situation?

106.   Give an example of when you had to work with someone who was difficult to get along with. How/why was this person difficult? How did you handle it? How did the relationship progress?

ANALYSIS: You want to know what type of behavior or personality is particularly challenging for the candidate to deal with, and then you need to know if the candidate has developed sufficient skills to deal with these types of people. The world of work is full of all sorts of people, and you need your employees to be able to get along with and communicate effectively with everyone. Be aware of candidates who list fairly innocuous habits as ones that disturb them.

Listen carefully to how the applicant discusses the scenario. People who truly know how to deal with challenging individuals will emphasize what was learned and how they came to appreciate interpersonal differences. People who still find it hard to deal with difficult people will talk more about the traits that made the person difficult and try to get affirmation that the person really was a creep.

107. What have you done in the past to build rapport and relationships with people?

108. Give me an example of a time when you deliberately attempted to build rapport with a coworker or customer.

109. Tell me about a time when you were able to establish rapport with a "difficult" person. How did you go about it? What were the results?

ANALYSIS: Rapport building is a specific skill that, if done effectively, can mitigate any future interpersonal difficulty. If you choose to ask this question, what you want to know is how well the candidate tries to find common ground with other people. Can the person empathize with people and understand where others are coming from? Rapport building is very important in positions that develop and maintain long-term relationships.

110. Describe a situation where you found yourself dealing with someone who didn't like you. How did you handle it?

ANALYSIS: This is a good question to ask if you sense the candidate is defensive or otherwise prone to volatile interpersonal relationships. When people answer questions about getting along with others, it is much easier to discuss situations where others are behaving in a challenging way. This question potentially uncovers areas of the applicant's personality that are challenging. Make sure to probe for details about why the other person did not like the applicant and how he or she contributed to the challenge and also facilitated a civil relationship. The biggest, and usually most transparent, red flag in this question is arrogance. Despite trying to put forth a best impression, an arrogant person will not be able to hide his disdain for someone who dared not like him.

111. Give me a specific example of a time when a coworker criticized your work in front of others. How did you respond? How has that event shaped the way you communicate with others?

ANALYSIS: Often the best lessons in interpersonal communication come from situations when we are at the wrong end of the communication stick. Pay attention to the details of the situation. A good follow-up probe is to ask if the candidate has ever criticized someone's work in front of other people.

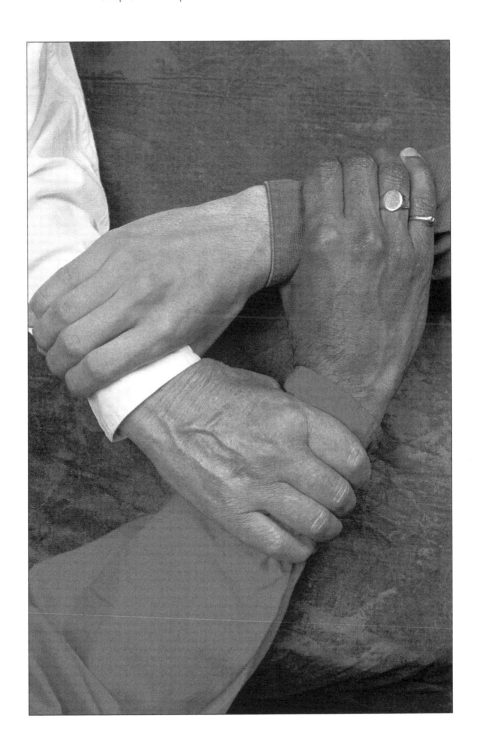

112. Give me an example of a situation when you demonstrated sensitivity to diversity issues.

113. Give me an example of your ability to communicate effectively and build relationships with people regardless of cultural differences.

ANALYSIS: Cultural differences are becoming more and more common-place in the work environment. With all the other challenges to working well with other people, you certainly don't need ethnicity or cultural discrimination coming into play. The desired answer to these questions is one that minimizes cultural differences and offers a tolerant view of the world and its people. Look for the candidate to use socially appropriate terms for other cultures and to speak inclusively of other cultures rather than an "us" and "them" type of response.

114. Your department is working on an important project. During the course of the project, you recognize a potential problem with its implementation. What do you do?

115. During the course of this same project, you have an idea that has the potential to improve the project but you are in a lower-level position that may not get respect from upper management. What do you do?

ANALYSIS: Assertiveness is an important consideration in interpersonal relationships. You want the candidate to be confident and willing to speak his or her mind in all situations. The ability to do this often stems from a well-developed method for dealing with opposition and even rudeness. Look for specific details that indicate the candidate is assured and confident with his or her own level of interpersonal ability.

> **116.**   One of your coworkers has a trait or habit that affects his relationships with other coworkers and customers. It is a difficult trait to mention but you feel it must be brought to his or her attention. How do you handle the situation?

ANALYSIS: This question deals with a candidate's honesty and straightforwardness when dealing with other people. What you want to pay attention to is whether or not the candidate can get his or her point across sensitively and considerately, making sure to preserve the other person's dignity in the process. There are many self-proclaimed "tell-it-like-it-is" people who are upfront with others, but they come across as rude and insulting. The effective communicator approaches the situation with empathy, putting himself or herself in the other person's shoes. The ineffective communicator just wants the other person to change regardless of that person's feelings or ability to change.

117. It is often necessary to adjust our method or style of communicating to meet the needs of the individual or group we are addressing. Give me an example of a time when you used a different approach or interpersonal style to more effectively communicate with a peer or subordinate.

118. Describe a situation in which you were able to effectively "read" another person and guide your actions by your understanding of their needs and values.

119. Describe an example of a time when you had to approach several people for support or cooperation, who you considered quite different from one another. What did you have to do differently with each person? How did you know what to do differently?

120. Describe a situation in which your first attempt to sell an idea failed. How did you react to this? What other approaches did you try?

ANALYSIS: The core of interpersonal skill is the ability to adjust one's responses to suit the situation and person with which one is dealing. What you ideally want to hear is an example that demonstrates the candidate can use a different style to deal with different people. If the candidate's previous examples involved using empathy and building rapport, then the answer to this question might involve the use of compassion or reason or active listening. What you want to know is whether or not the candidate has more than one or two tools in his or her interpersonal skill toolbox.

> **121.** Some situations require us to express ideas or opinions in a very tactful and careful way. Tell me about a time when you were successful in this type of situation.

Tact is so very important, and it is what constitutes the difference between honesty and rudeness. You need to know that your employees can assert themselves and communicate confidently but always with an eye to maintaining tact and professionalism. Cues for professional behavior are examples that exhibit keeping calm, mediating, compromising and placating when necessary.

> **122.** Describe a work situation that required you to really listen and display compassion to a coworker/ employee who was telling you about a personal or sensitive situation.

> **123.** Describe a recent situation in which what was really going on with someone else was much more complicated than it might have seemed on the surface.

ANALYSIS: In many workplaces, coworkers become an extended family of sorts, and despite every intention not to get too personal at work, it often cannot be avoided, particularly in supervisory or management roles when an employee needs coaching or even counseling. The key in this circumstance is to maintain a certain level of objectivity and distance. A good answer to this type of question is one that includes helping the person help himself rather than jumping in and trying to the solve the problem for him.

> **124.** What, in your opinion, are the key ingredients for developing and maintaining successful business relationships? Give me examples of how you practice these skills.

ANALYSIS: Figure out what the candidate values in terms of business goals. Ideally, you want the candidate to discuss various interpersonal skills that foster and enhance relationships, but the key to this question is the fact that it relates to business relationships, not personal ones. Probe to find out where profitability and strategy fit into the equation to make sure the candidate is not so relationship-focused that the overall needs of the business are compromised.

> **125.** Describe a situation in which you developed an effective win/win relationship with a stakeholder or client. How did you go about building the relationship?

ANALYSIS: It is important to establish whether or not the candidate appreciates the difference between compromising to solve a conflict or collaborating to get to a win/win relationship. What you don't want is an employee who compromises all over the place and calls it successful interpersonal skills. Effective interpersonal skills are those that get both

parties to a place of satisfaction without either having to give up anything to get there.

> **126.** Tell me about a time when you relied on a contact in your network to help you with a work-related task or problem.

ANALYSIS: Generally, people who have well-developed interpersonal skills also are well liked and well connected. Find out if the candidate keeps in touch with contacts. This is a very good clue that the relationship is solid and based on mutual respect and admiration.

> **127.** Give me an example of when you identified with someone else's difficulties at work. What, if anything, did you do to help them?

> **128.** Describe a situation when you were criticized for being too concerned about the difficulties of others.

ANALYSIS: Find out if the candidate equates interpersonal skills with meddling. The person who is forever concerned about everyone's welfare at work is more often the cause of conflict than the champion for change. Watch out for the candidate who emphasizes the problem his coworker was facing rather than his own actions in the situation. Solution-oriented people help the workplace develop and problem-oriented people look for things to gripe about.

129. Describe a time that politics at work affected your job. How did you handle it?

ANALYSIS: It is next to impossible to avoid workplace politics, and interpersonal skills are the best way to deal with the unfortunate reality. What you want to discover in this case is where the candidate draws the line between managing within a political environment and contributing to the office politics. A person with good interpersonal skills will try to stay as neutral as possible and behave professionally at all times.

Interview Questions for Assessing Conflict-Resolution Skills

130. In any field, conflicts will often arise between coworkers. How have you resolved a conflict with a coworker?

131. Describe a situation where you had a conflict with another individual, and how you dealt with it. What was the outcome? How did you feel about it?

132. Tell me about a situation where you were involved in a conflict. What did you do to resolve that conflict?

133. Tell me about the most memorable time when you had a personal conflict with another employee at work. How did you deal with the conflict? Why did you take this approach? How did your relationship with the person finally turn out?

134. Tell me about a difficult situation where it was desirable for you to keep a positive attitude.

ANALYSIS: Conflict is inevitable and relatively frequent. The actual conflict situation that the candidate chooses to relay is an excellent source of information about what really triggers his or her personal conflicts. What you need to determine is whether or not the candidate's triggers are more or less frequent in your workplace. If the scenario involves a difference of opinion or a slight miscommunication, that person may be less attractive as an employee than one who cites a time when he or she was the victim of outright deceit or grievous behavior.

Obviously, the resolution aspect of the question is important and the candidate can be counted on to use those skills in future conflicts, but what you want to avoid is hiring someone who views minor, everyday occurrences as conflicts requiring full-fledged conflict-resolution skills.

135. Describe the way you handled a specific problem involving others with differing values, ideas and beliefs in your current/previous job.

136. Tell me about a time when you had to resolve a difference of opinion with a coworker/customer/supervisor. How do you feel you showed respect?

ANALYSIS: A difference of opinion or core values is very often the basis of conflict and the type that is most difficult to resolve. The way a person sets out to work with people who are fundamentally different than himself or herself says a great deal about the person's ability to deal with differences in general. The bottom line in business is to maintain respect and professionalism at all times. These questions can yield valuable information about how the candidate deals with core personality and values differences. If he or she can provide a solid example in this category, then chances are his or her conflict-resolution skills are at least above average.

137. Give me a specific example of a time when you had to address an angry customer. What was the problem and what was the outcome? How would you assess your role in defusing the situation?

138. Describe a situation when a customer was frustrated with you because you didn't understand what he or she was saying. What did you do? What were the results?

> **139.** Give me an example of a time when you sensed that a customer or client was upset even though they did not specifically say so. What cues did you use to make that judgment? What did you do? What were the results?

ANALYSIS: Coworkers can be difficult but customers can sometimes be nasty. A customer does not have to face you the next day, or ever again, so he can be as rude as he wants, vent his anger however he wants, and be as disrespectful as he wants. Therein lies the reason that customers can frazzle even the most calm and collected employee. What you want to do is try to determine the candidate's breaking point. Where does the candidate draw the line between the customer always being right and the customer being downright wrong? Ultimately you want an employee who knows his or her limits and recognizes when the situation is best handled by someone in another position or with more authority. Probe until you are satisfied the employee went to appropriate lengths to resolve the situation without needlessly compromising the business or the relationship.

> **140.** Tell me about a conflict you have had with a superior. How did you resolve the conflict? How did you work towards mending the relationship with that superior?

> **141.** Tell me about the manager/supervisor/team leader who was the most difficult to work for. How did you handle this difficult relationship?

ANALYSIS: Conflicts with superiors should be kept to a minimum, and if and when they do occur, they must be handled with the utmost tact and respect. Egalitarian workplaces are espoused a great deal, but when push comes to shove, someone is in charge and is responsible for employee supervision. What you, as the interviewer, want to know is how well the candidate respects lines of authority, however informal, and how he or she operates within the system. It is also vital to know how long the conflict lingered before it was dealt with and how successful the relationship was after the attempts at resolution.

> **142.** Tell me about a time when you were assigned to a team that had a coworker you did not particularly like. How did you manage to make the team project successful while dealing with your personal feelings?

> **143.** Give me an example of a situation where you had difficulties with a team member. What, if anything, did you do to resolve the difficulties?

ANALYSIS: Interpersonal skills are all the more important when working within a team environment, so it is important to understand how the candidate deals with conflict in this particular situation. The information you are most interested in is the nature of the conflict between the team members. The resolution portion should be no different than when dealing with coworkers, in general, but what is quite revealing is the factors that led up to the conflict in the first place. Use the information given to assess whether or not the candidate is well suited to teamwork and probe to uncover his or her true feelings about teamwork.

144. Tell me about a time you had to "choose your battles carefully."

ANALYSIS: Even the most interpersonally gifted individual needs to know when to leave well enough alone. Just because a person can resolve a conflict when one arises does not mean he or she should go around looking for causes to champion. Effective interpersonal skills are evident when a person realizes that differences and conflict are natural aspects of human relations and learn to operate within a slightly conflicted environment. If a person made it her mission to solve all the conflict in a workplace, she would certainly have no time to do the productive work she is paid for, so knowing when to let it go is a valuable asset.

145. Tell me about a time when someone has lost his or her temper at you in a business environment.

ANALYSIS: A question that requires a candidate to discuss someone else's poor behavior is very revealing. The candidate is telling you what characteristics are most offensive to him or her; use that information to determine how well he or she will fit within your current work environment.

146. Tell me about a time when you saw a potential conflict between yourself and another coworker or between two of your coworkers. What did you do to help prevent the conflict?

ANALYSIS: This question is designed to determine whether a candidate believes "an ounce of prevention is worth a pound of cure." Astute individuals will pick up on conflict clues before the situation escalates and can use their skills to resolve the issue before it even has a chance to materialize. What you need to determine is whether or not the prevention was warranted and helpful. Probe to find out what the outcome was and whether or not the situation has reoccurred.

Don't let the candidate confuse actual resolution of a conflict with prevention. What you want to know is how the conflict was derailed before it even started.

Application: Interpersonal/Conflict-Resolution Skills Questions

APPLICANT: Charles Davenport

POSITION: Administrative Assistant

INTERVIEWER: "There are many employees in our organization and, as Administrative Assistant, you will work with many of them. Please tell me about the relationships you have with key people at your current workplace."

INTERVIEWEE: "Well, right now I work mainly with three people: my boss, the accounting clerk and the receptionist. My boss and I have a fabulous relationship—she really understands how I work and she lets me work as autonomously as possible, which is really helpful. She is also a generally positive person, so she doesn't bring the mood down if she having difficultly with something. My relationship with our receptionist is also very good—we are cross-trained on a lot of functions, so we help each other out and it's a very give-and-take relationship. The accounting clerk, on the other hand, is a little more difficult to get along with. She tends to be moody and quite focused on her own role and specific duties. Not so much a team player, which I prefer to work with. Having said that, though, we do have a respectful work relationship; it is just much more business-like and curt than other relationships I have at work."

INTERVIEWER: "Tell me more about this relationship you have with the accounting clerk. Can you describe the last time you encountered difficulty? What happened and what was the result?"

INTERVIEWEE: "It was last week actually. She was in crunch time because it was the end of our quarter, and her volume of work is much greater during key reporting periods. I knew that so I tried to do as much as I could without requesting help or information from her. However, my boss really needed some current expense figures broken down for a report she was working on and had asked me to do the round work. That was fine except I needed the overall figures and typical breakdown from Virginia, the accounting clerk. I e-mailed her first, hoping she would get to it when she had a spare moment, as it wasn't critical for me yet. When she didn't respond all day or the next morning, I went and asked her personally. I stood at her cubicle and waited until she noticed me, then I asked if she had a second. She snapped, "No, I don't have a second," and she asked me to not pester her when she was plainly concentrating on something. I apologized and left. Then at break I asked her if she had a few minutes for me in the afternoon. She exploded and said that she was on her break and did not want to be bothered with work details. I decided that I wasn't going to get anywhere with her so I talked to my boss and she decided that it was OK to leave the report information until after Virginia had a chance to catch-up."

INTERVIEWER: "OK, can you tell me about another time you had difficulties with someone on the job other than Virginia? What was the situation and how did you handle it?"

INTERVIEWEE: "Well, this guy in marketing started asking me to do a bunch of his correspondence, and I did it for a while because I had time. Then I got quite busy and I had to say that I couldn't do things for him anymore. He got quite peeved and started acting rude and condescending to me in front of other coworkers. Eventually I had enough, and I made an appointment to talk to my boss about the situation. She hadn't even known I was doing work for him in the first place so she was very glad I brought the situation to her attention. She went and talked to the Sales Manager and the guy hasn't bothered me since. They have also since hired a part-time assistant to help with administrative tasks in that department."

This portion of the interview yielded some very interesting facts about Charles and the way he deals with people. It seems he gets along very well with people when there are no issues to deal with or when the person is a good match for his personality. However, when he encounters difficulty, he hands over the responsibility of dealing with the problem to his superior. In the first scenario it was easy to see why he might have enlisted the help of someone else to work with Virginia.

The interviewer was very wise, though, to ask about another work conflict situation. With the second example you begin to get a fuller picture that this guy has not developed skills to deal with interpersonal conflict on his own. It also revealed some interesting information about his work priorities—he was doing unauthorized work and would have continued doing so until, presumably, his boss found out.

{ Probe, probe, and probe some more—you never know what gems of information you will pick up. }

Chapter 5

EMPATHY AND SERVICE ORIENTATION

Empathy is described as the ability to identify with and care about others. Customer service is the ability to serve customers in a manner that builds loyalty and repeat business. These two competencies are closely related, as one must have a well-developed sense of empathy in order to deal effectively and humanely with customers.

What you, as the interviewer, need to be concerned about is whether or not the person in front of you treats people with care and compassion without any expectation of rewards or benefit for himself or herself. In the workplace, employees deal with a variety of customers, or stakeholders, and each one must be dealt with in a manner that promotes respect and builds the relationship in preparation for future interaction.

The qualities that you are looking for include:

- Recognition that all people are different.
- Acceptance of those differences.
- Ability to see situations through different perspectives.

- Acknowledgment that treating people with dignity is an expectation of the job and does not require personal gain in return.

Understanding that great customer service is an expectation of the job and does not require personal gain in return.

While all workplaces will have different views on customer service and the exact administration of service, the common elements of empathy, respect and dignity are necessarily present in a sustainable work environment.

Interview Questions for Assessing Empathy

147. Give me an example of when you identified with someone else's difficulties at work. What, if anything, did you do to help them?

ANALYSIS: With a question like this, you are looking for answers that display genuine concern for the other individual. People with natural empathy will focus on what the other person was going through and will be able to pull you into the scenario, whereas people who are "faking it" will be less convincing and compelling. Trust your instincts with a question like this, and ask a lot of follow-up probes to make sure that the scenario being explained is real.

It is also important to evaluate the difficulty that is being described. Be wary of an example that deals with a fellow employee's personal life; better answers are ones that highlight how the candidate helped a coworker with a job-related task or issue.

> **148.** Give me an example of a time when a company policy or action hurt people. What, if anything, did you do to mitigate the negative consequences to people?

ANALYSIS: What you will be looking for is a candidate who clearly understands and recognizes the appropriate boundaries within organizations. While it is important to empathize with the plights of others, it is equally important to know when something is within your control or beyond it. Empathy is an important characteristic to demonstrate at all levels of a company and with all coworkers, peers and subordinates.

> **149.** Describe a situation when you were criticized for being too concerned about the difficulties of others.

ANALYSIS: Here, again, you are looking for a balance between wanting to help someone and making sure that the effort to do so is not wasted, inappropriate or counterproductive. Empathy is certainly important, but it cannot be allowed to overshadow one's day-to-day activities, duties or responsibilities. The effective application of empathy is such that it enhances the workplace, rather than deters from it.

150. Give me an example of when you went out of your way to help someone. What were your thoughts and feelings about that situation?

ANALYSIS: The candidate with a solid grasp of the notion of empathy will express thoughts and feelings such as self-satisfaction, accomplishment and enhanced self-esteem. People who generally embrace empathy do it for their own pleasure, rather than what they hope to gain from the situation. What you're looking for, as an interviewer, is a candidate whose answer emphasizes how good he or she felt about the experience, and who can demonstrate that his or her actions were well-received.

151. Give me an example of when you had to make a decision where the choices were either in favor of your own self-interest or someone else's. What were your thoughts and feelings? What did you do?

ANALYSIS: This is a very difficult question for candidates to answer. There is no clear right or wrong answer, and it is confusing as well as stressful. Your job will be to evaluate the response in relation to the culture within your own organization, the expectations placed on the position for which the person is applying, and your own sense of the honesty of the answer. What will be important in the answer is a well-thought-out and clearly articulated means for evaluating the two choices and a solid argument for why one choice was chosen over the other.

152. What positive contributions have you made to your community or society?

153. Give me an example of when you were given special recognition or acknowledgment for your contributions to the disadvantaged.

ANALYSIS: Depending on the culture or overall purpose of your organization, this may be an important factor when considering employment. Every company places a different value on community service, community involvement and other unselfish activities.

154. Can you recall a time when a person's cultural background affected your approach to a work situation?

ANALYSIS: Cultural differences are often at the root of many interpersonal conflicts at work. Regardless of the position for which you're hiring, the successful candidate must be able to demonstrate that he or she has a tolerance for differences in culture, as well as opinion. Listen carefully to the scenario being described. Be wary of answers that seem generalized or trivial. Very few people these days have not encountered a situation in which cultural differences played a significant role. Empathy is not something that can be faked or embellished— look for genuine concern and honesty. The more detailed the response and emotional the reaction, the higher the likelihood of the scenario being real.

155. Can you recall a time when you gave feedback to a coworker who was not tolerant of others?

ANALYSIS: People who display empathy in all aspects of their lives are sensitive to situations, where others are not acting particularly empathic. What is important in this answer is whether or not the person dealt with the coworker in a manner that would, in itself, be considered empathic. Remember, a person who is skilled in empathy will deal with all people and all situations with the utmost respect, dignity and compassion.

Interview Questions for Assessing Service Orientation

156. Describe the steps you would take if a customer came to you with a problem you could solve at your job level.

157. Tell me about a time when you did your best to resolve a customer or client concern and the individual still was not satisfied. What did you do next?

ANALYSIS: Customer complaints or concerns are perhaps the most difficult situations in which to display empathy, self-control and a commitment to service. However, these are the exact traits that are required for any position that deals with the general public or internal clients and customers. What you're looking for in the candidate's response to this question is the level of commitment he or she demonstrated while trying to resolve the customer's needs. Actually solving the problem is not as important in this answer as the steps the candidate took along the way. Evaluate the answer based on thoroughness and a commitment to understanding the client's concerns and then taking the appropriate action.

158. Tell me about a time when you exceeded a customer's expectations. How did it make the customer feel? How did it make you feel?

159. Describe a situation where you were given exceptional customer service. What made it stand out?

160. Give me an example of when you were given special recognition or acknowledgment for going the extra mile to satisfy a customer.

ANALYSIS: In order for a person to give excellent service, he or she needs to recognize what outstanding service truly entails. The best way to do this is to think about one's own experiences with customer service. What you're looking for is a candidate who places value on helping a customer to feel satisfied, dignified, respected, understood, and appreciated. Look for these types of emotional cues with the candidate's answer to determine whether or not the person has a solid understanding of the foundations of customer-service excellence.

Tell me about a time that you had to go out of your immediate network/job duties to help a customer.

161. Describe the steps you would take if a customer came to you with a problem that was beyond your knowledge and/or responsibilities.

162. Describe a recent situation when you didn't know with whom you needed to speak in organization to get something done. What did you do?

163.   Tell me about a time that you had to go out of your immediate network/job duties to help a customer.

164.   Tell me about a time when you didn't have the answer to a question that a customer wanted right away. What did you do? What was the final outcome?

ANALYSIS: Providing excellent customer service requires doing more than simply what you can do. Look for answers where the candidate recognizes his or her own limitations in terms of authority, responsibility or experience and how willing the candidate is to seek outside help. If an employee applies empathy to a customer-service situation, then he or she will be willing to do whatever it takes to satisfy the customer or at least make sure every option has been explored.

Another aspect to good service orientation is a thorough understanding of the resources available in order to satisfy a client. Make sure to evaluate the candidate based on desire to help as well as efficient and effective methods of attaining the help required.

165. Tell me about the worst customer you ever had and how you dealt with him or her.

166. Describe the steps you would use to calm an angry customer.

ANALYSIS: Some candidates may be reluctant to answer a question like this one, claiming that none of their clients were the worst or angry because they have always been successful at turning any situation into a positive one. If this happens, rephrase the question, making it clear that you're truly interested in hearing about one of the most difficult customers the candidate has ever had to deal with. Continue to probe until you get a specific answer.

What you're looking for in the answer is the specific triggers that the candidate may have in terms of behaviors he or she finds difficult to deal with. The less typical or common behavioral trigger, the lower the likelihood that the candidate will become flustered, stressed or agitated by consumers in general. You should also make sure that the qualities or behaviors mentioned are problematic for the average person. What you don't want in your workplace is an employee whose triggers include behaviors that are not expected to cause any difficulty.

The second aspect of this question is the actual steps the candidate took in order to resolve the situation. Look for answers that indicate the interviewee handled the situation on his or her own and only solicited outside help that was absolutely necessary. Evaluate the answer based on your own sense of how effective and appropriate the intervention was. Look for signs that the candidate's natural style of resolving customer difficulties is in line with the style espoused by your organization.

> **167.**   Tell me about a time that a customer came to you angry (not necessarily at you) and how you worked with that customer to solve the issue.

> **168.**   Have you ever had a customer get angry at something that wasn't your fault? If so, please explain.

ANALYSIS: Often when you work with customers, you are thrust into a situation where you need to deal with a problem that simply was not your fault. A natural tendency in situations like this is to abdicate your responsibility and refer the customer to the person who created the problem in the first place. Not only is this response unacceptable, it also displays a lack of empathy. The customer only wants his or her issue resolved; you need employees who understand this and are willing to take responsibility and help the customer become satisfied.

Look for answers that demonstrate the candidate took immediate action, took responsibility for the problem, and gathered whatever resources were necessary to resolve the situation.

> **169.**   Why is follow-up important in customer service?

170. A customer comes in with a small request. The small request is not a priority for you but you realize that they have the potential to use your services extensively in the future. How do you ensure that the customer has a good experience and will want to come back to you in the future?

171. Describe a situation when you took a stand for a customer.

ANALYSIS: What you looking for in answers to this question is the actual level of commitment the candidate has to providing excellent customer service. The employee never knows if a customer was satisfied or otherwise pleased with the service received unless he or she does something to verify that satisfaction.

The answer doesn't need to be an elaborate scheme, where the customer is phoned or contacted a few days or weeks after the incident. It can simply be escorting the customer to the door, engaging in pleasant small talk, acknowledging the customer the next time he or she comes in, or anything else that actively promotes a positive end to the situation.

172. Give us an example of a time when you used your customer service philosophy to deal with a perplexing problem.

ANALYSIS: This is a question that involves organizational fit. You want to know what the candidate's customer-service philosophy is, and whether or not that philosophy will work in your organization. A candidate's philosophy will be based on his or her values and principles, and it is important that your employees have similar methods for dealing with adversity and can embrace the company's philosophy without compromising their own ideals.

Application: Empathy/Service-Orientation Skills Questions

APPLICANT: Charles Davenport
POSITION: Administrative Assistant

INTERVIEWER: "In this role in administration you will be surrounded by a variety of people. Can you tell me about a time when you needed to understand another person's cultural background in order to work effectively with him or her?"

INTERVIEWEE: "Actually, at my current workplace we have a transfer student from Australia working with us for the summer. She is doing a lot of odd jobs and trying to learn about what it is like working in an American office. As a result, she does a lot of little projects for me, and at first her work ethic really bothered me. She was too relaxed and too methodical for me, and I found myself getting irritated. She was doing the jobs fine, she just wasn't doing them with the same zest that I would have, and I knew it was my issue, not hers. Since I'd never been to Australia or knew any Australians, I invited her over for dinner with our family and we got to talking about her culture and what life was like "down under." Turns out she was equally perplexed by our American vigor—things in Australia move at a slower pace and there is not that sense of urgency we experience here. I felt so good after talking with her, and now I understand where she is coming from."

INTERVIEWER: "As an Administrative Assistant you will often be asked to do things by a variety of internal clients. I'm interested in understanding your approach when dealing with people who may not be satisfied with your responsiveness."

INTERVIEWEE: "Hmmm, I must say that I am very responsive to people's requests. I think it is important to keep everyone satisfied, and as long as my boss is OK with the work I'm doing for other people, then I'm OK with it."

INTERVIEWER: "OK, but what I'm really interested in hearing is a specific incident where someone made a request of you that maybe you didn't have time for or couldn't get to. How did the negative feedback make you feel and what did you do?"

INTERVIEWEE: "There was this time when the sales department was getting me to run their monthly statistics. I really didn't like doing it and didn't think it was really my responsibility so I went to the sales manager and asked for a meeting with him as well as my boss. I knew I couldn't resolve the issue on my own and I knew he needed the stats run, so I was hoping we could all figure out a solution. Turns out the sales manager was considering hiring some part-time help and my boss agreed that I was too busy to be doing the work, so everything ended up fine. The sales manger appreciated my honesty and I felt good knowing that I just didn't dig in my heels but tried to work out a solution."

The interviewer did a good job of explaining the basis for asking the question. Often that explanation at the beginning of the question helps the candidate choose a relevant example and it also puts him or her at ease knowing you have a real reason for asking the question other than simply trying to trip him or her up.

Notice how Charles tried to avoid the "negatively" slanted internal customer question. This is a common avoidance technique, and the candidate will usually slip into a soapbox type answer that everyone is expected to agree with. The interviewer rephrased the question and probed for more information and it worked.

As we get to know more and more about Charles, it is becoming clearer what makes him tick and what his general outlook on life is. Turns out he is quite empathic. This is a bit surprising given his less than stellar interpersonal skills, but what it does indicate is that he has the foundation for resolving conflict and perhaps he just needs some specific training and more experience dealing with actual conflict.

{ Be on the lookout for areas where the candidate may simply require professional development in order to become fully competent in an area. }

Chapter 6

PROBLEM SOLVING

The ability to solve problems is a skill that oftentimes goes unrecognized. People who are good at solving problems often do so at an almost subconscious level. Your role in the interview is to draw out the automatic process that a candidate goes through when solving a problem and then evaluate the overall effectiveness of the approach.

Elements to look for when identifying good problem solvers include:

- Uses a systematic approach.
- Avoids jumping to conclusions.
- Gathers data and facts.
- Deals quickly with the immediate effects of the problem.
- Identifies the most likely cause and contributors to the problem.
- Recognizes that not all problems involve complex solutions.
- Looks at a problem from a practical standpoint first.
- Identifies alternative ways to deal with the problem.
- Uses resources (human and otherwise) to improve the process.
- Thinks pro-actively to avoid problems that have not yet been identified.

Interview Questions for Assessing Problem-Solving Skills

173. Describe a specific problem you solved for your employer. How did you approach the problem? What role did others play? What was the outcome?

174. Describe a difficult problem that you tried to solve. How did you identify the problem? How did you go about trying to solve it?

175. Describe a complicated problem you had to deal with. How did you identify it or gain a better understanding of it?

176. Describe a major problem you have faced and how you dealt with it.

177. Describe a work-related problem you had to face recently? What procedures did you use to deal with it? What was the outcome?

178. Think about a complex project or assignment that you have been assigned. What approach did you take to complete it?

179. Describe a time when you had to analyze a problem and generate a solution.

180. Tell me about a situation where you had to solve a problem or make a decision that required careful thought. What did you do?

ANALYSIS: What you are looking for is an answer that demonstrates the candidate applies a systematic problem-solving method. What you want to make sure of is that this person will not jump headfirst into the problem without taking the steps necessary to make sure that the actions are not going to exacerbate or in any way contribute to the problem. Problem solving is stressful, and sometimes the immediate reaction is to go into "fix it" mode. Unfortunately, a problem can't be fixed unless the causes and contributing factors have been identified.

Look for candidates who recognize that problem solving has two separate focuses: short-term and long-term. The short-term focus is on doing what needs to be done to get things up and running until the entire situation is dealt with. The long-term focus is on solving the problem and making sure it does not happen again.

You want indications that a potential employee is able to remain focused and concentrate on the task at hand and not get too caught up in either the short- or long-term end. The balance between the two is critical, and those people who can manage that balance will be invaluable in a problem-solving role.

181. Describe for me a major project that you worked on where things did not go exactly as planned.

182. Describe a time when you failed to solve a problem.

ANALYSIS: When you ask a question about a negative event, you want to make sure that the answer is not trivial or deceptive. Candidates don't like talking about their failures, but we all know that everyone has had disappointment, and what you want to know is how the candidate handled the adverse situation. What did he or she learn from the experience? Probe to find out whether a similar situation occurred after the experience and how the candidate's reaction was different. Did he or she apply what was learned from the first experience and how successful was the second attempt? The focus here is not so much on what they did wrong, but how they internalized that information and used it, hopefully, to improve their performance in the future.

183. Think of a time when you encountered a problem achieving a goal or objective. Tell me about the process you used to solve the problem.

ANALYSIS: Here, again, what you are looking for is the details to systematic explanation of the process the candidate uses when faced with a problem. Evaluate the approach based on your experiences within the organization and how well you think the approach will fit within the context. Be sure to look for clues to indicate frustration and/or stress levels that might be counterproductive to the problem-solving process. Encourage the candidate to talk about the emotional aspects of problem solving, and determine how well the person handles diversity in general.

184. Tell me about a time when you had to identify the underlying causes of a problem.

ANALYSIS: People often mistake quick fixes with good problem solving; your job is to determine what level of sophisticated problem solving the candidate possesses. Ask the candidate what it was about the situation that made him or her want or need to figure out the underlying causes and how successful the end result was because of it.

185. Tell me about a problem that needed a fast response and how you handled it.

186. Describe an instance when you had to think on your feet to extricate yourself from a difficult situation.

ANALYSIS: This question explores when and where the candidate uses good judgment in determining how quick of a response to a problem is needed. It's important for employees to know that the root causes of a problem need to be explored and rectified, however. There are times that call for quick action. Evaluate the example the candidate talks about to determine whether or not quick action was truly the best option. Other things to consider include the appropriateness of the action, the practicality of the solution, the reaction of other stakeholders, and the overall result. Because this is a problem-solving question, make sure to determine if further investigation was carried out or initiated by the candidate.

187. Tell me about a time when you recognized a problem or an opportunity before anyone else.

What happened? Have you ever recognized a problem before your boss or others in the organization? Explain.

188. Describe a time when you anticipated potential problems and developed preventative measures.

189. Describe a situation in which you forecasted a problem and prepared a strategy for handling it.

ANALYSIS: These types of questions highlight an important aspect of problem solving: pro-activity. Solving a problem after the fact is good, but averting a problem altogether is better. What you are looking for in the candidate's response is the type of clues the person looks for when identifying potential problem areas. Make sure the problem or opportunity discussed warrants the time and energy expended in the effort to avoid or prepare for it. What you don't want is an employee who looks for problems that may or may not be there and takes time away from more productive work. Make sure to ask for details of the outcome and whether or not the solution or opportunity was adequately addressed.

190. Tell me about a time when you missed an obvious solution to a problem.

ANALYSIS: What you are assessing in this question is the level of understanding the candidate has with regard to gathering facts and information before trying to solve a problem. It is very important that employees force themselves to understand the whole situation and think the options through before acting to solve the entire problem. What you are looking for is recognition from the candidate that he or she did not consider all possibilities or use judgment or logic to solve the problem, but rather relied more on instinct and gut feelings.

These things are tough for an interviewee to admit, so you are looking for candor and honesty as well as compelling evidence that the person learned from the situation. The best way to figure that out is to ask how they have performed in similar situations and how well they applied their new knowledge.

191. Tell me about a situation where when you were first presented a problem, you had absolutely no idea how to approach it and how you eventually solved the problem.

192. Tell me about a time when your manager was unavailable and you had to solve an immediate problem. What did you do and what was the outcome?

193. Describe a situation in which you effectively developed a solution to a problem by combining different perspectives or approaches.

ANALYSIS: Here you are looking for a candidate's ability to be creative and innovative in problem solving. Sure, they can have a tried-and-true method all worked out, but often life throws a wrench into the best-laid plans. What you are trying to assess is how well the person can adapt quickly and apply the same principles of systematic processes, logic and judgment to new and unfamiliar situations.

Be especially curious about the resources the person used to begin the problem-solving process. Who did they contact for help or advice and how useful was the information received? A very common element in solving problems is knowing who to turn to when you hit a road block. As always, make sure the end result was effective, and evaluate the candidate on his or her ability to perform a difficult task under trying circumstances.

194. Describe a recent situation in which you asked for advice.

195. Describe a recent situation in which you asked for help.

ANALYSIS: The key to problem solving is recognizing when you have a problem and need help. What you, as the interviewer, want to know is how open the candidate is to actually asking for assistance. It is important to know how to solve problems, but high-performing individuals are the ones most willing to ask for assistance or advice because they know doing so does not indicate weakness or ignorance; it simply acknowledges that they know they don't know everything.

In the same vein, make sure the example described is not one where the candidate was reasonably expected to perform the task on his or her own. If you are in doubt, make sure you probe for all the details and make sure to evaluate the candidate's tendency to ask for help with the overall expectations within your organization.

196. Describe a challenge or opportunity you identified based on your industry knowledge and how you developed a strategy to respond to it.

197. Describe a time when you used your business knowledge to understand a specific business situation.

ANALYSIS: Often specific business issues require specialized approaches. If you decide to ask this question it may because the job for which the candidate is applying requires a set, problem-solving approach. In other cases, you might be interested in finding out how the candidate incorporates technical or otherwise specific information in his or her problem-solving approach. When evaluating the answer, look for evidence that the person used his or her specialized skills to add value to the problem-solving process rather than further complicating the issue by adding irrelevant information.

Follow up with questions about the process and outcome to ensure that the example used was successful because of the candidate's involvement and expertise.

Application: Problem-Solving Skills Questions

APPLICANT: Charles Davenport
POSITION: Administrative Assistant

INTERVIEWER: "As an Administrative Assistant you will encounter many problems and setbacks: some minor and some quite significant. Can you describe for me the last problem you solved at work?"

INTERVIEWEE: "Yes, one of our employees was going on vacation the next week and we had recently changed our policy allowing employees to request their vacation pay before they went on vacation rather than waiting for the next scheduled payday. I know he filled out the request form because I personally received it and then forwarded it to my boss to confirm the employee had enough vacation hours to cover the request. I then returned the request form to the employee's boss for his final approval, and then he was to submit a check requisition to payroll and accounting. When the check didn't arrive, the employee came to me asking for it. I didn't know exactly what happened to the check but I did know he followed the correct process, and somewhere along the line the ball was dropped. I knew I had to get him his check. I called his boss and asked him if he had filled out the requisition. The boss had actually thought our department would fill out the requisition so the paperwork was still in his bin—untouched. I went immediately and got the boss to sign the requisition, and then took it personally to payroll and accounting and asked for a check. The employee had his check the next day and went on his vacation with no problem."

INTERVIEWER: "Was that the end of your involvement?"

INTERVIEWEE: "No, after I had dealt with the immediate problem, I got to thinking that if this type of mix-up happened once, it was sure to happen again, and the whole reason why we changed the policy was to make things easier for the employees, not more complicated and stressful, so I asked for a meeting with my boss and explained what had happened in detail. She knew the basics from my intervention the day before, but now we talked about it in depth. I suggested we re-examine our reasons for sending the request form back to the department manager for signature, and we eventually decided to take out that step and just streamline the process so that we receive the signed request, verify the hours, if the hours are sufficient, then we send the requisition in with a carbon copy to the department manager. The fewer steps in the process, the less chance for mistakes, and we haven't had a repeat problem since."

INTERVIEWER: "Tell me why you decided to intervene on the employee's behalf instead of concentrating on fixing the procedural problem."

INTERVIEWEE: "Well, the way I looked at it was, to fix the process may take a while—you have to analyze what went wrong and then put a plan in place to address it. This employee couldn't wait that long—he was going on vacation the next week. I guess I looked at the benefits versus the costs of helping the employee immediately and then dealing with the problem later, and it seemed the logical thing to do to make the situation right and then fix the whole thing when other people had a chance to get involved."

This time the interviewer started with a very broad question and then honed it down to get the answers he wanted. This is often a good technique because the interviewee does not know the direction the interviewer is going to go. This gives the interviewer a better chance of hearing a description that is less tailored to the situation and may reveal some potentially useful information: good or bad. Charles did a good job with the questions, and with each further prompt, he revealed important details about his problem-solving ability and the way he prioritizes issues during less than optimum conditions.

Notice that the prompts do not provide any clues for the candidate to judge whether his or her answer was good, bad or indifferent. This is an important characteristic of effective probes. Remember, you don't want to lead the candidate to an answer and you don't want the candidate to know whether or not you agree or disagree with the answer provided.

In order to get the most honest and forthright answers, you must give away very little in terms of your personal evaluation. Candidates will pick up on what you tend to approve or disapprove and censor (or augment) future answers accordingly. This doesn't mean you need to be stiff and unfriendly, just eliminate references to how you feel about certain answers, examples or responses.

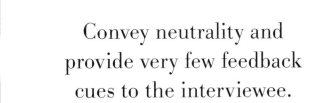

{ Convey neutrality and provide very few feedback cues to the interviewee. }

Chapter 7
ANALYTICAL ABILITY

The purpose of questions regarding a person's analytical ability is to uncover how well the candidate can gather information and extract relevant data. Today's workplaces are rife with information overload, so it is imperative that employees be able to make sense of and analyze vast amounts of information efficiently and accurately. Whether reaching conclusions, solving problems or making valid decisions, a productive employee needs strong analytical skills.

Your job is to determine whether the candidate sitting before you is a sharp thinker. Does he or she recognize the need for systematic analysis and how well does he or she apply it? What you're looking for in the responses are the details of the person's approach to analyzing information. Techniques to listen for include:

- Regularly consulting other sources of information such as the Internet or publications.
- Using visual aids to facilitate the analysis process, such as flowcharts, mind maps or diagrams.

- Conducting "what if" analyses to evaluate a variety of options and outcomes.
- Using established methods to analyze information or data as prescribed by the industry or company.
- Routinely verifying conclusions and the data they are based upon for reliability and validity.

Depending on the work environment, you may be interested in a candidate's analytical skills in individual work and teamwork. Tailor your questions accordingly, and be aware that people may use different strategies depending on the situation, so it is important to get more than one example.

Interview Questions for Assessing Analytical Skills

198. What kind of information have you been required to analyze?

ANALYSIS: This is a straightforward question but it gives you the information you need to determine if the candidate's experience with analytical thinking is suitable for the position.

Some people have experience analyzing numerical data but aren't comfortable with more theoretical and abstract analysis and vice versa; you need to decide if the person's exposure to analytical material is appropriate and sufficient.

199. Describe the project or situation that best demonstrates your analytical abilities. What was your role?

200. What steps do you follow to study a problem before making a decision? Why?

201. Describe a complicated problem you have had to deal with on the job. How did you identify or gain a better understanding of that problem?

ANALYSIS: What you are looking for in this answer is the candidate's overall familiarity and experience analyzing information. The more experience a person has with analysis, the more likely they will employ a lot of techniques to make sure the work is thorough. Probe to get details on the exact methods used and how the analysis contributed to a positive result.

> **202.** Describe a situation where you have gathered and analyzed facts to arrive at a decision.

> **203.** Tell me about a time when you used your fact-finding skills to solve a problem.

ANALYSIS: The less glamorous side of analysis is the actual fact-finding. Candidates may skim over this part of the process and focus more attention on what the findings meant and how they were used. By asking a specific question about gathering facts, you will be able to evaluate the thoroughness of the applicant's approach. You should also listen for enthusiasm and a willingness to participate in all stages of analysis.

> **204.** Can you tell me about a time when you presented complex information to a group of people? What techniques did you use in your presentation?

ANALYSIS: Here is a question where you can determine the candidate's comfort level with using and then presenting visual representations for analyzing information. The saying "a picture is worth a thousand words" definitely applies to analysis, and a candidate who can create visual images to explain analytical data is very competent with the entire process. Use this question to evaluate the level of expertise the candidate has, and compare that with the level needed for the position.

> **205.** Describe for me a time when you used a "what if" analysis of a situation. What was the issue and the outcome?

ANALYSIS: The ability to use "what if" analysis is key to successful analysis of many, if not all, situations. The "what if" process does not even have to be explicit or overly formal. The answers will range from a fleeting thought of, "What if this happens?" to a fully detailed and document-ed analysis. Regardless of the extent of the analysis, what you need to evaluate is the candidate's recognition that "what if" analysis is critical and whether the magnitude of the analysis was appropriate given the situation.

Some people are very analytical and will analyze a situation to death whether it needs it or not. Others will just breeze through the analysis to get to the decision making. Your job is to determine whether the candidate appreciates the value in "what if" analysis and to make sure that they don't engage in elaborate analytical exercises that are not necessary.

Probe for information about the results and how well-received the analysis was. You want to be able to get a good idea of whether or not other stakeholders saw the value in the analysis.

206. Tell me about a time when you had to analyze or interpret numerical or scientific information.

207. When have you been required to analyze detailed, numeric data while being under pressure or otherwise rushed?

ANALYSIS: Analyzing numbers is difficult at the best of times and requires a unique set of skills that are not required for non-numeric data. Numbers are concrete, and there is usually a right and wrong. What you want to know is how well a candidate deals with the precision required. Particularly telling is a situation where the person was under external pressure to complete the analysis. Probe to find out if corners were cut or some other sacrifice was made in order to make the deadline. Try to get the candidate to talk about the process he or she uses and what methods are used to verify accuracy and correctness.

Your job is to determine if the process is reliable. Ask for information regarding the number and type of revisions or corrections required. Does this figure change with work that is done under pressure, or does the candidate's skill and technique hold up under even the most difficult circumstances? What you need to determine is whether the candidate performs with this type of information and whether his or her experience is a good fit for the position.

208. Tell me about a time when you had to review detailed reports or documents to identify a problem.

ANALYSIS: Analyzing written information is another specific skill set that requires excellent reading comprehension and the ability to identify and answer missing elements. Ask what the analysis was for and how the candidate structured the analysis.

Often when analyzing written information, the volume of documents is staggering. What you want to know is how the person organizes the analysis. One approach would be to read through everything word for word, but that is highly time-consuming and costly. What you want to know is how adept the person is at extracting relevant information and then using that information to make a thorough analysis of the problem or situation.

209. Tell me about a time when you had to analyze information and make a decision or recommendation.

ANALYSIS: This is a general question designed to get the candidates talking about an analysis they were responsible for from start to finish. You want to get a complete answer that details the analytical process, and then take that to the next level by determining how confident the person is with the analysis he or she made. Eventually the analysis has to end and a decision or recommendation needs to be made. What you need to evaluate is the candidate's ability to recognize when sufficient analysis has been done and then how willing he or she is to rely on that analysis.

The second part of the question is determining how well the recommendation was received and information about the final outcome. Make sure you get the full scenario before evaluating the candidate. You will probably have to probe to get a full and complete answer. And be prepared for a question like this one to take a long time to answer. Examples of probes to use are: To whom did you make the recommendation? What was your reasoning? What kind of thought process did you go through? Why? Was the recommendation accepted? If not, why?

210. When have you found it useful to use detailed checklists/procedures to reduce potential for error on the job? Be specific.

211. What steps do you follow to study a problem in order to fully understand the situation?

ANALYSIS: Here, again, are technical questions designed to uncover the specific methodology used in analysis. Checking the accuracy and reliability of data is of paramount importance because many very critical decisions hinge on the outcome of a business analysis. You need to be confident that the candidate you choose recognizes the importance of this step and is not willing to compromise accuracy for speed.

212. Describe one of your most difficult analyses.

213.   Recall a time when you were assigned what you considered to be a complex project. Specifically, what steps did you take to prepare for and finish the project? Were you happy with the outcome? What one step would you have done differently if given the chance?

214.   What was the most complex assignment you have had? What was your role?

215.   Please describe a situation where you had to compile a large amount of information in order to complete a task or a project.

ANALYSIS: These questions are designed to get the candidate to reveal which aspects of analysis he or she is least confident with or experienced at. The situation a person feels is most complex or difficult is likely the one that brought up the most anxiety and feelings of doubt. What you are interested in is the outcome and how the situation contributed to the candidate's overall analytical ability to date.

Look for smart analysis of the person's own performance in the situation. If a person intuitively evaluates his or her own performance, that is a pretty strong indicator that analytical thinking is second nature and will be applied to all situations encountered at work and otherwise.

216.   Have you ever had to review proposals submitted by a vendor or by another team? Tell me about one of those situations.

ANALYSIS: Evaluating and analyzing coworkers' and peers' work is difficult. What you want to know is how the candidate prepares for the potential hard feelings or awkwardness once the analysis is complete. This type of question involves empathy and the ability to analyze data within the entire context of a situation and not see just the facts. Remembering that people's ideas and work are attached to those facts is important, and the candidate should be able to demonstrate a sensitivity to and understanding of the interpersonal dynamics at work in a situation like this. Evaluate the appropriateness of the analytical approach as well as how the results and/or recommendations were communicated.

Application: Analytical Skills Questions

APPLICANT: Charles Davenport

POSITION: Administrative Assistant

INTERVIEWER: "I'm wondering how much experience you have had with data analysis. Can you tell me about the last analytical task you performed?"

INTERVIEWEE: "Analytical? You mean solving a problem, like the last questions?"

INTERVIEWER: "Not exactly. Analysis of information deals with gathering together a bunch of information and extracting the relevant data to make a decision, come to a conclusion, or solve a problem. I'm looking for more information on times when you had to wade through large amounts of data and compare the information or make some kind of judgment about the information you collected."

INTERVIEWEE: "Oh, alright. That's easy. Just recently our photocopy lease was up for renewal and my boss needed to decide whether to continue with the current service or try out someone else. She asked me to gather information on different providers in the area and what they offered, their prices, that sort of thing. So I got her the information, and she ended up deciding to stick with our current guy."

INTERVIEWER: "I'd like a bit more detail. What information did you provide and how did it make her decision-making process easier? Walk me through what you did."

INTERVIEWEE: "I started with the Yellow Pages and made a list of all the services available in our area. I called the first company on the list and asked a bunch of questions and did the same thing with the next three or four companies. What I was finding was that I was getting slightly different information from each place, like some offered five-year leases and others three years, some included un-limited service calls; stuff like that. So because of these differences, their prices varied. What I ended up doing was making a master list of questions and then I created a spreadsheet where I was able to convert all prices to a per-year basis and then used the number of service calls we received over the last year as an average to figure out how much that would cost on a yearly basis. Eventually I came up with a pretty accurate yearly cost of the service for all of the compa-nies. I also included a column on reputation and years in business so it wasn't all just based on dollars. I explained my reasoning to my boss and she agreed with my process and then made a decision."

INTERVIEWER: "From what you learned during this process, what do you think is the most important aspect when doing an analysis?"

INTERVIEWEE: "Making sure you are comparing apples to apples. Gathering the information was just the first part; the critical aspect was breaking down that information and making it usable."

INTERVIEWER: "Now that you understand what I'm talking about when I refer to an analysis, what would you say is your overall experience level with analytical tasks?"

INTERVIEWEE: "Overall, I figure I've had moderate experience with it. This photocopy assignment was probably the largest analysis I've done, but I do break down training information and office costs, that sort of thing, for my boss pretty regularly. The big formal analysis is less frequent. I like it, though, and I think I have a good grasp on what it takes. My first big assignment turned out pretty well and I didn't get a lot of outside assistance so I feel confident in my ability to do analytical work, if that counts for anything."

With this scenario, the interviewer needed to explain a term in order to help Charles fully understand what was being asked of him. In this case, Charles gave an explicit clue that he wasn't clear on what analysis meant, but often you will have to pick up on an applicant's misunderstanding and quickly correct him or her. Don't feel awkward doing this; just explain that you're not getting the information you need, and place the responsibility for the misunderstanding on yourself. Never make the candidate feel ignorant or otherwise insulted; remember, it is your responsibility to extract the information you need to make a solid hiring decision.

After one prompt for more detail, Charles provided a very detailed account of the steps he took in his analysis. What the interviewer did next was ask opinion questions to get a sense of how Charles felt about his performance. The example was very clear and included a very well thought out and executed analysis. The interviewer didn't feel the need for more detailed explanations so he chose to get information on Charles' experience with analysis in a different way.

Opinion questions are just that—someone's opinion, which means they are neither right nor wrong, they simply are. However, in this case, the opinion questions gave the interviewer valuable information about analytical skills without getting into another detailed description of an analysis. You may want to use this technique for competencies that you are interested in but don't necessarily have time to cover completely. If you do choose to use opinion questions (or other non-behavioral questions), make sure you include them in your structured interview plan and ask them of all the candidates.

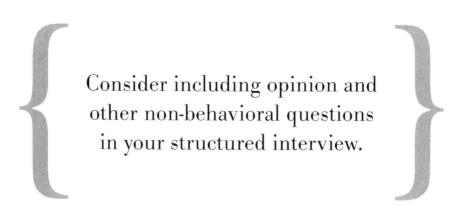

Consider including opinion and
other non-behavioral questions
in your structured interview.

Chapter 8
DECISION MAKING

The ability to make good decisions is a finely tuned skill that requires good judgment and self-confidence. Good judgment is the ability to know how to balance making decisions based on facts, data and observations versus using intuition and gut feelings. The more times a person makes a successful decision, the more confident he or she becomes in making decisions, and subsequent decisions are then made with more conviction. What you, as the interviewer, need to determine is where on the decision-making cycle the candidate is.

The questions to ask in the decision-making section should focus on the candidate's awareness of his or her own decision-making process. How much objectivity versus subjectivity goes into the decision, and was there a difference in emphasis when the decision turned out to be poor or excellent? Three components you are looking for are:

Judgment
Demonstration of a balance between reliance on facts and intuition.

Self-confidence

Demonstration of a belief in one's own capability to make a good decision.

Persistence

Demonstration of perseverance and stamina in the face of negative feedback or other adversity.

When evaluating candidates in this section, be on the lookout for confidence in the areas of judgment, analysis and instincts.

Equally important is the ability to make decisions under pressure or time constraints. The workplace is often fast-paced, and candidates who need to uncover every detail before taking action will hold back progress. Look for an appropriate balance between acting too hastily and not acting at all. Finally, you need to understand how the candidate will react in a situation where the decision is criticized or even turns out to be wrong. There is always an element of uncertainty in any decision, so choosing a candidate who can handle constructive feedback and take responsibility are crucial in the workplace.

Interview Questions for Assessing Decision-Making Skills

217. Tell me about a difficult decision you had to make. What information led you to make the decision that you made? What other possible solutions were there? What was the final outcome?

218. What was the biggest decision you made in the past three months? Tell me about the process you went through to make it.

219. What was the most difficult decision you made in the last six months? What made it difficult? How did you formulate this decision?

220. Give me an example of a time you had to make a difficult decision.

221. Give me a specific example of a time when you used good judgment and logic to make a decision.

222. What is the most difficult decision you've had to make? How did you arrive at your decision? What was the result?

ANALYSIS: Your intention with these types of questions is to get the candidate talking about how he or she goes about making decisions. What type of analysis does he or she use? Where does prior learning and experience fit in? Does the candidate have a track record of success? Ultimately, you want to hire a person who can and does make solid, well-thought-out decisions when faced with difficult circumstances.

223. Describe two examples of good decisions you have made in the last six months. What were the alternatives? Why were they good decisions?

224. Recall for me a time when you had to choose between several alternatives. How did you evaluate each alternative?

225. When you evaluate different choices, what are the criteria you use? Give me a specific example.

226. Tell me about the tools and techniques you use to help your decision-making process.

ANALYSIS: When evaluating decision making skills, it is important to get the full picture—sometimes people claim to make difficult decisions, but when all the details are uncovered, the decision itself wasn't difficult, rather the situation was. A difficult decision is one where there are valid alternatives from which to choose. What separates a good decision maker from an average, or even poor, one is the ability to choose the best option. Listen carefully to the alternatives described, and make a judgment about the actual difficulty of the decision. Also make sure to evaluate the candidate on how he or she ends up choosing a course of action. What you want to hear is the analytical and problem-solving processes the candidate employs.

227. Tell me about the riskiest decision that you have made.

ANALYSIS: Risk exponentially increases the difficulty of making a decision. Here what you are looking for is a sufficiently risky situation combined with a thorough analysis of the situation and a positive result. Risk also tends to delay decision making, so make sure to inquire about the timeline. This will enable you to determine if the candidate struck a good balance between analyzing the problem and taking action.

228. Describe a recent unpopular decision you made. How was it received? How did you handle it?

229. Tell me about a time when you made a decision and then had to justify that decision to your superiors.

230. Tell me about a time when you made a decision and then felt you had to defend your decision to coworkers or staff.

ANALYSIS: These questions will help you uncover the candidate's confidence in his or her decision-making skills. It is extremely difficult to make an unpopular decision or one that is doubted. The only way the decision is successfully defended is if the analysis has been done and the alternatives clearly evaluated. What you are looking for is whether or not the candidate did dot all the "I's" and cross all the "T's." Listen for how prepared he or she was for criticism.

Another important element of this question is interpersonal skills. It is difficult to keep composure when you feel attacked or questioned. Evaluate the candidate's method for dealing with the criticism and make sure it was appropriate and professional.

231. Give me an example of a time when you had to be quick in coming to a decision.

232. What kind of decisions do you make rapidly? What kind takes more time? Give examples.

233. Describe a situation where you handled decisions under pressure or when time limits were imposed?

234. Describe a situation where a prompt and accurate decision on your part was critical. What did you consider in reaching your decision?

235. Describe a situation in which you had to draw a conclusion quickly and take speedy action.

ANALYSIS: Time pressures provide a prime influence for making fair or even poor decisions. What you want to know is how much time the candidate has taken and if he or she is willing to take shortcuts with the analysis portion to come to quicker decisions. Sometimes, however, a situation calls for quick action. What you need to determine is whether the speed of the action was justified and what steps the candidate took to do a thorough analysis after the fact and/or run damage control if necessary. Quick decision making is one thing, preparing for and handling the consequences is quite another. Listen and probe for details about what happened after the decision was made and what the ultimate outcome looked like.

> **236.** Give me an example of when taking your time to make a decision paid off.

ANALYSIS: Here you want to know why the decision-making process was emphasized over the timeliness. Make sure the length of time was a result of the situation rather than the candidate's reluctance to actually make a decision.

> **237.** Describe a time in which you weighed the pros and cons of a situation and decided not to take action, even though you were under pressure to do so?

> **238.** Tell me about a time when you took a public stance on an issue and then had to change your position?

ANALYSIS: This is another question that judges a candidate's commitment levels to their decision-making processes. Those who use a well-planned, thorough and well-executed process have no reason to second-guess themselves. What you are looking for is overall conviction as well as information about how the candidate handled the opposition. Do they continue to make efforts to keep all the stakeholders informed and satisfied, and do they handle criticism or negative feedback with professionalism?

239.   Give me an example of a time when there was a decision to be made and procedures were not in place? What was the outcome?

240.   Tell me about a time when you had to make a decision without all the information you needed. How did you handle it? Why? Were you happy with the outcome?

241.   Give me an example of a time when you had to keep from speaking or making a decision because you did not have enough information.

ANALYSIS: While there is always a level of uncertainly in decision-making, sometimes a person is forced to make a decision even when there is a glaring hole in the analysis. This is the type of question where you will be evaluating the candidate's overall experience with decision-making. The process will not be thorough so the candidate needs to demonstrate how well he or she can depend on judgment and past experience to make reasonable decisions. This type of competence comes with experience, so probe to find out how often the person is confronted with situations like these and what his or her overall success rate is.

242.   Tell me about a decision you made in the past that later proved to be a wrong decision. Why was it wrong? What would you do differently now, if anything, in making that decision?

243. Tell me about a situation where you made a poor decision and had to live with the consequences?

244. Give me an example of when your work contributed to making a wrong decision. What was the outcome? What, if anything, would you do differently?

ANALYSIS: Accepting responsibility for a poor decision is hard, and no candidate wants to admit in an interview that he or she actually made a poor decision. However, what you need to know is how the candidate dealt with the consequences. Listen for any sign of excuses or attempts to spread the blame. What you want in an employee is someone who can stand behind good decisions as well as bad ones.

To alleviate the candidate's discomfort, shift focus to the learning process the candidate went through. Has he or she used what was learned to make future decisions? Try to determine if the setback affected the candidate's confidence. It's OK to be leery of making decisions for a while, but you don't want to hire an employee who is constantly second-guessing himself or trying to avoid important decisions altogether.

Application: Decision-Making Skills Questions

APPLICANT: Charles Davenport

POSITION: Administrative Assistant

INTERVIEWER: "Charles, can you tell me about a time when you had to make a decision very fast? What was the situation and outcome?"

INTERVIEWEE: "Oh gosh, fast decisions scare me, but I know sometimes you have no choice. Well, certainly the decision to help that employee get his vacation check was done quickly, but it turned out well in the end because I followed up on it."

INTERVIEWER: "In our office we work with production schedules that change with sales forecasts. Sometimes that means taking whole new directions at the last minute. Can you think of an example where you had to make a decision to completely shift focus?"

INTERVIEWEE: "The only thing I can think of is when we get behind with a project. I know that I have my own tasks and responsibilities, but sometimes those have to be altered for the benefit of the department and company. In those situations I make a decision to help out my coworkers, knowing that I will be swamped later on, but the consequence is worth it."

In this situation, the interviewer recognizes quickly that Charles' experience with quick decision making is not completely relevant to the position. Since the interviewer has already had a chance to evaluate analytical and problem-solving skills, he decides to cut this section short and move on. While structured interviews are set up so that every candidate is asked the same questions, if you know that a candidate does not have relevant experience in that one area, it is futile to belabor the point.

What the interviewer did was ask the question and then use a specific work explanation in order to assist the candidate to come up with a more relevant example. Clearly, Charles has not worked in an environment that required him to make quick decisions, and that may be due to the level of responsibility and authority he has had. The interviewer knows how he makes decisions based on his answers to previous questions and it is also quite unlikely a "real" interview would examine these three interrelated competencies separately. Remember that behavioral interviews are time-consuming, so you must determine which competencies are most critical to job success, and then ask detailed questions in those specific categories.

{ Focus your interview on the five
or six competencies most critical
for success in the position. }

Chapter 9
TEAMWORK

Working in a team environment is almost a mainstay of modern work. Whether the team is formally recognized, long-term, short-term, or simply a group of people working toward a common goal, the ability to work with others is imperative. Working within a team context is unique in that all members are equally valued, and it is the sharing of resources and expertise that makes for enhanced production. It is also a prime situation for differences in opinions, styles of work and other interpersonal issues to surface.

What you are looking for is a person who recognizes the value of teamwork and understands that to be effective, all members must collaborate. The result of this collaboration is called synergy—where the team's output is better than the performance of the strongest individual team member. Questions in the teamwork section focus on what the candidate believes to be true about effective teams and what role he or she has played on effective and ineffective teams. Look for the following:

- Recognition of what a team is.
- Understanding of synergy.

- Willingness to accept other opinions.
- Openness to different processes and procedures.
- Ability to persuade others.
- Ability to think objectively.
- Ability to motivate.

Some people mistakenly think teamwork happens when employees are willing to help each other out, cover for each other, occasionally provide input and advice, etc. True teamwork is much more complex than that and involves people working together because they truly appreciate that a collective of talents, expertise and ideas will produce superior results.

Interview Questions for Assessing Teamwork Skills

245. Describe a time when you were a member of a team or group that had to achieve a goal or solve a problem. What type of team or group was it? What was the team or group trying to do? What was your role? How did you contribute to the team or group? Was the team or group successful?

246. Can you give me an example of a team decision you were involved in recently? What did you do to help the team reach the decision?

247. What have you done in past situations to contribute toward a teamwork environment?

248. Describe a project you were responsible for that required a lot of interaction with people over a long period of time.

249. Tell me about a time when you had to rely on a team to get things done.

250. Describe a situation in which you were involved in a project as part of a team.

251. Describe the types of teams you've been involved with. What were your roles?

252. Describe a team experience you found rewarding.

253. Tell me about a course, work experience or extracurricular activity where you had to work closely with others. How did it go? How did you overcome any difficulties?

254. Tell me about a time that you had to cooperate with members of other departments to solve a problem.

255. Think of a time when you worked effectively in a team situation. Describe how you felt about the contributions of the others on the team.

256. Tell me about a time when, if it hadn't been for teamwork, your goal might not have been achieved.

257. Give me an example of one of the most significant contributions you made as a member of a high-performing team. What, in your opinion, made it a high-performing team?

ANALYSIS: All of these questions are designed to get the candidate talking about what being a member of a team means to him or her. Notions of teamwork are very diverse, and you need to determine if the person's experience with teamwork is adequate for your company's work environment. As mentioned, not all perceptions of teamwork are the same, so you need to figure out if the candidate will fit in well within the type of team environment evident in the company.

Look for indications of the extent of teamwork; what the candidate thinks teamwork is; the candidate's idea of cooperation; what role does the candidate assume in a team situation; what qualifies as an effective team; what makes a team experience enjoyable; etc.

Listen closely for indications of the candidate's true commitment level to working in a team as well as his or her enthusiasm to do so. Most people realize that teamwork is expected, but not all people appreciate the difficulties that are involved with teamwork. Sometimes it's easier to accomplish a task on your own, but the result will not be as good as the one that an effective team accomplishes. Determine for yourself whether the candidate is "talking the talk" or if he or she "walks the walk."

258. Tell me about one of the toughest teams/groups you've had to work with. What made it difficult? What did you do?

259. Sometimes it can be frustrating when trying to get information from other people so that you can solve a problem. Please describe a situation you've had like this. What did you do?

260. Tell me about a time when you worked with a classmate or colleague who was not doing their share of the work. How did you handle it?

261. Tell us about a time in the past year when you had to deal with a difficult team member and describe what you did.

262. Give me an example of a situation where you had difficulties with a team member. What, if anything, did you do to resolve the difficulties?

263. Tell me about a time when you had to work on a team that did not get along. What happened? What role did you take? What was the result?

264. Describe a team experience you found disappointing. What would you have done to improve the outcome?

265. Tell me about a time when you were on a team and one of the members wasn't carrying his or her weight. What did you do to try to prevent this?

ANALYSIS: Teamwork is rife with conflict, disillusionment and frustration. Working closely with other people who have different values, styles, expertise, experience, perceptions, work ethics, etc., is very difficult. What you need to determine is what triggers frustration in the candidate and what he or she does to get over it. Listen for the use of interpersonal and conflict-resolutions skills that preserve a professional working environment but that make sure everyone in the team is heard and understood.

Be alert for clues that might indicate the candidate is more the cause of the conflict than part of the solution. These people typically discuss what other people did and take little or no responsibility for the difficulty. They concentrate their answers on what went wrong and may even express disgust or disdain for the actions of others. Effective team members present conflict as a shared dynamic and focus more on the solutions than the problems.

266. Give me an example of when you were on a team that failed to meet its objectives. What could the team have done differently?

ANALYSIS: This question is designed to get the candidate to think objectively about the team's overall performance. Make sure the candidate takes adequate responsibility for the failure and discusses his or her performance and how it contributed to the ineffectiveness. What you don't want is a candidate who focuses on what other people did wrong and maintains a righteous view of the situation. Also look for indications that the candidate espouses a team approach when discussing what should have been done differently. You'd be surprised at the number of people who will say things like, "If they had done it the way I'd suggested…" as part of their answer to the solution.

267. Gaining the cooperation of others can be difficult. Give a specific example of when you had to do that and what challenges you faced. What was the outcome? What was the long-term impact on your ability to work with this person?

268. Describe how you felt about a decision the team wanted to make that you didn't agree with.

269. Describe a situation where the team was having trouble agreeing on a decision and what you did to facilitate consensus.

270. Describe a situation where others you were working with on a project disagreed with your ideas. What did you do?

271. Describe a situation in which you had to arrive at a compromise or help others to compromise. What was your role? What steps did you take? What was the result?

ANALYSIS: One of the main challenges of working within a team is getting and maintaining cooperation. The whole idea of teamwork is to bring together different opinions and perspectives in the hopes of creating a better outcome than any one person could come up with. These interpersonal differences are what make coming to a consensus so difficult. What you are evaluating is the candidate's appreciation of these differences and what strategies he or she uses to handle the mixture constructively. Of particular interest is the role the individual plays in the situation. Do they tend toward mediator, reconciliatory, judge, compiler, evaluator, etc.? Evaluate the answer in terms of fit with the current team as well as appropriateness of the role.

> **272.** Tell me about a time where you were a member of a team and had to encourage everyone to participate.

> **273.** Give me an example of something you did that helped build enthusiasm in others.

ANALYSIS: With these inquiries, you are trying to determine how much spirit and enthusiasm the candidate brings to a team situation. Some people are very comfortable in a motivational or inspirational role and others are not. Use this information to again evaluate overall fit with the current team and demands of the role.

> **274.** Tell me about a team where you were the leader. How did you promote the effectiveness of your team? What were the results?

275. When dealing with individuals or groups, how do you determine when you are pushing too hard?

ANALYSIS: Use these questions if the candidate is applying for a role that is expected to take on a leadership role within a team. While most teams have specified leaders, it is also true that some people emerge as a leader due to their expertise or experience and will fluctuate between roles depending on the project. Listen for signs of leadership but with a definite tendency toward egalitarian methods of gaining cooperation and buy-in. An autocratic leadership style is not conducive to teamwork, so make sure to evaluate the fit and appropriateness.

Application: Teamwork Skills Questions

APPLICANT: Charles Davenport
POSITION: Administrative Assistant

INTERVIEWER: "We work as a team in our office with everyone pitching in and helping out. Occasionally we also work on larger projects that require a team effort. Can you tell me about a project-specific team that you worked on?"

INTERVIEWEE: "Sure, it was when we were putting together the new policy and procedure manual. There were four of us working on the project—we needed to get input from the various departments to make sure the policies made sense and were actually practical. The whole reason for the revamp was because some of the policies were out of date and others were not even relevant. We met every week for a month and a half, and we each had our own responsibilities that we put together to create the finished manual. It was a lot of work and I know I couldn't have done as thorough a job if it was just myself and my boss working on it."

INTERVIEWER: "What role did you take on within the team?"

INTERVIEWEE: "Well, at first I was kind of the leader. It was my overall responsibility to complete the manual but whomever had the most expertise in the area we were discussing ended up being the leader for that section. Because we all had very different experiences with the manual, and reasons for wanting it updated, it worked out well."

INTERVIEWER: "Can you tell me about any conflicts you had during the process, how it was resolved, and what the outcome was?"

INTERVIEWEE: "The conflicts were a result of our differences in focus. Because I'm part of the admin group, my main concern was clarity and ease of use, while the other people were more concerned about the specifics of the policy and how it would affect the department or specific jobs, so we had a few heated discussions about wording and relevance, but one person in the group was always able to take the role of mediator and help us work through it. I think what made it such a strong team was that not everyone had a strong interest in every section so there was always someone who could be objective and help set the priorities."

INTERVIEWER: "What I'd like is some detail on a specific conflict you were faced with and how you handled it."

INTERVIEWEE: "Well, this other guy and I were at odds a few times over quality of work. Like I said, we each had certain responsibilities that we were expected to complete for each meeting. This guy was obviously completing his stuff minutes before the meeting and it was sloppy, unorganized and incomplete. Because this was a team effort, I thought we should discus it as a team. At the beginning of the next meting I added "quality of work" to the agenda and opened the topic up to comments. Everyone else had the same problem with the guy, so I didn't have to be the bad guy, and peer pressure worked to get him to improve his reports and assignments. It worked out really well."

INTERVIEWER: "So, in a team environment when there is conflict between two members, how do you deal with it?"

INTERVIEWEE: "I think that it is up to them to deal with the problem directly. If you have a problem with someone, you should be able to discuss it openly and work it out. That's what we did with the guy who was doing sloppy work and it worked out."

What we see in this scenario is the interviewer probing to affirm what he already suspected about the candidate's interpersonal skills. Charles' answers were quite vague and general, so he was prompted to provide specifics. What he revealed was confirmation that he does not deal with conflict directly but gets others to intervene. In this case he made a personal issue part of a team meeting in hopes that others would deal with the issue and allow him to avoid the responsibility.

The interview used a final probe to get Charles' opinion about dealing with interpersonal conflict and he again slipped into a generalization that was in line with what we are "told" is the right way to deal with conflict. What this proves is that behavioral interviewing is the key to finding out what a candidate really does, rather than what they know they should do. Remember to probe for as much specific detail as you need to uncover a candidate's actual behavior. If the candidate tries to generalize or give opinions when you want real examples, gently but firmly ask for specifics. You might have to ask a few times, but make sure you persist. As you can see, real examples will reveal the most insightful and relevant information.

{ Continue to probe for specific details that will confirm your opinion about a candidate's competency in a certain area. }

Chapter 10
ORGANIZATION

An efficient employee is an organized one. The ability to establish a course of action for yourself (and/or others) is essential for accomplishing goals thoroughly and on time. Organization requires proper planning of assignments and allocating resources. Time spent organizing and planning will ensure steps are not missed, timelines are met, and tasks are prioritized. To be well organized, a person must employ particular tools and techniques. Look for evidence that the candidate uses a variety of strategies to remain focused. Examples include:

- Daytimer
- Planning calendars
- To-do lists
- Flow charts
- Visual planning software (e.g.,. GAANT charts)
- Timelines
- Scheduling software
- Whiteboards
- Filing systems
- Regular meetings

What you are looking for is examples of when these types of tools have been used and how well they have helped the candidate improve the efficiency and completeness of his or her work. Evaluate the candidate's answer on how well and often they use organizational tools, how well they prioritize tasks, and how they deal with deadlines. The purpose of organization is to avoid the stress and pressure associated with time crunches and procrastination, so make sure these are not problem areas for the candidate.

Interview Questions for Assessing Organization Skills

276. Are you able to schedule your time? How far ahead can you schedule?

277. Can you walk me through last week and tell me how you planned the week's activities and how the schedule worked out?

278. How do you schedule your time? Set priorities?

279. Describe a time in school when you had many projects or assignments due at the same time. What steps did you take to get them all done?

280. What have you done in order to be effective with your organization and planning?

281. Give me an example of when your ability to manage your time and priorities proved to be an asset.

282. Tell me about a project that you planned. How did you organize and schedule the tasks? Tell me about your action plan.

ANALYSIS: With these questions you are establishing the candidate's preference for and use of organizational tools. Which tools does the candidate use? Evaluate whether or not the tool is sufficient for the magnitude of the project. While a to-do list might be adequate for a project with a timeline of a few days, large projects require schedules and timelines and other long-term planning tools. Try to find evidence that the candidate uses a variety of planning tools and is flexible enough to adapt to the situation at hand.

Another avenue to explore is how much time the candidate spends planning. Neglecting the planning phase is detriment to productivity but so is over-planning. People who plan every detail may have trouble adapting to changes in schedules, priorities, etc., and may spend more time organizing their work than actually doing their work. If you have doubts, use probes to determine if the candidate strikes a healthy balance between the two extremes.

283. Describe a time when you had to handle multiple responsibilities and how you managed it.

284. How do you handle doing twenty things at once?

285.   We often have multiple tasks to accomplish in a day. Tell me about a time when you had to handle many competing priorities. How did you plan your time? What were the results?

286.   Describe a situation that required things to be done at the same time. How did you handle the situation? What was the result?

287.   How do you prioritize projects and tasks when scheduling your time? Give me some examples. How do you determine priorities in scheduling your time? Give me an example.

288.   Tell me about a time when you were particularly effective at prioritizing tasks and completing a project on schedule.

289.   If you are faced with two pressing projects and only have time to complete one, how will you decide which one to complete? Try to use an example from real life.

290.   How do you decide what gets top priority when scheduling your time?

291.   How do you determine priorities in scheduling your time? Give examples.

ANALYSIS: With this line of questioning what you are trying to determine is whether or not the candidate is willing and able to prioritize. When there are competing tasks and deadlines it is very difficult to determine which projects get worked on and when. What you want to hear about are specific situations when the candidate had to prioritize tasks and on what basis the determination was made. Without any express planning and forethought, often the more enjoyable or easier tasks are worked on. What you want to know is how the candidate goes about filling his or her work schedule. What considerations are made for competing deadlines and large workloads?

> **292.** We all have had times when we just couldn't get everything done on time. Tell me about a time when this has happened to you.

> **293.** We have all had occasions when we were working on something that just "slipped through the cracks." Can you give me some examples of when this happened to you and what were the results?

> **294.** At one time or another we've all forgotten to do something important for a customer. Tell me about a time this happened to you recently. What did you forget? Why? What happened?

ANALYSIS: Even the most diligent of planners will miss a deadline or forget to do something. What you are interested in is what circumstances led to the mistake and then how the situation was corrected.

The purpose of asking this question is not to embarrass the candidate or make him or her feel uncomfortable, so make sure you put more emphasis on the final outcome and what was learned. What you are trying to determine is how the candidate's experience has made him or her a better organizer or planner.

295. Has your time schedule ever been upset by unforeseen circumstances? Give me a recent example. What did you do then?

296. Tell me about a situation you observed or were a part of where there were time and/or resource constraints. What happened? Why?

ANALYSIS: The best-laid plans are inevitably put to the test. What you want to know is whether or not the candidate anticipates this type of change. Does he or she build in contingency plans or extra time to accommodate change? Listen carefully for how well the candidate prepared for and then dealt with the unforeseen circumstance. Probe for more examples and determine how well the candidate responds to change in general.

297. What objectives did you set for this year? What steps have you taken to make sure you're making progress on all of them?

ANALYSIS: This question deals with a candidate's ability and willingness to set long-range plans for himself or herself. It is not uncommon for employees to get too task-oriented and their planning calendars are just a long laundry list of to-do items. A candidate who recognizes the power of planning will use those same tools to set professional goals. What you are looking for is whether or not the candidate takes a more strategic outlook to their day-to-day tasks and sees how his or her accomplishments fit into the company's big picture.

298. Tell me about a time when you were given a deadline by someone of higher authority which could not possibly be met. How did you handle it?

299. Tell me about the last project you worked on that had a fixed deadline.

300. Describe for me a time when you missed a deadline. What was the result and what did you learn from the experience?

301. Can you tell me about a time when you rushed the completion of a project, sacrificing quality for efficiency?

ANALYSIS: Deadlines are inevitable and can be stress inducing if you don't plan adequately for full completion of a project. What you want to know is how well the candidate responds to deadlines and what factors contributed to missed deadlines. Of equal importance is the recognition that quality and completion should not be rushed just to make a deadline.

Communication is important in all projects, and you should look for evidence that the candidate keeps all stakeholders informed about the progress and status of a project. This type of process will more often result in modified deadlines rather than missed ones.

302. Give me an example of when you were able to meet the personal and professional demands in your life yet still maintained a healthy balance.

303. Describe a time when you had to make a difficult choice between your personal and professional life.

ANALYSIS: This is an interesting line of questioning that helps you determine overall fit with the company and its values and ideals. Of course, a balanced lifestyle is the ultimate goal but some workplaces have more of an emphasis on this than others. If your workplace is fast-paced, go, go, go, then you need employees who are willing to sacrifice their personal life for certain periods of time or under certain circumstances, and the opposite is true as well. Planning and organization will help a person maintain balance but, ultimately, personal and professional lives will collide. You have to use your best judgment to determine a candidate's fit with your company.

> **304.** Tell me about a time when you needed to keep a wide variety of people updated or informed on an on-going basis. What steps or process did you use to accomplish your task? What were the results?

ANALYSIS: With this question you are evaluating the communication processes a candidate builds into his or her overall project plan. As mentioned in another question, keeping stakeholders up to date on your progress is the best way to ensure no one is surprised with a result. Look for specific evidence that the candidate plans to communicate and then follows through with the communication. Determine whether the communicating method used was appropriate and sufficient, and question the candidate about how well the information was received and understood (refer to the communication skills section for more ideas).

Application: Organization Skills Questions

APPLICANT: Charles Davenport

POSITION: Administrative Assistant

INTERVIEWER: "Needless to say, the job of an administrative assistant requires excellent planning and organization skills. Tell me how you planned your last week of work."

INTERVIEWEE: "Typically what I do is sit down with my boss every Monday morning and we review what needs to be done. I make notes and then plan out my week's activities. What I like to do is use a Daytimer that has all the days of the week on one open page. That way I know what is coming up and what to prepare for."

INTERVIEWER: "What exact types of activities do you track in your Daytimer?"

INTERVIEWEE: "I use it to write deadlines or meetings or when certain projects are supposed to be complete. I like to have those reminders so I don't forget to do something important or miss a deadline or meeting or something."

INTERVIEWER: "Well, that brings me to my next question. Can you describe for me a time when you did miss a deadline? What happened and what was the result?"

INTERVIEWEE: "Well, it doesn't happen very often but a few months ago when we were in the final stages of putting together that new policy and procedure manual, I was a few days late submitting our employee's benefit claims. The project was in my Daytimer so I did plan to complete it but unfortunately I got so busy that I didn't even see it. I was concentrating so heavily on my other project. Thankfully, I was able to call and fax the claims directly to the person responsible for processing, and she was able to process the requests on time. What I've done since then is use bright yellow highlighter to mark each of my deadlines and other important dates in my Daytimer. I can't miss the yellow and it leaps up at me from the page every week."

INTERVIEWER: "Besides your Daytimer, do you use any other planning tools on a regular basis?"

INTERVIEWEE: "No, not really. My Daytimer is really all I need. It works for me and now that I can't miss seeing my deadlines, I haven't had a problem. I am a naturally very organized person—you should see my desk—so my Daytimer is my way of backing up the information that I store in my brain."

INTERVIEWER: "Can you relate for me a time when you had to cut corners in order to complete a project on time?"

INTERVIEWEE: "I'm not the type who cuts corners. There are times when I realize I didn't get everything done in a day that needed to be done so I just stay late and complete the work properly. I am very committed to my job and I will put in whatever time is necessary to complete the job properly. I have a strong work ethic, and I don't see myself ever being able to sacrifice quality for speed."

The interviewer sets up this section with a note about how important organizational skills are to the job for which the candidate is applying. When the candidate doesn't provide enough information in response to the first question, the interviewer asks specifically for more details. The interviewer immediately recognizes a flaw in the candidate's organizational skills—he relies on a Daytimer to plan deadlines and major events but there is no daily task planning or prioritization mentioned, so the interviewer probes further to make sure this initial evaluation is valid. When the interviewer receives confirmation that the candidate has only one organizational tool, his red-flag concerns are confirmed.

The warning signs were there, and the interviewer capitalized on the situation making sure to provide the candidate with more opportunities to fully explain his planning techniques. With this interview, it is interesting to note that the last question in the section affirms why effective planning is so important. If the candidate did use a daily to-do list or some other prioritization process, he would not have to stay late to complete work. Use each section of the interview to confirm or deny opinions you've formed and evaluations you've made. The more supporting evidence you can gather for your final decision, the more confident you will be when making the decision.

{ Use each section of interview
questions to confirm or
deny previous evaluations
you have made. }

Chapter 11

MOTIVATION

An employee's motivation is one of the most important factors in employee productivity. A paycheck only motivates to a certain degree; after that, other factors need to be present to drive an employee to perform good work. Those other factors are the activities and responsibilities that provide personal satisfaction as well as job satisfaction. What you are looking for is an employee who is motivated to do a good job because he or she derives intrinsic satisfaction from knowing that a job was done well.

Signs that an employee is internally motivated to do good work and accomplish high levels of productivity include:

- Active goal setting.
- Understanding how their role fits into the big picture.
- Determination.
- Persistence.
- Participation in professional development.
- Willingness to learn new things.
- Positive approach to challenges.

- Task initiation rather than acceptance.
- Providing a positive influence in the workplace.

What you need to assess in this section is how likely the candidate is to need external rewards and other forms of explicit recognition in order to do a good job. Obviously, what you want is an employee who is self-motivated to do excellent work and who does not accept any less, regardless of the accolades received or recognition given. Ultimately you will have to evaluate the fit of the candidate's motivation needs with the motivational elements provided by the company.

Interview Questions for Assessing Motivation

305. Tell me about an important goal that you set in the past. Were you successful? Why?

306. Give me an example of the most significant professional goal you have met. How did you achieve it? What were the obstacles? How did you overcome them?

307. Give me an example of when you have worked the hardest and felt the greatest sense of achievement.

308. Give me an example of an important goal that you have set in the past, and tell me about your success in reaching it.

309. Give me an example of when you took a risk to achieve a goal. What was the outcome?

310. What are your future professional goals? How do you plan to achieve them? What might keep you from achieving them?

311. Tell me about a time when you set and achieved a goal.

312. What were your objectives for last year? Were they achieved? How?

313. Tell me about a performance standard that you have set for yourself. How are you working towards meeting that standard?

314. Tell me about a time when you overcame great obstacles to achieve something significant.

ANALYSIS: With these questions you are trying to determine how goal-oriented the candidate is as well as how likely he or she is to actually set goals for himself or herself. Some people are very good at achieving goals that are set for them, but those people who actively set their own goals are the ones who are continuously striving to improve and perform at higher levels than expected. On the other hand, you want to be sure that the candidate is not the type who sets goals but doesn't actually follow through with them. Make sure you get a complete picture of the goal-setting process as well as the result.

The other portion of these questions you need to consider is how the person actually tracks his or her progress. This is another valuable indicator of how motivated the person is by goal setting. Evaluate how well the candidate keeps track of his or her goals and whether there are intermediate steps along the way that are recognized as achievements. Highly motivated individuals use these short-term accomplishments to bolster their drive to the end.

> **315.**   Describe a situation when you were able to have a positive influence on the actions of others.

> **316.**   Relate a scenario where you were responsible for motivating others.

> **317.**   Describe a situation when you were able to have a positive influence on the action of others.

ANALYSIS: Motivating yourself is one thing, motivating others is quite another. What you want to know is whether the candidate is able to remain upbeat and enthusiastic about company-wide goals and if that enthusiasm is infectious. Use these inquiries to determine if the candidate is likely to take on a "championing" role within your organization and help motivate others to accomplish company-wide objectives.

> **318.**   How would you define "success" for someone in your chosen career?

> **319.**   What are your standards of success in your job/ school? What have you done to meet these standards?

320. In your position, how do you define doing a good job?

ANALYSIS: This question will provide invaluable clues into what motivates the candidate to perform at an exemplary level. Use the answer to determine if the candidate is more or less motivated by extrinsic factors than intrinsic ones. The employees who will require less maintenance and attention are the ones who use internal feelings of satisfaction and pride to gauge when a job has been performed successfully. Listen for examples where the candidate did not receive external recognition but still knew he or she was successful.

321. Give an example of when your persistence had the biggest payoff. Give me an example of when you achieved something by your persistence that others couldn't.

322. Please describe a time when you were successful at an activity only after repeated attempts.

323. Describe a situation in which you persevered with an idea or a plan even when others disagreed with you.

ANALYSIS: Persistence in the face of challenge or adversity is the mark of a highly motivated individual. What you need to determine is whether that persistence is channeled in an appropriate manner. There are people who persevere even when the end result is so longer valid or relevant. These people, though highly motivated, are misguided and may not be the most productive people on your team. What you need to determine is whether the persistence paid off in terms of benefit to the company or benefit to the individual. What you want is an employee who works tirelessly to achieve corporate objectives and doesn't lose sight of the overall goal just to prove a point or meet a personal challenge.

> **324.** Give examples of your experiences at school or in a job that were satisfying.

> **325.** For what kind of supervisor do you work best? Provide examples.

> **326.** Give me an example of a time when a project really excited you.

> **327.** Tell me about the things you like about your current or most recent job.

> **328.** Under what conditions do you work best?

ANALYSIS: These questions are designed to uncover what external factors the candidate considers motivating. Self-motivation is wonderful but we all need to work in an environment that is pleasing and enjoyable. Figure out what it is about a situation that makes it satisfying for the candidate, and then compare those characteristics to what the workplace offers and determine if there is a good fit. Since motivation is one of the keys to productivity, you are best to start off with employees who will find your company a desirable place to work.

329. Tell me about a time when you were given an assignment that was distasteful or unpleasant.

330. Tell me what your least favorite part or parts are of your current or most recent job.

331. Your supervisor asks you to complete a task that you cannot stand doing. How do you react to him or her?

ANALYSIS: It's easy to get motivated by a project or situation that is interesting and exciting, but the true test of one's motivation is how one reacts when the circumstances are less than inviting. The purpose of these questions is twofold: determine what the candidate dislikes and how he or she reacts to an undesirable situation. It is good to know upfront what duties or circumstances are unpleasant for a candidate and then evaluate the likelihood of encountering those situations in your workplace. More people leave positions for reasons of fit than all other reasons combined, so it is critical to make sure the candidate you hire has a fighting chance from the start.

The other aspect is, of course, how the candidate approaches situations that are least favorable. Every job carries a certain number of elements that are less than optimum, and you need to determine if the candidate approaches these tasks with negativity and disdain or if he or she is able to dig "way down deep" and find something motivating about the situation even if it is just the thought of finishing.

332. When was a time that you were most dissatisfied with your work?

333. All jobs have their frustrations and problems. Describe some examples of specific job conditions, tasks or assignments that have been dissatisfying to you.

334. Give examples of your experiences that were dissatisfying.

ANALYSIS: What you are trying to evaluate with this type of question is how the candidate reacts to and recovers from disappointment or dissatisfaction. Again, we are talking about attitude, and what you are looking for is a genuine ability to see the positive in any situation. Look for candidates who focus more on what they learned from the experience and are able to see the benefit of the situation. Those who concentrate on the negative aspects of the situation tend to be stuck in the negative and are not as likely to motivate themselves to recover, learn and move on.

335. Describe a really tough or long day and how you dealt with the situation?

336. How have you motivated yourself to complete an assignment or task that you did not want to do?

337. Describe a time when you were unmotivated to get a job done?

338. Have you found any ways to make school or a job easier or more rewarding?

ANALYSIS: These are direct questions designed to uncover a candidate's ability to self-motivate. You will learn what the candidate values and feels is important for his or her own satisfaction. Evaluate your work environment against those factors to determine the level of fit for the organization. Certainly anyone who is successful at self-motivation is well suited to most positions, but the better the overall fit, the better the chances of developing a long-term employee.

339. Describe a situation where you were asked to assume responsibility for something you had never handled before.

ANALYSIS: Here is a question that involves motivation and confidence. Answers you want to hear are ones that include some trepidation but overall excitement and honor at being given the responsibility. High motivation levels are excellent but they have to be kept in check by a realistic sense of what one is and is not capable of doing with the skills and resources available. Look for answers that include seeking outside assistance and expertise to complete the task as well as the typical strategies of goal setting and intrinsic rewards. There is a fine line between being motivated and "up" for anything and biting off more than one can chew. It is your job to determine if the person in front of you has a healthy respect and understanding of his or her own abilities and limits.

Application: Motivation Questions

APPLICANT: Charles Davenport

POSITION: Administrative Assistant

INTERVIEWER: "Charles, I'd like to switch gears a bit and get to know a little more about you and specifically what you find motivating."

INTERVIEWEE: "I love responsibility. I am really motivated when I know my boss trusts me to complete my work and doesn't feel the need to check up on me or hover over me. Not that I don't take direction well, because I do. I just work my best when the onus is more on me to ask for questions and clarification rather than my boss assuming I need help or assistance when I don't. I think I'm also like a lot of other people in that I like to hear that I'm doing a good job or that my work is appreciated. No one needs to take out a big ad in the paper but a genuine 'thank you' every once in a while certainly makes we want to work extra hard."

INTERVIEWER: "So, tell me about the last time you felt really unmotivated to do something."

INTERVIEWEE: "Well, I guess every month when I know the filing has to be caught up I cringe a little inside. It's not my favorite task but I know it has to be done so I set up a little competition with myself. I went to my boss with the idea when I realized I was letting the filing slip more and more. I set a time that I have to have all the filing done—there are no excuses and no second chances—if I get it done in time, I can come to work 30 minutes later one day in the next month. We've been doing it for over a year and I only missed one month."

INTERVIEWER: "Describe for me the things you have liked about your workplaces."

INTERVIEWEE: "As I said before, responsibility and autonomy are really important. It's also important that the people in the office are respectful and professional. We had a receptionist for a while that was rude and foul-mouthed and it really brought the whole office morale down, so pleasant people are important. And it may sound silly but it's important that the office be clean. When I was in college I temped at a few places that were dirty and it really turned me off. For me to do a good job I need to know that the boss or owner takes as much pride in his operation as I do in my work."

INTERVIEWER: "Our office is based on the team approach, so I would like to hear about a situation where you motivated others to complete an assignment or do a good job."

INTERVIEWEE: "I think I motivate others just with my optimism and positive outlook. I really try not to bring negativity into the workplace and I know others see me as a role model, of sorts, when it comes to the right attitude for the job."

INTERVIEWER: "Can you describe a specific situation where you did something overt, or beyond just displaying a positive attitude, to motivate someone else?"

INTERVIEWEE: "I guess what I do is use a lot of praise and encouragement and try to pay extra attention to the person in order to cheer them up. Like last week our receptionist was feeling down because her husband had left on a three-week business trip. What I did was invite her to dinner with my wife and I one night and I also made sure to be extra helpful and appreciative of the things she did. After the first week, I noticed her attitude changed and she thanked me for being so considerate. That felt good."

This section is very insightful. The interviewer is discovering more personal aspects of Charles' personality and preferences that will allow him to make a valid assessment of Charles' ability to fit into the company culture. Notice that she starts off with an opinion question rather than a behavioral one. This is a deliberate attempt to get Charles thinking about what motivates him. Often we are unaware of our motivations so it helps to stimulate the thought process early on in the questions in order to avoid weak or incomplete answers later.

You'll also notice that Charles has more difficulty with this line of questioning than the others and, again, that is likely because motivation is a competence that has an ethereal quality to it. It's hard for a candidate to give a specific answer to what he or she finds motivational, so it is your job to pull the information out of him or her with effective, and perhaps numerous, probes. It is common for candidates to revert to opinions and generalizations when the questions get a little deep and personal. That's OK; just make sure you are prepared to probe further, and don't relent until you get the information you need.

The final issue to consider with competencies that are considered essential to most jobs is the candidate's anticipation of these exact questions.

Charles did offer responses that could be considered canned, pre-prepared or even coached. Always be leery of generalizations, and make sure you insist on getting detailed, specific examples of times when the competency was actually demonstrated. Be understanding of the candidate's unfamiliarity with behavioral interviewing but don't let up until you have an answer with which you are satisfied.

{ Be on the lookout for canned or coached answers, and insist on specific, detailed examples for all of your behavioral questions. }

Chapter 12
INITIATIVE

Initiative is often confused with motivation, and although the two competencies are related, they are unique. Initiative refers to an employee's ability to be a self-starter and see work without explicit directions or prompts. Initiative is generally what separates an average employee from an exceptional one. The average person satisfies the job description, and the exceptional one sees it as a starting point for future responsibility.

You want to hire people with initiative because you know and trust that task will be accomplished with minimal levels of supervision and direction. Highly self-directed employees understand how their roles fit into the mission and vision of the company and they find ways to enhance the company with every task or project they take on. Characteristics to look for include:

- Proactive
- Capable
- Risk-taker
- Visionary
- Dedicated

- Strategic

Your goal with these questions is to determine how well the candidate recognizes the importance of going beyond what is expected and doing what is needed. There is no room for "that's not in my job description" comments, so you have to be diligent in determining how far above and beyond the call of duty the applicant is really willing and able to go.

Interview Questions for Assessing Initiative

340. What did you do to prepare for this interview?

ANALYSIS: Here is a question most candidates are not expecting—they expect to be asked what they know about the company but not what they did to prepare. The beauty of it is the fact that you can easily verify if they did what they claimed by asking for a few facts they should have uncovered.

Aside from the element of surprise, this question is an ultimate initiative question. How much further than checking out the company Web site did the candidate actually go to understand what the company was about? A candidate with a strong answer to this question almost qualifies for an "Advance to 'GO' and collect $200 (or get the job)" card.

341. Give an example of a time when you went above and beyond the call of duty.

342. Tell me about some projects you generated on your own. What prompted you to begin them?

343. Tell me about a time when you did more than was expected of you.

344. Give me an example of a time when you were given a project and did more than was required in order to exceed someone's expectation.

345. Describe a time when you decided on your own that something needed to be done, and you took on the task to get it done.

346. Give me examples of projects/tasks you started on your own.

347. How have you demonstrated initiative? Tell me about a time when you demonstrated the most initiative.

348. Tell me about a project you initiated. What did you do? Why? What was the outcome? Were you happy with the result?

349. What have you done in your present/previous job that went beyond what was required?

ANALYSIS: These classic initiative prompts will provide valuable information about what specific activities a candidate feels are "above and beyond the call of duty." Some people think taking his or her coffee of cup to the sink is a stretch, while others stay late, pick up the slack, identify new projects, etc. You need to evaluate whether the candidate's idea of initiative and supporting examples are worthy of being considered exceptional.

350. Describe for me two improvements you have made in your job in the past six months.

351. Describe any significant project ideas, etc., you have initiated or thought of in the past year. How did you know they were needed and would work? Where they used? Do they work?

352. Give me an example of time when you made a suggestion that would improve operations, either through cost cutting, increasing profits, streamlining a system, etc.

353. What have you done in the past that demonstrates your commitment to continuous improvement?

354. What proactive steps have you taken to make your workplace more efficient and productive? Specifically describe a policy, project or system you created or initiated.

355. Tell me about a suggestion you made to improve the way job processes/operations worked. What was the result?

356. Tell me about a time when you improved the way things were typically done on the job.

357. Describe something you have done to improve the performance of your work unit.

358. Describe something you have done to maximize or improve the use of resources beyond your own work unit to achieve improved results.

359. Describe how you have improved the productivity of your most recent assignment.

ANALYSIS: Many employees do what they do the way they do it because that's the way it's been done for years and years. An employee with initiative and drive will think critically about the way things operate and come up with suggestions to improve efficiency, productivity or both. Employees who see how things ought to be done are the type of people who that make positive contributions to the workplace.

360. What are some of the best ideas you have ever sold to a superior? What was your approach?

361. Describe some projects or ideas (not necessarily your own) that were implemented or carried out successfully primarily because of your efforts.

362. Tell me about a time when your initiative caused a change to occur.

363. Give me an example of a situation that could not have happened successfully without you being there.

364. What was the best idea you came up with during your professional or college career? How did you apply it?

ANALYSIS: This is your opportunity to determine how useful the candidate's suggestions for improvement really were. There is a difference between constructive change and changing simply for the sake of it. Your job is to determine how practical and well founded the candidate's ideas and plans were. You don't necessarily want someone who is too radical or intent on transformation unless that is the sort of work environment your company encourages.

365. Tell me about a situation where you attempted to improve something and you were met with resistance. How did you handle the situation?

ANALYSIS: These negative situation questions are always very revealing. You need to get a complete understanding of the situation and then try to understand what exactly about the idea was poorly received. Perhaps it was premature or not well planned or maybe the consequences weren't fully explored; whatever the reason, what you want to know is how the candidate dealt with the reaction and how it impacted his or her motivation to initiate projects in the future. Be sure to explore what the candidate learned from the situation and how it impacted the process used to evaluate and present other new ideas.

366. Give some instances in which you anticipated problems and were able to influence a new direction.

367. Describe a situation in which you recognized a potential problem as an opportunity. What did you do? What was the result? What do you wish you had done differently?

ANALYSIS: Often initiative is born out of necessity, and while the average employee will sit back and let the boss deal with problems down the road, the employee who is driven and sees the big picture will recognize the opportunity and devise a plan to address it. What you want to know is how successfully the candidate developed a proactive solution to a problem before it even became a problem. Candidates who provide solid answers to these types of questions deserve serious consideration; however, recognize that not all interviewees will be able to come up with appropriate or relevant answers. Work with what you get and make the best evaluation you can.

Application: Initiative Questions

APPLICANT: Charles Davenport

POSITION: Administrative Assistant

INTERVIEWER: "We were just talking about motivation, and now I'd like to focus on initiative. Please tell me what initiative means to you."

INTERVIEWEE: "Initiative means seeing work that has to be done and doing it without having to be asked."

INTERVIEWER: "Give me an example in the last week where you demonstrated initiative."

INTERVIEWEE: "It's kind of silly but around our office it is really a big deal. We don't have a coffee service so we supply our own coffee and make it in the company's coffee maker. By the end of the week it is an atrocious mess and, like I said, I hate dirty workplaces so I often take it upon myself to clean it up midweek before the cleaning company comes in on the weekends. It doesn't take much time and it is a good way for me to use my spare time, when I have any. I often go out of my way to do little things like that around the office that no one else thinks to do."

INTERVIEWER: "Can you describe for me a time when you suggested an improvement in a process or system that was implemented by the company?"

INTERVIEWEE: "Well, that whole policy and procedure manual update was my suggestion. Since I'm the one who deals with most of the forms, I realized that the information on lots of them was no longer relevant. I knew it would be an involved task but I also knew there would be a lot of time saving once all the new policies were in place. So I went to my boss and explained the situation, she had me present the idea to the owner and he agreed it was time for a revamp so we went ahead and did it. I actually got a lot of positive feedback about the new manual and many people said they had the same idea but never wanted to tackle such a large task."

INTERVIEWER: "Tell me about a suggestion you made that wasn't well-received or implemented. How did you feel and what did you do?"

INTERVIEWEE: "You know, I don't think there ever was a time that I made a suggestion that wasn't implemented. I'm pretty good at analyzing the outcome and all the possible problems before I make a suggestion. If anything, I guess I'm cautious. I see where change is necessary, but unless I'm pretty sure my idea has merit, I don't talk about it."

INTERVIEWER: "Tell me about some ideas you've had that you haven't presented."

INTERVIEWEE: "I did want to revamp the payroll system. We use such a manual process and I thought we could improve it. I sat on the idea for a few months and then my boss announced that we were getting a new software system for payroll and all human resource functions. Whether my idea would have sped up the process, I'm not sure, but I know I wasn't in a position to suggest a new software system because changes that involve that kind of money are left up to management."

INTERVIEWER: "Tell me more about that. What other sorts of decisions are best left to management?"

INTERVIEWEE: "Certainly anything to do with significant amounts of money. Other decisions include staffing. I wanted to suggest the sales department get some part-time help a long time before they did, but I kept quiet about my helping them because I didn't think it was my place to say anything. I try to go to my boss when I'm having difficulty with another employee—the whole discipline and performance area is another thing left for management. Some people are so belligerent that the only ones who will get through to them are mangers."

Charles's answers to the first part of this section are very impressive, but he opens the door to some close examination of his beliefs and perspectives on management vs. staff roles. It seems Charles' reliance on management to solve interpersonal issues stems from his deep-rooted sense that that is their job. This may or may not be an attitude you choose to work with, but the interviewer was very astute and probed for more details even though her questions deviated from the realm of initiative. It is important not to get so focused on your questions that you miss opportunities to get impromptu bits of information that reveal more about a candidate than any prepared question could.

The whole idea of interviewing is that it is a structured conversation. Keep in mind that the structure comes from standard questions; the conversation element relies on a natural flow of questions and answers. If the candidate is heading in the wrong direction, reel him or her in; if the candidate heads into a different direction than expected, evaluate the usefulness of the information and proceed as appropriate. No information is bad information; your job is to extract the most relevant information, and if a candidate offers something that is potentially beneficial, you need to be flexible enough to capitalize on the situation.

{ Remain flexible throughout the interview and be open to probing for information outside the competency being investigated. }

Chapter 13
STRESS MANAGEMENT

Stress and pressure are in abundance in today's workplace, and the presence of either often brings out employees' worst behaviors, habits and attitudes. Some stress is motivating, yet too much stress can be debilitating, not to mention a serious health concern. What you, as the interviewer, need to assess is whether the candidate has developed mechanisms to cope with stress and whether the strategies are successful.

Some of the more common stress-management tools to be aware of include:

- Identifying stress triggers.
- Eliminating stressors.
- Reducing the intensity of emotional reactions to stress.
- Moderating physical reactions to stress.
- Building physical reserves.
- Maintaining emotional reserves.

Be aware that most people know what they should do manage stress in their lives; your job is to determine if they actually can and do manage it.

Interview Questions for Assessing Stress-Management Skills

368.   Tell me about a high-stress situation when it was desirable for you to keep a positive attitude.

369.   Tell me about a decision you made while under a lot of pressure.

370.   Narrate a situation in which you experienced a particularly high level of stress.

371.   Describe a time where you were faced with problems or stresses that tested your coping skills.

372.   Give me an example of a high-pressure situation you have faced this past year and how you resolved it.

373.   Describe a time when you were in a high-pressure situation.

374.   Give me an example of a time you worked under extreme stress.

375.   Tell me about a stressful work situation you have experienced and how you dealt with it.

376. Describe a project or goal that has caused you frustration.

377. Give me an example of a high-pressure situation you have faced this past year and how you resolved it.

378. What kinds of pressures did you feel in your job? Tell me about them. How did you deal with them?

379. Describe situations that you have been under pressure in which you feel you handled well.

ANALYSIS: All of these questions are designed to help you understand the candidate's acknowledgment of stress, and determine what types of situations induce stress. What you want to hear are details and specifics. Everyone will say they take stress in stride or they try to "get it out of their system," but your job is to uncover what exact strategies the candidate uses to actually accomplish this. It may take some persistent probing, but you really need to assess the candidate's ability to perform under pressure.

Critically examine the coping tactics used and determine how practical they are. Potential interviewees usually anticipate stress questions, so you have to make sure the answer you get is not rehearsed or designed to be impressive. Make sure to ask for a few examples, and the more recent the situation, the more likely the strategy will be used in your workplace.

380. Describe the level of stress in your job and what you do to manage it.

381. What do you do to manage stress?

382. How do you manage stress in your daily work?

383. Describe how you work when you are under pressure.

384. Tell me about the work pace at your previous job?

ANALYSIS: These questions are important because they allow you to evaluate whether or not the stress level at your company is more or less intense than what the candidate is used to. It is certainly more difficult to adapt to a more stressful environment, but if the candidate has strong coping strategies, then that will mitigate the situation. Overall, these are fit questions, and you will have to determine if the candidate is suitable for the expected work environment.

385. What are your stress triggers?

386. How do you know when you are under stress?

ANALYSIS: Often the first and most important component of dealing with stress is recognizing the early warning signs. Candidates that have developed techniques to counteract the early signs of stress are more likely to effectively combat stress in general. Use these question as lead-ins to the questions that specifically ask for stress-management techniques.

387. Who do you go to for support when you are stressed or under pressure at work?

388. After a difficult day, how do you alleviate your stress?

389. Tell me about a time when you were under stress and a coworker stepped in to help you.

ANALYSIS: What you are trying to evaluate here is the extent that the candidate uses external resources to help fight stress. Having outlets for stress relief is very important, and you need to know if the candidate is able to ask for and use the assistance available to him or her. Coworkers and family members are common sources of stress relief but exercise clubs or other hobby groups are often useful as well. Try to determine how varied the candidate's approach to stress management is. The more resources the person employs, the higher the likelihood of success.

390. Tell me about a time when your boss was under a lot of pressure. What did you do?

ANALYSIS: Recognizing when others are under pressure is an important element of a strong team player. Using others for support is helpful but offering your own support is invaluable. A candidate who can give and receive support during stressful situations will be a valuable addition to your team.

391. How do you handle the pressure of dealing with a very irate customer, coworker or other person you encounter on the job?

392. Describe a time when you lost your temper.

393. Describe a situation when you had to exercise a significant amount of self-control.

ANALYSIS: Professionalism is so hard to maintain when a person is stressed and feeling attacked. Use this type of question to find out how the candidate behaves in the most stressful and uncomfortable situations. What are the things that cause the lid to blow? Don't penalize the person for being honest, and be suspicious of the candidate who replies he or she has never behaved poorly. Focus on what was learned, and use the answers to other stress-related questions to determine the likelihood of it happening again.

394. Describe a recent situation that you just couldn't handle.

ANALYSIS: It's important to know a candidate's breaking point before making a hiring decision. Everyone has different levels of coping, and you need to know what situations the candidate just can't deal with, and then make a fit evaluation based on that information. Obviously, the situation should be something that most people who find unbearable. If the candidate expresses an inability to handle a moderate amount of stress, then he or she is not a very strong choice as an employee. As always, evaluate the answer in context and ask for details to make sure you understand the full situation.

> **395.** Describe a time where stress from your personal life threatened to interfere with your work. What did you do?

ANALYSIS: Personal and professional lives often mix, but when stress from home affects work, that is a huge problem. Focus your attention on the coping mechanisms and strategies used rather than the personal issue that was causing the stress. You don't want to get into the details of someone's personal life, but you want to know what was done to make the situation bearable at work.

Application: Stress-Management Skills Questions

APPLICANT: Charles Davenport

POSITION: Administrative Assistant

INTERVIEWER: "Finally, I want to talk about stress management. Can you tell me what your current workplace is like in terms of stress and pressure?"

INTERVIEWEE: "There are times like when quarterly or year end reports are due or if we have a large deadline to adhere to. Mostly it's pretty casual and we all get along fairly well, so there's not a lot of stress happening between us."

INTERVIEWER: "Can you tell me about a particularly stressful time that you encountered recently and how you handled it?"

INTERVIEWEE: "We have a client who has been dealing with our company for over five years. He wasn't happy about an invoice that was sent to him and I happened to be covering for payroll and accounts that day. Well, this guy is tearing a strip off me on the phone and I can hardly get a word in edge-wise to tell him that I'm not familiar with the invoice but I'll investigate and get back to him. I hadn't ever been talked to like that in a professional capacity so it was all I could do to remain calm. Eventually I was able to get him to agree to wait until I found the invoice and reviewed it. I looked up the invoice and couldn't find anything wrong with the amount but I knew I wasn't going to be able to deal with him when he realized he wasn't going to get any satisfaction, so I explained the situation to the accounting supervisor and he handled the phone call. I'm not even sure how it all ended up because the next day I was back at my own little desk, happy that I didn't have to deal with irate customers in my job."

INTERVIEWER: "Tell me about what triggers stress for you. Use a specific example."

INTERVIEWEE: "Well, that irate customer sure got my dander up. I knew I was getting stressed because my heart started beating fast and I could feel my face turning red. I just couldn't believe someone would attack the way he did. Other times when I've been stressed I've started to shake and I could feel the adrenaline rushing inside me. Luckily, I'm an avid jogger so I can get all the tension out on a regular basis that way."

It was pretty obvious from the start of this topic that Charles' ability to handle stress is not that great. His tendency to pass difficult interpersonal issues on to someone else was also evident. The interviewer received answers that confirmed other information she had about Charles and so she chose not to probe further or ask for more details. Interviewing is time-intensive so there is not point in getting more information than you need.

{ Know when you've gathered
enough detail to make a defensible
evaluation of the competency
and of the candidate overall. }

Chapter 14

SUMMARY OF INTERVIEW TIPS

You've followed Charles' interview through 11 competencies. What should be clear is that interviewing is a conversation that is set within pre-identified boundaries. Be open and flexible with the flow of conversation and remember that you are in control. Your goal is to get the information you need, so ask as many follow-up questions as necessary.

Here is a summary of the key tip or technique identified in each section of Charles' interview:

- Use explanatory lead-ins to supplement your behavioral questions, making them relevant to your company and the position.
- Probe, probe and probe some more—you never know what gems of information you will pick up.
- Be on the lookout for areas where the candidate may require some professional development in order to become fully competent in an area.
- Convey neutrality and provide very few feedback cues to the interviewee.

- Consider including opinion and other non-behavioral questions in your structured interview.
- Focus your interview on the five or six competencies most critical for success in the position.
- Continue to probe for specific details that will confirm your opinion about a candidate's competency in a certain area.
- Use each section of the interview questions to confirm or deny previous evaluations you have made.
- Be on the lookout for canned or coached answers and insist on specific, detailed examples for all your behavioral questions.
- Remain flexible throughout the interview and be open to probing for information outside the competency being investigated.
- Know when you've gathered enough detail to make a defensible evaluation of the competency and of the candidate overall.

Chapter 15
OTHER COMPETENCIES

The interview with Charles covered 11 competencies—double what a typical interview would cover—and there are many more competencies that could have been presented in detail. The next section is a compilation of interview questions for seven more areas of competence that you may choose to evaluate. Use the list of questions to develop your own behaviorally based structured interviews.

Ethics and Integrity

What you are assessing with ethics and integrity question the degree of honesty and trustworthiness a candidate displays, as well as the likelihood that the person will take responsibility for his or her actions and make decisions that are in the best interest of the company rather than for personal gain.

Use these questions to uncover the following:

- Does the candidate have the character required to avoid unethical, inappropriate and illegal behavior in the workplace?
- Will this person adhere to his or her values and principles in the face of significant pressure to compromise?
- How easily will this person cave into pressures and act in ways that are not appropriate or even illegal?
- How honest is the candidate?
- Is this person loyal?
- Is this person reliable?
- Does this person respect confidentiality?

Ethics and Integrity Questions

396.   Tell me about your level of integrity.

397.   What will your references tell me about your integrity?

398.   Describe a politically sensitive situation that you were in and how you handled the situation.

399.   Tell me about a time when you knew you made a mistake but there was little chance of anyone else finding out. How did you handle the mistake and what was the resolution?

400. Tell me about a time when you bypassed your supervisor and went to your supervisor's supervisor to handle a situation.

401. Tell me about a situation that illustrates your ability to exercise good judgment.

402. Describe a situation where you had to keep information confidential.

403. Describe a situation in which you promised more than you could deliver. How did you handle it?

404. Give me an example of time when you chose to be completely honest, even when doing so was risky and potentially damaging for you.

405. Tell me about a time when you believe someone broke unwritten rules or violated acceptable business behavior. What was your role and what happened?

406. Can you tell me about a situation when you had to bend the rules to get the job done?

407. Tell me about a time when someone challenged your integrity. How did you handle it?

408. Describe a recent moral or ethical dilemma you have encountered.

409. Recall for me a time when you were aware that a fellow employee did something inappropriate, unethical or illegal? What did you do?

410. Explain to me a situation where you withheld information from your supervisor. What was the reason and the outcome?

411. Tell me about a time you may have taken credit for someone else's work.

412. Tell me about a time when you did the bulk of the work for a team assignment. How did you handle the team recognition versus personal recognition?

413. Describe the types of personal activities you do on work time.

414. If you knew your company was committing a serious legal violation, what would you do?

415. Have you ever resigned from a position because you felt company ethics were not being adhered to? Tell me about the situation.

416. Tell me about a time when honesty was not the best policy.

417. On what occasions have you been tempted to lie?

418. Describe for me a time when your boss gave you an order that violated company policy.

419. Have you ever been fired? Tell me about it.

420. Tell me about a specific time when you had to handle a tough problem which challenged fairness or ethical issues.

421. Discuss a time when your integrity was challenged. How did you handle it?

422. Tell me about a time when you experienced personal loss or disadvantage for doing what was right. How did you react?

423. Tell me about a situation when you were asked to do something that you thought was a conflict of interest. How did you deal with the situation?

424. Please relate for me an experience where you found out a coworker was taking work supplies for personal use. What did you do?

425. Have you ever intervened on behalf of an employee who was not being treated fairly? Tell me about it.

Chapter 16
WORK ETHICS AND PROFESSIONALISM

These questions assess the likelihood that the candidate will perform at high levels of productivity long after the initial "best first impression" phase is over. What you are looking for is a candidate who performs his or her work with professionalism and makes decisions that are in the best interest of the company. Attributes addressed include:

- Accountability
- Commitment to quality
- Composure
- Dedication
- Dependability
- Diligence
- Positive attitude
- Responsibility

Work Ethic and Professionalism Questions

426.   Tell me about a last-minute assignment that put you under a short deadline. How did you accomplish the task on time? How accurate was your end result?

427.   After being given an assignment, how do you prepare to "tackle" the assignment?

428.   Tell me about a time when you were sick or had other personal commitments that got in the way of completing an assignment on time.

429.   What is the best job you have ever done on an assignment? What do you use as your own personal benchmark for success?

430.   Tell me about a time that you exceeded a coworker's or boss's expectations.

431.   It is 30 minutes before the end of the official workday. You have just finished a large project. What do you do in those last 30 minutes of the day?

432.   Is there a particular experience that stands out as one you never want to repeat because you did not meet your normal standards of performance? Explain the situation.

433. Tell me about a time when you were asked to complete a task that you didn't know anything about. How did you complete the task? What was the result?

434. Describe a time when you went above and beyond the call of duty.

435. Recall for me a time when you made a personal sacrifice in order to help a coworker meet his or her deadline or job responsibility.

436. Tell me about a time when you were late or absent to work. How did you communicate that to your supervisor? How many workdays have you missed in the last year?

437. Tell me about the most challenging task you have ever been faced with. What did you do to meet that challenge?

438. Would you describe yourself as someone who goes the extra mile? Tell me why.

439. Would you describe yourself as task-oriented or concept-oriented? Tell me about it.

440. Describe for me a time when you filled in for someone who had different or lower-level responsibilities than your own?

441. Recall for me the last opportunity you took to keep informed or up to date professionally.

442. Describe something you have done that demonstrated professionalism.

443. Tell me about your last performance review. What areas were exemplary and what areas needed improvement?

444. Tell me how you compose yourself after things have not gone as planned or expected.

445. Give me an example of how determined you are.

446. Has anyone ever criticized your work? If so, how did you handle it?

447. Give me an example of how you saw a project through despite numerous obstacles.

448. Tell me about one of the most difficult work experiences you have ever had.

449. Tell me about a time when your diplomacy skills were really put to the test.

450. Tell me about a time when you felt you did not perform to expectations.

{ Some workplaces are more structured than others, but there is always a fundamental set of rules and regulations that apply. }

Chapter 17

COMPLIANCE

All workplaces operate within a set of rules. Some workplaces are more structured than others, but there is always a fundamental set of rules and regulations that apply. Some rules are explicit and others may be more cultural or "that's the way it's done around here." The compliance section allows you to determine a candidate's respect for and adherence to these rules. Your job is to assess the following:

- Ability to follow established guidelines.
- Understand and respect for policies and procedures.
- Recognition of the importance of consistency.
- Level of impulsive behavior.
- Ability to stick to a routine.

Compliance Questions

451. Give a specific example of a policy you conformed to with which you did not agree.

452.   Tell me about a recent business problem you solved. How did you utilize organizational structure (policies, systems, etc.) to solve the problem?

453.   Tell me about a time when you knowingly disregarded an organizational policy. Why did you choose to disregard the policy? What happened?

454.   Tell me about a time your organization was unable to keep a commitment you made. What happened?

455.   Give me an example of a time when you made a decision only to find out later that it was rejected. Why was it rejected? Why, do you think, was it not approved through your systems?

456.   Give me an example of a time when a company policy or action hurt people. What, if anything, did you do to mitigate the negative consequences to people?

457.   Recall for me a time when a coworker violated a company policy. What was your reaction and what was the outcome?

458.   What is the farthest you have to bend your standards in order to succeed?

459.   Tell me about a time when you had to follow a superior's orders when you did not agree with them.

460. Describe a time when you were given specific procedures to complete your job but knew that if you skipped some of the formalities, you could complete your job more quickly. What did you do?

461. Tell me about a time when you discovered a quality issue. What did you do to address the problem?

462. Recall for me a time when you ignored a safety violation or broke a safety rule in the name of improved efficiency.

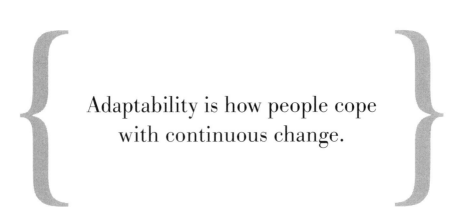

{ Adaptability is how people cope
with continuous change. }

Chapter 18

ADAPTABILITY

I'm sure you have heard that "the only constant is change." Adaptability is how people cope with continuous change. Some organizations change rapidly and frequently, while others are less intense. For those companies where change is a permanent fixture, assessing a candidate's level of flexibility and adaptability is crucial.

Questions within this area of competency are designed for you to assess a candidate's ability to deal with the following situations:

- Ambiguity
- Constraints
- Rapid change
- Frustration
- Shifting priorities
- Multiple demands
- Frustrating circumstances
- Identifying other's needs
- Putting other's needs first

Adaptability Questions

463. What do you do when your schedule is suddenly interrupted? Provide an example.

464. Describe a time you had to be flexible in planning a workload.

465. Describe a time when you were working on a project that suddenly changed in mid-stream.

466. Tell me about a situation when you had to adjust quickly to change in organizational/departmental or team priorities. How did the change affect you?

467. Tell of some situations in which you have had to adjust quickly to changes over which you had no control. What was the impact of the change on you?

468. How was your transition from high school to college? Did you face any particular problems?

469. Tell me about a time that it was crucial for you to remain focused on the task at hand but you kept getting interrupted. What did you do to ensure your focus was where it needed to be?

470. Tell me about a time when you changed your priorities to meet others' expectations.

471. Describe a time when you altered your own behavior to fit the situation.

472. Tell me about a time when you had to change your point of view or your plans to take into account new information or changing priorities.

473. Tell me about a time when you worked with a person who did things very differently from you. How did you get the job done?

474. By providing examples, demonstrate that you can adapt to a wide variety of people, situations and/or environments.

475. Tell me about a time when you had to adjust to a classmate's or colleague's working style in order to complete a project or achieve your objectives.

476. Has your job ever changed because of re-organization? Please explain how you handled the situation.

477. Recall a major change you went through at work. How did you handle it?

478. Describe a change you have made to your work environment.

479. Tell me about a time you had to change your work priorities to respond to other company matters.

480.   Can you give me an example of how you helped others effectively handle a changing environment?

481.   Tell me about a time when rapid change created a problem for you.

482.   Tell me about a time when you changed your priorities to meet others' needs.

483.   Tell me about a time when you had to change your plans to take into account new information.

484.   Describe a time when you adapted guidelines or procedures in order to get the job done.

485.   Tell me about a time when you adjusted to a colleague's practice or procedure because it was proven to be a more effective method.

486.   Describe a time when you identified and communicated a need for change in your department or organization. What did you do?

487.   Describe a time when you changed a long-term strategy to address a new situation.

488.   Tell me about a time you had to adapt to a new supervisor or manager. What did you do?

489.   What do you do when your schedule is suddenly interrupted? Give a specific example.

490. Have you ever had an experience where you found it impossible to adapt to a changing circumstance? Tell me about it.

491. Tell me about a time you may have been asked to completely change jobs in order to stay employed with your company.

492. Tell me about a time you had to be flexible in arranging your work schedule and your personal life.

Chapter 19

LEADERSHIP

Not all positions require formal leadership, but the characteristics of effective leaders are often desirable across a variety of positions. The important issue for you to uncover is the candidate's personal beliefs around what an effective leader does and how he or she goes about doing it. Whether the position is management or staff, you need to evaluate the candidate's ability to motivate and positively influence others in the workplace.

Leadership questions focus on the following characteristics:

- Open and accessible communicator
- Team player
- Values diversity
- Fosters creativity
- Shares information and expectations
- Welcomes ideas
- Values all contributions
- Facilitates participation
- Acknowledges mistakes

- Demonstrates enthusiasm
- Offers feedback
- Acts as a role model
- Empowers others

Leadership Questions

493. Describe your management philosophy and management style. Provide examples.

494. What leadership positions have you held? Describe your leadership style.

495. Tell me about a time when you coached someone to help them improve their skills or job performance. What did you do?

496. Describe a time when you provided feedback to someone about his or her performance.

497. Describe a situation where you helped someone establish his or her objectives.

498. Give me an example of a time when you recognized that a member of your team had a performance difficulty/deficiency. What did you do?

499. Please describe a situation in which you were responsible for organizing the training of other people, in addition to being responsible for your own daily tasks.

500. Tell me about a time when you prepared for and led an important meeting.

501. Were you ever responsible for the outcome of someone else's efforts? Please tell me about it.

502. Tell me about the time you demonstrated your best leadership abilities.

503. Give me an example of your leadership style.

504. Give me an example of a situation where you took charge.

505. Tell me about the characteristics that you demonstrate that make you a good leader. Give me an example where you used that characteristic.

506. What are three effective leadership qualities you think are important? How have you demonstrated these qualities in your past/current position?

507. Can you tell me about a time when you pushed your staff to complete a project on time even though the outcome was less than optimal?

508. Describe a time when you tried to persuade another person to do something that he or she was not very willing to do.

509.   Provide an example of a time when you had to persuade people to do something that they didn't want to do.

510.   What is the toughest group that you have had to get cooperation from? Describe how you handled it. What was the outcome?

511.   Have you ever been a member of a group where two of the members did not work well together? What did you do to help them get along?

512.   Tell me about a time when you coached someone to success on a task or project.

513.   Tell me about a team project when you had to take the lead or take charge of the project? What did you do? How did you do it? What was the result?

514.   Describe a leadership role of yours. Why did you commit your time to it? How did you feel about it?

515.   What is the toughest group that you have had to get cooperation from? What were the obstacles? How did you handle the situation? What were the reactions of the group members? What was the end result?

516.   Have you ever had difficulty getting others to accept your ideas? What was your approach? Did it work?

517. Tell me about a time when you delegated a project effectively.

518. Of the people you have encountered or know about in public positions of leadership, who do you look to as a role model and why?

519. Tell me about a situation in which you supervised someone whose performance was substandard.

520. Describe a situation where you helped motivate someone to improve his or her performance.

521. Tell me about a time when you had to conduct a particularly difficult employee counseling or corrective session. How did you prepare for the session? Did you delay having it? How long?

522. Tell me about a time when an employee you supervised disagreed with you about a work issue and suggested an alternate way the issue might be addressed. How did you handle that?

523. Give me an example of a leadership experience you have had.

524. When have you felt most comfortable as a leader?

525. How do you ensure that your team is working effectively?

526.   How do you reward employees?

527.   What techniques do you use to motivate others?

528.   Have you patterned your management style after someone in particular? Tell me about it.

529.   Describe a situation where you contributed to a team effort when you were not the leader.

530.   Describe a time when you had to change your leadership style.

531.   How have you demonstrated leadership by example?

532.   What methods do you use as a leader to foster open communication?

533.   What event made you least proud to be a leader?

534.   What steps have you had to take in disciplining an employee or group member?

535.   Have you ever had to overcome weaknesses as a manager? If so, how did you overcome them?

536.   How do you handle an employee who is not doing his or her work correctly?

537. Tell me about some of the people who have become successful as a result of your management. What was your role in their development?

538. What was your most recent mistake leading a team, and how did you repair the situation?

539. Describe a situation that required you to inspire excitement and enthusiasm in your team or direct staff.

Chapter 20
CREATIVITY

Creativity is not limited to artistic people. Creativity can be found in one's ability to generate creative or original solutions to problems and find innovative ways to solve old problems. Creativity is a valuable competency because it demonstrates an ability to think beyond a job description and see how a role impacts coworkers, supervisors and the overall performance of the company.

The types of questions you should ask yourself when approaching creativity questions are:

- Is this person capable of bringing fresh and inventive ideas to light?
- Will this person bring original thinking to the company?
- Is the person's creativity tempered with practicality?
- Has this person improved processes?
- Does this person challenge the "that's the way it has always been done" mentality?

Creativity Questions

540.   Describe something you have done that was new and different for your organization that improved performance and/or productivity.

541.   Tell me about a time when you identified a new, unusual or different approach for addressing a problem or task.

542.   Tell me about a recent problem in which old solutions wouldn't work. How did you solve the problem?

543.   Describe for me the most innovative idea or approach that you were able to implement successfully on the job.

544.   Tell me about a time when an idea you brought to fruition did not live up to your expectations.

545.   Describe a situation in which you took a creative approach to finding the resources needed to accomplish a goal.

546.   Tell me about a time when you created a new process or program that was considered risky. What was the situation and what did you do?

547.   Describe the most significant or creative presentation/ idea that you developed/implemented.

548. When was the last time you thought "outside the box" and how did you do it? Why?

549. Tell me about a problem that you've solved in a unique or unusual way. What was the outcome? Were you happy or satisfied with it?

550. Give me an example of when someone brought you a new idea that was odd or unusual. What did you do?

551. Please describe a situation where you used your creativity to solve a problem.

552. Tell me about a time when your innovative approach convinced someone to try something new.

553. Did you ever develop a creative solution to a problem? Tell me about it.

554. Give an example of a time when you had to teach someone a skill and how you went about it.

555. Are you the type of person who likes to "try new things" or "stay with regular routines"? Give an example.

556. What would you regard as being the most creative activity you have engaged in? Did it bring you recognition, financial reward or personal satisfaction?

557. What would you say has been the most creative accomplishment in your last position? Be specific.

558. Are you an innovator? Provide examples.

559. Tell me about a technical problem you have solved.

560. Have you ever been recognized or rewarded for your creativity? Tell me about it?

561. Can you tell me about a non-artistic situation or problem which required creativity?

562. What types of creative work give you the most satisfaction?

563. Give an example of how you have had to overcome an obstacle in a creative way.

564. Tell me about a time an existing process was not working and you found a solution.

565. Tell me about an improvement you personally initiated.

566. Describe a time when you came up with a solution when others couldn't.

567. Describe how you feel when you find solutions to problems that others did not recognize?

568. Describe an instance when you had to think on your feet to extricate yourself from a difficult situation.

569. Describe an idea that was implemented successfully because of the efforts you made.

570. Have you found any ways to make your job easier or more rewarding? Describe them.

571. Tell me about a time your company was facing a challenge and you came up with an innovative solution.

Chapter 21
SKILL-BASED BEHAVIORAL QUESTIONS

The final area of competency questions relates to specific skills, abilities and qualifications. In addition to "soft" skills that are required for general job success, there are "hard" skills that are required in order to perform specific jobs. Many of the skill-based competencies can be sufficiently evaluated from information on the résumé. There are instances, though, when you need or want to confirm the level of expertise a candidate claims to bring to the table. In those instances, skill-based questions provide an excellent and efficient method.

Some employers choose to conduct pre-employment tests to evaluate qualification and skill level, but time and resource constraints often mean that those competencies are evaluated during the structured interview process.

Use and adapt the following skill-based competency questions for your specific workplace and functional position:

Skill: Computers

572. At what computer programs are you proficient?

573. Tell me about the types of activities for which you use your computer.

574. What was the most complex problem you used your computer to help you solve?

575. Explain to me the process you went through to design your last database.

576. When you have a task that requires analyzing large amount of data, what computer programs or resources do you use to assist you?

577. What percentage of your time at work is spent working on a computer?

578. Describe a recent project where you used the Internet as a valuable resource tool.

579. What is your experience level with e-mail and Intranets?

580. Tell me about your experience in network administration.

581. Tell me about a time when you assisted someone else with a computer-related problem.

582. With what programming languages are you proficient?

583. Tell me about the most challenging application you worked on.

584. What techniques and tools do you use to ensure that a new application is as user-friendly as possible?

585. What steps do you use to check the accuracy of your code? Use a specific example.

586. Describe for me the last problem involving computer hardware that you solved.

587. What are the various tools and measures that can be implemented to secure data?

588. Recall for me a time when you were responsible for securing electronic data. How did you determine what needed to be done and what was the result?

Skill: Accounting

589. Tell me about your experience with accounts receivable.

590. Explain for me an experience you had involving collections.

591. What process do you go though to prepare a bill for services?

592. Tell me about your experience with accounts payable.

593. Recall for me a time when you discovered a discrepancy in an invoice. What did you do and what was the result?

594. Describe the types of financial reports you have prepared.

595. Describe your experiences with cash flow analysis

596. How familiar are you with variance analyses?

597. What experience do you have with cost accounting? What systems have you worked with?

598. Explain the depth of your accounting responsibility at your current job.

599. Describe for me your experience with budgeting.

600. What experience do you have with tax accounting?

601. How involved have you been in the auditing process at your company?

602. Recall for me what you did the last time your figures did not balance?

603. What is our experience with setting up accounting systems?

604. What role do you play in monitoring the accuracy of accounts?

Skill: Teaching

605. Describe a situation where you had to "think on your feet" to handle an emerging unexpected situation.

606. What specific approaches or ideas do you have for dealing with at-risk students?

607. What strategies do you use to improve reading skills of students who are far below grade level?

608. Describe the process you would use to deal with a student who was disrupting the class.

609. Describe the parts of your portfolio that best indicate your teaching style and beliefs.

610. What provisions do you make for meeting the range of skills and needs commonly present in a classroom?

611. Describe a team project you have done and your role.

612. What steps have you taken prior to parent-teacher conference to ensure its success?

613. Describe your experiences working with a diverse student body.

614. Explain a difficult situation, how you handled it, what you learned from it, and what would you do differently now.

Skill: Customer Service

615. Is the customer always right?

616. Tell me about a situation with a very demanding customer that you handled well.

617. Tell me about a situation with a very demanding customer that you handled poorly. What went wrong? What would you do differently?

618. Recall for me a time when you provided superb customer service.

619. Give me an example of a recognition (formal or informal) you received for quality service.

620. When you move to a new company, how have you become proficient with the company's products and services?

621. Tell me about how you handled a dissatisfied customer.

622. Describe the last time a customer interrupted you when you were in the middle of completing an assignment for your boss. What did you do?

623. Recall for me a time when a customer was abusive with you. What did you do? What was the outcome?

624. What experience do you have with developing customer surveys or other feedback tools?

625. Describe for me a time when you noticed a coworker having difficulty with a customer. What did you do? What was the outcome?

Skill: Supervision

626. Describe your supervisory experience.

627. In your role as supervisor, what had been your greatest challenge?

628.   What one supervisory experience stands out as the most rewarding?

629.   Tell me about a time when your role as supervisor was least enjoyable.

630.   Describe for me the last conflict between two of your employees that you got personally involved in. What was the situation and result?

631.   In your role as supervisor, when have you felt it necessary to involve your boss in a decision or problem? What was the outcome?

632.   What is the most difficult aspect of supervision?

633.   Tell me about a time when you had to delegate supervisory responsibility to one of your employees. How did you decide who was given authority? What was the reaction?

634.   Tell me about the most difficult personal problem you helped an employee work through.

635.   Describe for me a time when you were part of the decision to fire an employee.

636.   What is your method of employee correction or discipline? Provide examples.

637. Have you ever been involved with discrimination or harassment issues? Tell me about your role and what the final outcome was.

638. Recall for me a time when you had to deal with excessive absenteeism. What did you do? What was the result?

Skill: General Office

639. How many words do you type per minute?

640. With is your experience with dictation?

641. What types of reports and documents have you been responsible for preparing?

642. Describe for me a time when you had an unexpected office visitor. What did you do?

643. Recall for me a time when there were many people waiting for appointments. What did you do and what was the result?

644. Tell me about a time when you were given competing directions from two people. How did you determine what to do?

645.   Describe a time when you were responsible for handling your boss's schedule. What strategies do you use to keep him or her informed?

646.   Tell me about a time your boss got frustrated or short with you. How did you react? What was the outcome?

647.   What is the best experience you have had as an office assistant?

648.   Tell me about a time when you let your boss down? What happened? What would you do differently?

649.   How do you determine the best form of communication? For instance, when do you use a letter versus a memo or e-mail versus a notice on the bulletin board?

650.   What types of business documents are you responsible for preparing?

651.   Walk me through your process to make sure all correspondence is accurate?

Skill: Sales

652. Is your current compensation commission or salary or a combination? What do you like best and least about the compensation structure?

653. Tell me about a time when you spent a great deal of time with a customer and you did not get the sale.

654. Recall for me a time when a coworker snatched a sale from under you. What did you do? What was the outcome?

655. What steps do you take to overcome a prospect's sales resistance? Use an example.

656. Tell me about the longest sale you ever completed? Why did it take so long? What could you have done differently?

657. Tell me about your closing technique. Provide a few examples.

658. Tell me about a time when you used deception in order to finalize a sale.

659. Recall for me the largest sale you lost? What happened? What did you learn from the experience?

660. What is your strategy for dealing with buyer's remorse? Use an example.

661. Where do you generate your best leads?

662. Tell me about your most loyal customer.

663. Tell me about a time when you failed to meet your sales goal. What went wrong?

664. Tell me about a time when your actual sales far exceeded your projected sales. What contributed most to your success?

665. What percentage of your sales comes from current customers and how much comes from new leads?

666. Describe for me the most outrageous thing you did to close a sale.

Skill: Marketing

667. Describe for me your most successful marketing plan.

668. Describe for me your least successful marketing plan.

669. How do you see marketing differentiates from sales?

670. To what extent are you responsible for developing and monitoring a marketing plan. Use an example.

671. Tell me about a time when you identified a growth market and provided a strategy to move into that market.

672. What sorts of variables do you consider before developing a marketing plan?

673. Tell me about the last marketing plan you put together.

674. Recall for me the best marketing strategy you put together.

675. Recall a time when you failed to foresee a significant consequence of your marketing plan. What happened? What would you do differently?

676. Describe your approach to market research.

677. What have you done to familiarize yourself with new industries and emerging markets?

678. Tell me about a promotion campaign you were directly involved in.

679. Describe your involvement with focus groups and other direct means of gathering market information.

680. Tell me about a success you experienced in niche marketing.

Skill: Human Service

681. What experiences and unique perspectives do you bring to this agency?

682. Tell me about specific individuals you worked with that had multiple difficulties. How did you manage the case? What was the outcome?

683. What inspired you to choose a career in human services?

684. What kind of experience have you had with different populations (i.e., women, youth, terminally ill, etc.)? Use examples.

685. Explain why you are interested in working with our specific client population.

686. What was the most difficult case you worked on?

687. Tell me about a time when you and other human service professionals disagreed on the best treatment of a mutual client. How did you handle the situation? What was the outcome?

688. Tell me about the one case that you will never forget? What made it unforgettable?

689. Explain the specific strategies and techniques you use in crisis-intervention work.

690. Tell me about a situation in which you crossed your professional boundaries? What happened?

691. Recall for me the most frustrating individual you worked with. What made the situation so frustrating and what was the end result?

692. Tell me about a time when you declined to work with an individual. How did you make your decision?

693. How have you dealt with a lack of professional resources needed to do your job?

694. What is the most recent professional development activity you participated in?

695. Tell me about a time when you suffered from professional burnout. How did you cope? What was the end result?

Chapter 22
FINAL WORDS

Well, you've made it to the end of the questions but your job has just begun. Take the time to analyze the position you are attempting to fill. After you have decided which competencies to evaluate, go through each section and choose the questions that are most applicable to your workplace. Some will work as is and others will need a bit of modification. After reading though and becoming familiar with the behavioral interview approach, you will be confident to develop your own questions tailored specifically for each position in your company.

Follow This Succinct Recipe for Interviewing Success

1. Keep in mind the Golden Rule of behavioral interviewing

The Best Predictor of Future Behavior is Past Behavior

2. Ask yourself with every question:

Did the candidate's answer give me specific details about actions, responses and outcomes?

3.   (a) If your answer is "yes," then you have what you need to make an evaluation.

   (b) If your answer is "no," then you need to probe further.

Index

A

B

C

D

S0-BDP-060

C I T Y P A C K
Florence

By Susannah Perry

2ND EDITION

Fodor's Travel Publications, Inc.
New York • Toronto • London • Sydney • Auckland

WWW.FODORS.COM

Contents

About this book

Citypack Florence is divided into six sections to cover the six most important aspects of your visit to Florence. It includes:

- The author's view of the city and its people
- Itineraries, walks, and excursions
- The top 25 sights to visit—as selected by the author
- Features about different aspects of the city that make it special
- Detailed listings of hotels, restaurants, stores, and nightlife
- Practical information

In addition, easy-to-read side panels provide fascinating extra facts and snippets, highlights of places to visit, and invaluable practical advice.

CROSS-REFERENCES

To help you make the most of your visit, cross-references, indicated by ▶, show you where to find additional information about a place or subject.

MAPS

The fold-out map in the wallet at the back of the book is a comprehensive street plan of Florence. All the map references given in the book refer to this map. For example, the Church of San Lorenzo on Piazza San Lorenzo has the following information: ✚ bII—indicating the grid square of the map in which the Church of San Lorenzo will be found.

The city-center maps found on the inside front and back covers of the book itself are for quick reference. They show the top 25 sights, described on pages 24–48, which are clearly plotted by number (**1** – **25**, not page number) from west to east.

FLORENCE
life

5

INTRODUCING FLORENCE

Neighborhoods

The heart of Florence is the square grid of streets laid out by the Romans: here the religious center, Piazza del Duomo, is closely linked to the political center, the Piazza della Signoria. In the east, Santa Croce is historically the blue-collar area, while the ultra-glamorous Via de' Tornabuoni is in the west. Across the river, the Oltrarno (literally "beyond the Arno") is the site of the Pitti Palace and the Boboli Gardens. It is also the most relaxed part of town, least touched by tourism.

Mention Florence and the words "cradle of the Renaissance" trip off the tongue. Works of art inextricably associated with Florence, such as Botticelli's *Birth of Venus* and Michelangelo's *David*, are potent symbols not just of the extraordinary flowering of creativity fostered in Florence in the 14th and 15th centuries, but also of the spirit of humanity itself. Florence's reputation precedes it, and many travelers go burdened with weighty expectations of great beauty. However, much of its architecture is stern, stolid and forbidding; its uncompromising beauty is a subtle working of mathematical proportion and harmony. And faced with an overwhelming artistic richness, you'll find a vacation easily becomes torture by culture. With not a patch of green in sight, the streets can be noisy and dusty, and you can spend hours in line just to see the Uffizi.

It is therefore essential to go beyond the tourist circuit: the Duomo, Piazza della Signoria, Santa Croce. Cross the river and wander through the Oltrarno, where artisans have their workshops. Visit the Boboli Gardens. The trick is to combine the modern with the historical, the frivolous and

The cradle of the Renaissance: a panoramic view

the serious in the way, one suspects, the greats of the Florentine Renaissance would have done.

Florence has certainly seen its share of greats. The poet Dante Alighieri (1265–1321), father of Italian literature, and the famous artist Sandro Botticelli (1445–1510) were not Florence's only sons to make a worldwide reputation for themselves: sculptor Donatello was born here in 1386; Fra Filippo Lippi in 1469; and Masaccio in 1401. Attracted by the patronage of the leading Medici family, other artists, thinkers, and scientists flocked to the city. Galileo Galilei (1564–1642), from Pisa, spent much of his life in Florence as the Medici court mathematician. Leonardo and Michelangelo created some of their most famous works here. And modern Florentine creativity has made its mark on the fashion industry—Gucci, Pucci, and Ferragamo all started here. It is no wonder that today's Florentines harbor no doubt that they live in the greatest center of culture in the world and are quietly appreciative if you show the right degree of reverence.

However you take it—whether you fall in love with its self-confidently restrained charm, find it a beautiful but heartless museum or a tourist-packed zoo—it's difficult not to develop strong feelings about Florence.

Local loyalties

The hugely proud Florentines consider themselves Italians only once every four years—for the soccer World Cup. Otherwise their loyalty is fiercely local.

Everywhere you go you will see the lily, the emblem of Florence, usually on a soccer pennant celebrating Fiorentina, the soccer team also known as "I Viola" (The Purples), who are the subject of fervent adoration.

A Day in the Life of Florence

Florence is primarily a city for walkers

Left-leaning

Tuscany is probably the only place in Europe where you will still find affectionate posters of Stalin on the street corners. Florence, the capital of Tuscany, is no exception, and many Florentines cling tenaciously to the icons of their left-wing identity.

Like most Italians the Florentines are light breakfasters. They will rise relatively early and start work between 8AM and 9AM after a frothy cappuccino and an airy pastry, taken in a bar. Many people walk or bicycle to work, although, in a break with the past, an increasing number of people who work in the city now live in the villages outside and commute to work by car.

Most people in Florence are employed in work related to tourism. This might be a direct involvement, for example, guiding and hotel work, or else retail or arts and crafts that are ultimately patronized by tourists and represent a continuity with Florence's artistic past. Attempts to make the city less tourism-dependent can be seen in the growth of high-technology industry in the outskirts, with companies such as Nuova Pignone and Galileo. The university is also an important employer, as is the government, not just of Florence, but also of the region of Tuscany.

A good key to understanding any group of people is their attitude toward food. In Florence there is a delicious contrast between the refined sophistication of the city's art and the earthiness of Tuscan food. Drop into one of the *vinaii*, little old wine bars (once found all over the city, now dying out in the face of the threat from fast-food empires), where salami and pungent cheeses are served on unsalted bread and washed down with Tuscan wines.

A rest for weary feet

Traditionally lunch is a substantial affair followed by a siesta, but many people now do not return home for lunch and instead grab a sandwich and get on with their work. Most of the city still shuts down from about 1:30PM until 4PM—when people return feeling refreshed and work until about 7:30PM. In the evening, as in all of Italy, families and groups step out for the *passeggiata*, the evening stroll, which might well be punctuated by a meal or drink at a bar.

FLORENCE IN FIGURES

History

- 10th century BC—Italic tribes settle at the crossing-point of the River Arno, near the present-day Ponte Vecchio
- 5th century BC—Etruscans settle in hills to the north; their colony becomes Fiesole
- 283 BC—Fiesole first defeated by Rome
- 59 BC—Caesar's agrarian law creates the conditions for Florence's establishment
- AD 1001—becomes the capital of the Margraves (princes)
- 1115—becomes an independent city-state
- Early 15th century to 1743—dominance of the Medici banking dynasty
- 1865–70—Florence briefly serves as the capital of the Italian state

Geography

- Latitude: 43° 46 minutes north—the same as Toronto, Canada and Sapporo, Japan
- Longitude: 11° 14 minutes east
- 160 feet above sea level
- 172 miles north of Rome
- 185 miles south of Milan

Climate

- Hottest months: July and August—average temperature 77°F
- Coldest month: January—average temperature 43°F
- Average annual rainfall—35 inches
- Rainiest month: October—average rainfall 5 inches
- Driest months: June and July—average rainfall 1½ inches

People

- Population in June 1997: 380,000
- Population in June 1995: 385,969
- Population in December 1994: 388,304 (one of the lowest birth rates in Italy, which has the lowest national birth rate in the world)

Tourism

- Number of tourists per year—3 to 5 million
- Most visited museum: the Uffizi—1,150,093 visitors (1995)
- Number of visitors spending a night or more in Florence (1997)—more than 3,300,000
- Number of visitors visiting the city without staying—1 million

A CHRONOLOGY

59 BC	Florence starts to grow as a result of a law passed by Julius Caesar.
AD 541–4	Byzantine walls added to the Roman walls, as protection against the Ostrogoths. Walls also built in 9th, 11th, 12th and 13th centuries.
570	Tuscany taken by the Lombards, who set up their administration in Pavia and Lucca.
781–786	Charlemagne, King of the Franks, pays visits to Florence, which becomes part of the Carolingian Empire (later the Holy Roman Empire), ruled by Margraves based in Lucca.
1115	Death of the last Margrave, Matilda, followed by the formation of the first *comune* (the city state) in which Florence is run by a 100-strong assembly.
1235	Florin first minted in silver and then, in 1252, in gold; used as the standard coin in Europe: evidence of the pre-eminence of Florence in European finance.
1250–60	The *Primo Popolo* regime dominated by the trade guilds.
1265	Birth of poet Dante Alighieri in Florence.
1296	Building of the Duomo begun under Arnolfo di Cambio.
1302	Dante exiled by Charles of Valois.
1340s	Economic crisis, due in part to the bankruptcy of the Peruzzi and Bardi by Edward III of England, and also partly a result of the Black Death (plague), during which the population is halved.
1378	Uprising of the *ciompi* (wool carders); high point of labor unrest.
1406	Florence captures Pisa, gaining direct access to the sea.

1458	Cosimo de' Medici recognized as ruler of Florence.
1469–92	Rule of Lorenzo the Magnificent; artistic high-point.
1469	Birth of Machiavelli.
1475	Birth of Michelangelo.
1478	Pazzi conspirators scheme to have Giuliano and Lorenzo de' Medici murdered in the cathedral. Giuliano is killed but Lorenzo escapes by hiding in the sacristy.
1494	Surrender of Florence to Charles VIII of France at Sarzana.
1498	Savonarola burned at the stake after four years of rule.
1502	Republic of Florence retakes Pisa.
1570	Cosimo I creates Tuscan state free from Pope and the Holy Roman Empire.
1616	Church condemns Galileo Galilei as a heretic; he takes refuge with the Medici.
1743	Death of Anna Maria Luisa, last of the Medici. Florence then ruled by the house of Lorraine under Francis Stephen.
1799–1814	Tuscany occupied by Napoleon's troops.
1865–70	Florence is made capital of Italy. King Vittorio Emanuele installed in Pitti Palace.
1944	On August 4, Germans blow up all the bridges in Florence except the Ponte Vecchio.
1966	River Arno bursts its banks: Florence flooded.
1993	Bombing of the Uffizi Gallery.
1996	G7 meeting held in Florence.

PEOPLE & EVENTS FROM HISTORY

Capital of Italy

Florence was briefly capital of Italy, from 1865 to 1870, with King Vittorio Emanuele in the Palazzo Pitti and the Parliament and Foreign Ministry seated in the Palazzo Vecchio. Rome was still in the hands of the Papacy and defended by French troops. After the defeat of the French in the Franco-Prussian war, Italian troops marched into Rome, which within months became the capital.

SAVONAROLA

A firebrand preacher who attempted to put the fear of God into the pleasure-loving Florentines, Girolamo Savonarola was a Dominican friar and prior of San Marco. He rebelled against the Medici and founded the Florentine Republic at the end of the 15th century. Convinced that Florence was the new Jerusalem, he fulminated about standards of public morality, closing taverns, prohibiting gambling and mobilizing the young in religious processions. Savonarola was excommunicated and then burned at the stake on May 23, 1498, in Piazza della Signoria. The Republic staggered on until 1530 when it collapsed under siege from the Medici.

THE MEDICI

A family of bankers, the Medici were Florence's royal family in all but name from the 14th to the 18th century. The greatest Medici was Cosimo il Vecchio (the Old; 1389–1464), a military leader, politician, and patron of the arts. His son Lorenzo il Magnifico (the Magnificent; 1449–92) was another great patron of the arts and humanist thought, although he lacked his father's economic acumen. After Florence's flirtation with republicanism, and the period when the Medici Popes, Leo X and Clement VII, ruled Florence from Rome, the Medici returned to power in Florence in 1537 under Cosimo I, who became Grand Duke of Tuscany in 1570. By this time, the dynasty was in decline, the rulers becoming increasingly decadent, while Austria and Spain were the powers of real importance. Gian Gastone, the last male Medici died in 1743 without heir; his sister, Anna Maria Luisa, bequeathed the entire Medici fortune to Florence in perpetuity—becoming the basis of the Uffizi Gallery collection.

Cosimo I

FLORENCE
how to organize your time

ITINERARIES

To get the best out of Florence, you may find it makes sense to do as the Italians do, and have a siesta after lunch: most of the sights and stores are shut until 4PM and Florence is small enough for you to be able to return to your hotel.

ITINERARY ONE	**THE MEDICI AND THE MARKETS**
Morning	Visit the church of San Lorenzo (➤ 31) and the Cappelle Medicee (➤ 30), which are part of the same building but entered through Piazza della Madonna degli Aldobrandini.
Lunch	The Mercato Centrale (➤ 60) is near by: here you could buy the ingredients for a picnic or get a good cheap lunch at Da Sergio (➤ 64).
Afternoon	Visit the Palazzo Medici (➤ 32). Shopping in the Mercato San Lorenzo (➤ 60). From here walk through Piazza del Duomo on the Via dei Calzaiuoli to Piazza della Signoria and the Palazzo Vecchio (➤ 41).
ITINERARY TWO	**THE OLTRARNO**
Morning	Cross the Ponte Vecchio (➤ 28) and take the second left for Santa Felicita (➤ 53). Continue up Via Guicciardini to the Palazzo Pitti (➤ 26). Visit the Galleria Palatina and Museo degli Argenti, then go to the Boboli Gardens (➤ 27) and have coffee in the Kaffeehaus (➤ 68).
Lunch	At Piazza San Felice take Via Mazzetta to Piazza Santo Spirito for a good lunch at the Antica Trattoria Oreste (➤ 63) or eat a pizza at Borgo Antico (➤ 66).
Afternoon	Continue along Via Sant'Agostino, crossing Via dei Serragli into Via Santa Monica which leads into Piazza del Carmine. Visit the Cappella Brancacci (➤ 24, closes at 5) in Santa Maria del Carmine. Return to Via dei Serragli for antiques and crafts and onto Via Maggio for elegant antiques (➤ 77).
Dinner	Quattro Leoni (➤ 63).

ITINERARY THREE	AROUND THE VIA DE' TORNABUONI
Morning	Visit the Museo della Casa Fiorentina Antica (➤ 29), then head for the Via de' Tornabuoni. You might like to take a break and have a coffee at Giacosa (➤ 68), or, for gourmets, truffle sandwiches and a glass of wine at Procacci (➤ 66). Go window-shopping in Via de' Tornabuoni and Via della Vigna Nuova.
Lunch	If you are dressed for the part, have an elegant lunch at Cantinetta Antinori (➤ 62); if you are looking for something simpler, try Garga (➤ 63) or Belle Donne (➤ 64).
Afternoon	Take the Via della Vigna Nuova toward Piazza Rucellai, where you could pay a visit to the Museo Fratelli Alinari (➤ 51, closed Wed). Go back to Via de' Tornabuoni and Santa Trinita (➤ 53). Just opposite Santa Trinita you will find Salvatore Ferragamo (➤ 70), which has a fascinating shoe museum (➤ 51, reserve ahead). Enjoy the wonderful views from the Ponte Santa Trinita (➤ 59).
Dinner	Coco Lezzone (➤ 63).
Evening	Take a leisurely stroll along the banks of the Arno (➤ 59).
ITINERARY FOUR	THE HEART OF THE CITY
Morning	Climb to the top of the cathedral dome (➤ 35) for breathtaking views. Visit the Baptistery (➤ 33) and also the Museo dell'Opera del Duomo (➤ 36). From the Piazza del Duomo take the Via dei Calzaiuoli and visit Orsanmichele (➤ 37) and its museum (➤ 55).
Lunch	Just opposite is the Via Tavolini where you will find the Cantinetta dei Verrazzano (➤ 66) for a snack lunch followed by delicious ice cream at Perchè No! (➤ 67), just across the road.
Afternoon	Take a stroll through the Piazza della Signoria (➤ 40) to the Ponte Vecchio (➤ 28) for another window-shopping session. Visit the Galleria degli Uffizi (➤ 38, closed Mon) and include a stop at the café for the views.

15

WALKS

THE SIGHTS

- Ponte Vecchio (➤ 28)
- Santa Felicita (➤ 52)
- Forte di Belvedere (➤ 55)
- San Miniato (➤ 48)
- Piazzale Michelangelo (➤ 55)

INFORMATION

Distance 1¼ miles
Time at least 2–3 hours
Start point Ponte Vecchio
🚌 bIV
🚍 B, C
End point Piazzale Michelangelo
🚌 J7
🚍 12, 13

Below: a 19th-century painting shows a wedding party emerging from the church of Santa Margherita de' Cerchi (➤ 17)

Right: city views from Piazzale Michelangelo

PONTE VECCHIO TO PIAZZALE MICHELANGELO

In summer this walk can be baking hot and it is best to start either very early in the morning or in the afternoon, about 4. Take a bottle of water along with you. In the spring or autumn plan a midday picnic at the Forte di Belvedere.

Start at the Ponte Vecchio and cross over to the Oltrarno. The first square on your left is Piazza Santa Felicita where you will find Pontormo's *Deposition* in the church of Santa Felicita (➤ 53). As you come out, take the road on the left of the church, the Costa di San Giorgio, where at No. 19 Galileo once lived. Continue up its steep slope, passing through the Porta di San Giorgio (1260), the oldest of the city's gates, which has a carving of St. George slaying the dragon.

Turn right into the Forte di Belvedere (➤ 55), which dates from 1590 and is a good place for a rest or a picnic. Follow the Via del Belvedere, which descends sharply along the city walls. At the bottom of the hill turn right into Via del Monte alle Croci. Follow it to its end then cross Viale Galileo Galilei to take the steps flanked by cypress trees and reliefs of the stations of the cross that continue up toward San Miniato (➤ 48). After your visit, go back to Viale Galileo Galilei, turn right and follow it to Piazzale Michelangelo for marvelous views. A 12 or 13 bus will take you back into the center of town.

Bust of Dante

THE SIGHTS

- Baptistery (➤ 33)
- Duomo (➤ 35)
- Santa Margherita de' Cerchi
- Casa di Dante
- Badia Fiorentina (➤ 52)
- Bargello (➤ 42)
- Santa Croce (➤ 47)

INFORMATION

Distance ⅔ mile approx
Time 1 hour including visits
Starting point Baptistery
🚩 bIII
🚌 1, 6, 7, 11, 12, 14 (in the pedestrian zone)
End point Santa Croce
🚩 cIV
🚌 12, 14, 19, 23, 31, 32

DANTE'S FLORENCE

Start at the Baptistery, where the poet Dante Alighieri was baptized and which he called his *bel San Giovanni*. In his day it was not covered with the marble facing. According to tradition, Dante watched the construction of the cathedral from the Sasso di Dante, a stone (marked) in the wall between Via dello Studio and Via del Proconsolo, opposite the Duomo.

Take the Via dello Studio. Turn left when you reach the Via del Corso and take the first right into Via di Santa Margherita. This leads to the Casa di Dante, which houses exhibits relating to 13th-century Florence. Immediately opposite is the church of San Martino del Vescovo, where Dante's family worshipped, and back towards Via del Corso is the church of Santa Margherita, where his lifelong muse, Beatrice, went to Mass. Inside are paintings relating to Dante's life.

From Santa Margherita turn left into Via Dante Alighieri for the entrance of the Badia, where Dante often saw Beatrice. The Badia's bell would have punctuated Dante's daily life. Exit and turn onto Via del Proconsolo, past the Bargello, which was being built in Dante's time. Take Via dell'Anguillara until you come to Piazza Santa Croce. Outside Santa Croce there is a large 19th-century statue of Dante. His sarcophagus, inside, is empty: Dante was buried, a political exile, in Ravenna.

The Bargello's courtyard

17

EVENING STROLLS

The evening passeggiata *along Via dei Calzaiuoli*

THE LUNGARNO AND PONTE VECCHIO

There are few open spaces in Florence, so people flock to the roads alongside the river (Lungarni). You can walk a long or a short distance, depending on how you feel. The Ponte Vecchio (▶ 28) is the natural hub of activity, with well-groomed Florentines rubbing shoulders with more raffish types. If you walk from the Ponte Vecchio beyond the Ponte alle Grazie on the Oltrarno side, you will come to the Piazza Demidoff, now a meeting place for chic Florentine youth. In the other direction, the prettiest bridge is the Ponte Santa Trinita, which gives wonderful views of the Ponte Vecchio.

VIA DEI CALZAIUOLI AND PIAZZA DELLA REPUBBLICA

The street that links the Piazza del Duomo with the Piazza della Signoria (▶ 40) is the place to be seen of an evening. Here you will see Florentines in all their finery engaged in that most Italian of activities, the *passeggiata*, or evening stroll. The purpose is to see and be seen; the pace is slow—essentially nobody is going anywhere. In Piazza della Repubblica expensive cafés are frequented by tourists and elderly Italians, and there is usually a side-show from aging Italian men rapt in animated discussion in the center of the square.

GUIDED TOURS

BY BUS
CAF (Consorzio Agenzie Fiorentine) ✉ Via Roma 4 ☎ 055 210612/283200; SITA ✉ Via Santa Caterina da Siena 15r ☎ 055 483651 and Lazzi ✉ Piazza della Stazione ☎ 055 287118 excursions can be reserved through American Express or travel agencies, such as CIT. The following tours are offered:

- Morning sightseeing, including a visit to the cathedral (➤ 35) and the Accademia (➤ 43) to see the *David* and then to Piazzale Michelangelo (➤ 55).

- Afternoon sightseeing, including Fiesole (➤ 20), Santa Croce (➤ 47), and the Palazzo Pitti for the Palatine Galleries (➤ 26).

- Afternoon tour to Pisa, to see the leaning tower, the cathedral, and the baptistery.

The Leaning Tower of Pisa

- Afternoon excursion to Chianti (➤ 21) for wine tasting. Gourmet tours of the surrounding area also offer tastings of other local produce such as olive oil.

- Full-day tour to San Gimignano and Siena (➤ 20, 21).

- Private custom tours—designed to suit your own interests.

CONOSCERE FIRENZE VILLAS AND GARDENS
Each year from May to October the municipal government of Florence organizes tours of sumptuous private villas and gardens—an irresistible glimpse of the contemporary wealth of Florence and the houses of the city's great families (not just the Medici) as well as castles in satellite towns such as Settignano. For details, pick up a leaflet at the tourist information center (➤ 90). Make reservations through the Ufficio Cultura ✉ Via Sant'Egidio 21 ☎ 055 288049.

Carriages

Outside the Duomo and in Piazza della Signoria, horse-drawn carriages tour the center, where cars and buses are banned. Before setting off, establish the duration of the tour and settle a fair price (per carriage or person).

Seeing the sights from a horse-drawn carriage

EXCURSIONS

INFORMATION

Fiesole
Distance 5 miles
Journey time 20–30 minutes
🚌 7 (regular bus departures from the train station or San Marco)
ℹ️ Piazza Mino 37 ☎ 055 598720

Siena
Distance 41 miles
Journey time 1–2 hours
🚌 Regular departures from Santa Maria Novella station
ℹ️ Piazza del Campo 56 ☎ 0577 280551

The Piazza del Campo, seen from the Torre del Mangia

FIESOLE

Fiesole is a charming hill town just above Florence, and more important than Florence for much of the Roman period. It has a Roman theater and impressive Etruscan remains. A delightfully quiet place to escape to from Florence, it is very easily accessible. The bus from Florence arrives in Fiesole's Piazza Mino. (The last bus returns to Florence at 1AM, allowing an evening visit to admire the lights in the city below.) The Roman ruins are clearly signposted, and the ticket includes access to the Roman and Etruscan museum. There is a small Romanesque cathedral dating from the 11th century. Walk up the Via di San Francesco for wonderful views of Florence in the valley below. Walk or take bus No. 7 down the hill to the village of San Domenico, and from there walk to the Badia Fiesolana, a pretty Romanesque church with an inlaid facade.

SIENA

One of the loveliest towns in Italy, with great museums, fabulous stores, and many hills, Siena is best reached by train. At Siena station take the shuttle bus to the center and spend the rest of the day on foot. The focal point is the fan-shaped Piazza del Campo, which slopes down to the bell tower. The Gothic cathedral was built between 1136 and 1382. Outside there is a vast unfinished nave begun in 1339 with the intention of making this the world's largest cathedral but abandoned during the plague. Look for the animal symbols of the town's 17 *contrade* (districts) that take part in the famous *Palio*, a fearsome horse race held annually in the Piazza del Campo on July 2 and August 16 (► 83).

The rooftops and towers of San Gimignano

INFORMATION

Car rental (▶ 91)

Chianti
Distance 93 miles
Journey time 3–5 hours
Start point Head south out of Florence on the Via Senese, going past La Certosa and take the N2, not the expressway. San Casciano is a good place to start taking back roads.

Museo Leonardiano
✉ Castello dei Conti Guidi, Vinci
☎ 0571 56055
🕐 Mar–Oct: daily 9:30–7:30. Nov–Feb: daily 9:30–6
💶 Moderate

Poggio a Caiano
Distance 11 miles
Journey time 35 minutes
Start point Piazza Santa Maria Novella (see below)

Villa Medicea
✉ Piazza dei Medici 12, Poggio a Caiano
☎ 055 877012 (COPIT service)
🕐 Grounds Apr–Oct: Mon–Sat 9–6:30; Sun 9–1:30. Nov–Mar: Mon–Sat 9–4:30; Sun 9–1:30. Villa daily 9–1:30. Closed 2nd and 3rd Mon of month
🚌 COPIT service departing every 30 minutes from Piazzo Santa Maria Novella
💶 Moderate

THE TUSCAN COUNTRYSIDE

A country drive is a real treat. Much-visited San Gimignano, set on a hill with a collection of medieval towers. Its Palazzo del Popolo houses a gruesome museum of torture. For lovely pots, stop in Montelupo, where many of Florence's ceramics have been made for centuries. On your way back visit Vinci, to the west of Florence, the birthplace of Leonardo da Vinci (1452–1519); it is home to a museum about his life, art, and inventions. Spend some time enjoying the views and perhaps buy some olive oil and wine direct from a farm. You might like to have a swim: the village of Sambuca, near Tavarnelle, for example, has an excellent outdoor pool.

VILLA MEDICEA DI POGGIO A CAIANO

The Medici had a series of villas around Florence where they would go when the city became unbearable. The best preserved of them is set in English-style gardens in the village of Poggio a Caiano, northwest of Florence. A farmhouse remodeled by Giuliano da Sangallo for Lorenzo the Magnificent in 1480, it was the first country villa built since Roman times. It has an outstanding two-story *salone* with frescoes by Andrea del Sarto and Jacopo da Pontormo, in which the Medici appear dressed as Romans.

WHAT'S ON

January	*Pitti Immagine Uomo, Pitti Immagine Bimbo*: Fashion shows at the Fortezza da Basso.
February	*Carnevale*: Florence's carnival is a low-key version of Venice's annual extravaganza.
March	*Festa dell'Annunziata* (Mar 25): Traditionally this was the Florentine new year and a fair is held to celebrate in Piazza Santissima Annunziata. *Scoppio del Carro* (Explosion of the Cart): The Easter Sunday service at the Duomo culminates in an exploding carriage full of fireworks.
April	*Mostra Mercato Internazionale dell'Artigianato*: An important international arts and crafts festival in the Fortezza da Basso.
May	*Maggio Musicale*: Florence's international music and dance festival at various locations. *Festa del Grillo* (first Sunday after Ascension Day): Crickets are sold in tiny cages and then released in the park of Le Cascine (➤ 56).
June	*Calcio in Costume*: An elaborate soccer game between town districts usually played in medieval costume over three days in late June in Piazza Santa Croce (➤ 47, 83); preceded by a procession. *Festa di San Giovanni* (Jun 24): The feast of the patron saint of Florence; fireworks are set off in Piazzale Michelangelo. *Estate Fiesolana* (mid-Jun through Aug): A Fiesole arts festival, often spreading to Florence with music, art, drama, and film (➤ 80).
September	*Festa del Rificolona* (Sep 7): Children carry paper lanterns in Piazza Santissima Annunziata to honor the birth of the Virgin. *Mostra Mercato Internazionale dell'Antiquariato* (Sep–Oct alternate years): An antiques show.
October	*Amici della Musica* (Oct–Apr): Concerts run by Teatro della Pergola ☎ 055 608420.
November	*Festival dei Popoli* (Nov–Dec): A film festival held in the Palazzo dei Congressi, showing subtitled international films.

FLORENCE's
top 25 sights

The sights are shown on the maps on the inside front cover and inside back cover, numbered **1–25** *from west to east across the city*

23

CAPPELLA BRANCACCI

1

INFORMATION

- ✚ H7
- ✉ Santa Maria del Carmine, Piazza del Carmine (enter through the cloisters)
- ☎ 055 238 2195
- ◷ Mon, Wed–Sat 10–5; Sun 1–5
- 🄱 B
- ♿ Acceptable
- 👜 Moderate
- ↔ Santo Spirito (➤ 53)

Part of the thrill of the Cappella Brancacci is the sensation that you are seeing the opening phases of the Renaissance, observing in Masaccio's frescoes the same power of expression and technical brilliance that inspired the Florentine painters of the 15th century.

The chapel   The Cappella Brancacci is a tiny chapel reached via the cloisters of the otherwise rather dull Santa Maria del Carmine. Two layers of frescoes commissioned in 1424 by Felice Brancacci, a wealthy Florentine merchant and statesman, illustrate the life of St. Peter, shown in his orange gown. The frescoes were designed by Masolino da Panicale, who began painting them with his brilliant and promising pupil, Masaccio. In 1428 Masaccio took over from Masolino but died that year, aged 27, and the rest of the frescoes were completed in the 1480s by Filippino Lippi.

Restoration   In the 1980s the chapel was superbly restored, with the removal of accumulated candlesoot and layers of an 18th-century egg-based gum (which had formed a mold). The frescoes now have an intense radiance that makes it possible to see very clearly the shifts in emphasis between Masolino's work and that of Masaccio; contrast the serenity of Masolino's *Temptation of Adam and Eve* with the excruciating agony of Masaccio's *Expulsion of Adam and Eve from Paradise*. The restoration has also highlighted Masaccio's mastery of *chiaroscuro* (light and shade), which, combined with his grasp of perspective, was marveled at and consciously copied by the 15th-century Florentine painters. His depiction of St. Peter healing the sick (left of the altar as you face it, lower register) showed beggars and cripples with revolutionary realism.

Masaccio's Expulsion of Adam and Eve from Paradise

SANTA MARIA NOVELLA

The decorative marble facade of Tuscany's most important Gothic church incorporates billowing sails (emblem of Alberti's patron Giovanni Rucellai) and ostrich feathers (emblem of the Medici). Inside are immense artistic riches, donated by numerous wealthy patrons, many of whom had chapels named after them.

Origins The church of Santa Maria Novella was built between 1279 and 1357 by Dominican monks. The lower part of the marble facade, Romanesque in style, is believed to have been executed by Fra Jacopo Talenti; the upper part was completed between 1456 and 1470 by Leon Battista Alberti.

The interior Inside, the church is vast and looks even longer than it is, thanks to the clever spacing of the columns. Facing the altar, on the left-hand side is a fresco of the *Trinità* (c1428) by Masaccio, one of the earliest paintings to demonstrate mastery of perspective. The Strozzi Chapel (left transept) is dedicated to St. Thomas Aquinas and decorated with frescoes (1351–7) by Nardo di Cione depicting *Heaven and Hell*: Dante himself is represented in the *Last Judgment* just behind the altar. The Tornabuoni Chapel contains Ghirlandaio's fresco cycle of the life of St. John the Baptist (1485) in contemporary costume.

The Dogs of God The Cappellone degli Spagnoli ("Spanish Chapel") was used by the courtiers of Eleanor of Toledo, wife of Cosimo I. In the frescoes *Triumph of the Doctrine* (c1365) by Andrea da Firenze, the dogs of God (a pun on the word Dominican—*domini canes*) are sent to round up lost sheep into the fold of the church.

HIGHLIGHTS

- Marble facade
- Masaccio's *Trinità*
- Cappellone degli Spagnoli
- Tornabuoni Chapel

INFORMATION

- ✚ alll
- ✉ Piazza di Santa Maria Novella
- ☎ Church 055 210113. Museum 055 282187
- 🕐 Church Mon–Sat 7–noon, 3–6; Sun 8–noon, 3:30–5. Museum Mon–Thu, Sat 9–noon; Sun 8–1
- 🚊 5 minutes' walk from the railroad station
- ♿ Good
- 🎟 Church free. Museum moderate
- ↔ Duomo (► 35), Battistero (► 33), Campanile (► 34)

3

PALAZZO PITTI

HIGHLIGHTS

- Frescoed ceilings by Pietro da Cortona, Galleria Palatina (rooms 5, 6, 7, 8, 10)
- Raphael's *Madonna of the Chair* (c1516) (room 8)
- Titian's overtly sexual *Mary Magdalene* (c1531) (room 5)
- Van Dyck's *Charles I and Henrietta Maria* (c1632) (room 5)
- Titian's *Portrait of a Gentleman* (1540) (room 5)

Raphael's Madonna of the Chair

INFORMATION

- ✚ alV
- ✉ Piazza Pitti
- ☎ Galleria Palatina 055 238 8611. Museo degli Argenti 055 238 8709
- 🕐 Galleria Palatina Tue–Thu, Sat 8:30–6:45; Sun 8:30–2; Fri 8:30–11 (last admission 30 minutes before closing)
- 🚌 B, C, 11, 36, 37
- ♿ Good
- 💶 Expensive
- ↔ Giardino di Boboli (➤ 27)
- ❓ 1-hour guided tour of the Galleria del Costume

The Pitti Palace, with its four museums, is unremittingly grand, opulent, and pompous. Its saving grace is the outstanding art collection in the Galleria Palatina.

Origins The Palazzo Pitti was built in 1457 to designs by Filippo Brunelleschi for banker, Luca Pitti. He wanted it to be bigger and better than the Medici Palace: the result has been likened to a "rusticated Stalinist ministry." Ironically, the Medici bought the Palazzo Pitti in 1550 when the Pitti lost their fortune, and thereafter it remained the residence of the rulers of Florence.

Art The Galleria Palatina contains Renaissance and baroque works from the Medici collection as important as those in the Uffizi. Highlights include masterpieces by Titian, Raphael, and Van Dyck displayed in an apparently haphazard way that reflects the taste of the Medici, who had so many valuable works of art that they didn't worry about hanging them in any order. The *Appartamenti Monumentali* (state rooms) are entered through the Galleria Palatina.

Silver The Museo degli Argenti represents a triumph of Medici wealth over taste. Rooms are full of ghoulish reliquaries, rare Roman glass, and the Roman and Byzantine *pietra dura* (inlaid decoration made of marble and semi-precious stone pieces) vases that belonged to Lorenzo the Magnificent. Upstairs is an attractive display of cameos and intaglios, as well as a 17th-century Crucifixion scene made out of colored glass that is in such appalling taste as to be hilarious.

Costume and Modern Art The Galleria del Costume reflects 18th- and 19th-century court fashions while the Galleria d'Arte Moderna shows Italian art from the late 19th to the early 20th centuries, not its greatest period.

GIARDINO DI BOBOLI

The Boboli Gardens are, quite literally, a breath of fresh air: the only easily accessible reservoir of greenery and tranquility in Florence, and a lovely retreat after a hard day's sightseeing.

Renaissance origins The Boboli Gardens were created for the Medici when they moved to the Palazzo Pitti in 1550. They represent a superb example of Italian Renaissance gardening, an interplay between nature and artifice expressed in a geometrical arrangement of fountains, grass, and low box hedges. In 1766 they were opened to the public, and in 1992 an (unpopular) entrance charge was imposed.

Ampitheater Just behind the Palazzo Pitti is the amphitheater, built where the stone for the Palazzo Pitti was quarried. It was the site of the first-ever opera performance and is surrounded by maze-like alleys of fragrant, dusty bay trees. Go uphill past the Neptune Fountain (1565–8) to reach the Giardino dei Cavallieri, where roses and peonies wilt in the summer sun. The pretty building nearby houses the Porcelain Museum (no charge).

Island The Viottolone, an avenue of cypresses planted in 1637 and studded with classical statues, leads to the *Isolotto*, an island set in a murky green pond dotted with pleasantly crumbling statues. In the center is a copy of Giambologna's *Oceanus* fountain (1576), the original of which is in the Bargello (▶ 42).

Luxury garden shed Do not miss *The Limonaia*, built in 1785 to protect rare citrus fruit trees from frost. Now it is a huge rococo garden shed, used for storing gardening equipment.

HIGHLIGHTS

- *Bacchus* fountain (1560)
- *La Grotta Grande*, a Mannerist cave-cum-sculpture gallery (1583–8)
- *The Kaffeehaus* café (1776) (▶ 68): superb views
- Views of the hills from the Giardino dei Cavallieri
- *Limonaia*
- The *Isolotto*

INFORMATION

- ✚ aIV; H7
- ✉ Piazza Pitti
- ☎ 055 218741
- ◷ Daily 9–1 hour before sunset (last admission 30 minutes before closing)
- 🚌 B, C, 11, 36, 37
- ♿ Good
- 💰 Inexpensive
- ↔ Palazzo Pitti (▶ 26)
- ❓ Free maps (Italian) available at entrance on request

Statue of Bacchus astride a tortoise

5

PONTE VECCHIO

No visit to Florence is complete without a saunter down this bridge; lined with old shops jutting precariously over the water, it is difficult to believe you're on a bridge and not just strolling down a narrow street.

History Near the Roman crossing, the Old Bridge was, until 1218, the only bridge across the Arno in Florence. The current bridge was rebuilt after a flood in 1345. During World War II it was the only bridge that the fleeing Germans did not destroy; instead, they blocked access by demolishing the medieval buildings on either side. On November 4, 1966, the bridge miraculously withstood the tremendous weight of water and silt when the Arno burst its banks.

Private path When the Medici moved from the Palazzo Vecchio to the Palazzo Pitti, they decided they needed a connecting route from the Uffizi to the Palazzo Pitti on the other side of the river that enabled them to keep out of contact—heaven forfend!—with their people. The result was Vasari's *Corridoio Vasariano*, built in 1565 on top of the buildings lining the bridge's eastern parapet.

Stores Shops have been on the Ponte Vecchio since the 13th century: initially all types— butchers and fishmongers and later tanners, whose industrial waste caused a pretty rank stench. In 1593, Medici Duke Ferdinand I decreed that only goldsmiths and jewelers be allowed on the bridge, and in the center stands the bust of the 16th-century goldsmith Cellini (1900). When the shops close at night, their wooden shutters make them look like suitcases. As one of the places that Florentines come to for the *passeggiata*, it also has a reputation for being where local drug dealers meet their clients—but you have to be in the know to recognize them.

Window-shopping on the Ponte Vecchio

MUSEO DELLA CASA FIORENTINA ANTICA

In contrast to Florence's other museums, which are packed with important works, this restored 14th-century palace contains everyday artifacts used by rich Florentines from the 14th to the 18th centuries, giving an intriguing insight into their lives.

History The Palazzo Davanzati was built (*c*1330) for the Davizzi, who were wealthy wool merchants. From 1578 to 1904, it was owned by the Davanzati family who were also merchants. In 1904 it was restored to look like a 14th-century palace; in 1910 it was opened as a museum; and in 1951 it was acquired by the State. The palace is arranged around a courtyard.

Water on site A staircase links the courtyard to the Palazzo's three floors and an elaborate system of pulleys transports water from the well, a great luxury in an age when most people had to collect their water by bucket from a public fountain. Pulleys were also used to transport goods to the kitchen which was on the top floor so that, in the event of a kitchen fire, only the upper part of the palace would be burned.

The siege mentality Other signs of wealth are the sheer size and style of the building which, as was necessary at the time, could be converted to a fortress in times of strife, famine or plague; supplies of grain, oil and other food would have been stored in the rooms off the courtyard. The facade has remained much as it was when it was first built, although the original battlements were replaced by a loggia, used for banquets and entertainments, in the 16th century. The sumptuous upper rooms are currently closed for restoration, but a selection of the lace, handwarmers and other treasures from the museum's collection are on show in the temporary first floor gallery.

HIGHLIGHTS

- Sala dei Pappagalli (Parrot Room)
- Kitchen
- 17th-century shoe-shaped handwarmers
- Camera dei Pavoni (Peacock Room)

INFORMATION

- ✚ alll
- ✉ Palazzo Davanzati, Via Porta Rossa 13
- ☎ 055 238 8610
- 🕐 Tue–Sun 8:30–2. Closed alternate Sun and Mon. (Currently only the first floor is open)
- ♿ (Details not available at time of publication, but likely to be part of the refurbishment)
- 🚶 In the pedestrian zone
- 🎫 Moderate
- ⟷ Orsanmichele (➤ 37), Piazza della Signoria (➤ 40)

CAPPELLE MEDICEE

INFORMATION

➕ all
✉ Piazza Madonna degli Aldobrandini
☎ 055 238 8602
🕐 Mon, Wed, Sat, Sun 8:30–4; Tue, Thu, Fri 8:30–2 (last admission 30 minutes before closing). Closed 1st, 3rd, and 5th Mon of the month
🚆 Pedestrian zone near station
♿ Poor
👋 Expensive
↔ San Lorenzo (➤ 31)
❓ Regular guided tours to see charcoal drawings

Of all the places in Florence associated with Michelangelo, Medici Chapels, the mausoleum of the Medici family, are the most intriguing: here are his sculptures for the tombs of Lorenzo and Giuliano, his Madonna and Child, *and even sketches.*

Mausoleum The mausoleum of the Medici family is in three distinct parts of the church of San Lorenzo (➤ 31): the crypt, the Cappella dei Principi, and the Sagrestia Nuova.

Crypt The crypt was where the bodies of minor members of the dynasty were unceremoniously dumped. Tidied up in the 19th century, it now houses numerous tomb slabs.

Chapel of the Princes In the Cappella dei Principi is a huge dome by Bernado Buontalenti, begun in 1604 and not completed until the 20th century. The inner surface is decorated in a heavy, grandiose way that speaks of political tyranny: the Medici coat of arms is rarely out of view. The tombs of six Medici Grand Dukes are in the chapel beneath the dome.

The tomb of Grand Duke Ferdinand

New Sacristy Right of the altar, the Sagrestia Nuova, built by Michelangelo between 1520 and 1534, is a reminder that the Medici were enlightened patrons. Michelangelo sculpted figures representing *Night* and *Day*, and *Dawn* and *Dusk* to adorn the tombs of Lorenzo, Duke of Urbino (1492–1519), and Giuliano, Duke of Nemours (1479–1516). The figure of *Night*, with moon, owl, and mask, is regarded as one of his finest works. The *Madonna and Child* is also by Michelangelo. In a room left of the altar are charcoal drawings found in 1975 and attributed to Michelangelo.

SAN LORENZO

San Lorenzo is the parish church of the Medici, and together with the Cappelle Medicee, it is a monument to their artistic patronage and dynastic grandeur.

History San Lorenzo was rebuilt by Filippo Brunelleschi in 1419, on the site of one of the city's oldest churches (consecrated in AD 393). Its rough-hewn ocher exterior was to have been covered with a facade by Michelangelo: this was never added, but a model can be found in Casa Buonarroti (➤ 54). San Lorenzo is the burial place of the Medici and it's filled with art commissioned by them; the most bizarre is the white statue of Anna Maria Luisa (*d*1743), the last of the dynasty, found—like a displaced Limoges porcelain figure—outside the back of the church.

Interior Brunelleschi's design, with its *pietra serena* (gray sandstone) columns, is cool and airy. The bronze pulpits (*c*1460) that depict the Resurrection and scenes from the life of Christ are Donatello's last work. Savonarola (➤ 12) preached his hellfire-and-brimstone sermons from here. Bronzino's fresco (facing the altar, left) of the *Martyrdom of St. Lawrence* (1569) is an absorbing Mannerist study of the human body in a variety of contortions. Inside Brunelleschi's geometrically precise and esthetically pleasing Sagrestia Vecchia (Old Sacristy, 1421) are eight *tondi* (circular reliefs) by Donatello depicting the evangelists and scenes from the life of St. John.

Biblioteca Laurenziana The Laurentian Library houses the Medici's collection of manuscripts. This extraordinary example of Mannerist architecture by Michelangelo is left of the church approached by a curvaceous *pietra serena* staircase via the cloisters. The readers' desks, which sit at a precipitous angle, are also by Michelangelo. The terra-cotta floor and wooden ceiling are by Tribolo.

HIGHLIGHTS

- Biblioteca Laurenziana
- Staircase by Michelangelo
- Bronzino's *Martyrdom of St. Lawrence*
- Pulpits by Donatello
- Brunelleschi's Sagrestia Vecchia

INFORMATION

- ✚ bII
- ✉ Piazza San Lorenzo
- ☎ 055 216634.
  Library 055 230 2991
- 🕐 Daily 7:30–noon, 3:30–6:30.
  Library Mon–Sat 9–1
- 🚌 In the pedestrian zone
- ♿ Poor
- 🎫 Free
- ↔ Cappelle Medicee (➤ 30), Duomo (➤ 35), Battistero (➤ 33), Palazzo Medici (➤ 32)

Market stands outside San Lorenzo

31

9

PALAZZO MEDICI RICCARDI

HIGHLIGHTS

- Gozzoli's fresco cycle of the Journey of the Magi

INFORMATION

- ✚ bII
- ✉ Via Cavour 1
- ☎ 055 276 0340
- ◷ Mon, Tue, Thu–Sat 9–1, 3–5:15; Sun and hols 9–1
- ▣ 1, 6, 7
- ♿ Good
- ▣ Cappella dei Magi moderate
- ⬌ San Lorenzo (► 31)
- ❓ The Palazzo houses the Museo Mediceo, used to house temporary exhibitions

The Medici ruled with a strange mixture of tyranny and humanity. This is reflected in the imposingly rough facade of their main headquarters, with its fearsome lattice of window bars and slightly incongruous built-in bench at seat height, where passers-by could, and still can, sit and relax.

History The Palazzo Medici Riccardi, now mostly government offices, was the seat of the Medici family from its completion in 1444 until 1540 when Cosimo I moved the Medici residence to the Palazzo Vecchio and this palace was bought by the Riccardi family.

Exterior The Palazzo Medici, designed by Michelozzo, was widely imitated in Florence, for example in the Palazzo Strozzi and the Palazzo Pitti. It is characterized by huge slabs of stone, rusticated to give a roughly hewn rural appearance. The courtyard is in a lighter style, with a graceful colonnade and black and white sgraffito decoration of medallions, based on the designs of Roman intaglios collected by the Medici and displayed in the Museo degli Argenti (► 26).

Detail from Gozzoli's 15th-century fresco, Journey of the Magi

Chapel Steps right of the entrance lead to the Cappella dei Magi. In this tiny chapel you will find the dazzling fresco cycle showing the *Journey of the Magi* (1459–63) that Piero de' Medici commissioned from Gozzoli in honor of the Compagnia dei Magi, a religious organization to which the Medici belonged. Portraits of the Medici are believed to have been incorporated into the cast of characters, while the procession recalls the pageantry of the Compagnia dei Magi and includes enchanting little animals: leopards, monkeys, and a falcon whose claws pierce the entrails of a hare.

BATTISTERO

Perhaps the most loved of all Florence's edifices is the Baptistery, referred to by Dante as his "bel San Giovanni," and dedicated to St. John the Baptist, the patron saint of Florence. With its octagonal, marble exterior and fabulous bronze doors, it is one of the city's most beautiful buildings.

Roman origins The Baptistery is one of the oldest buildings in Florence: the remains of a Roman palace lie under it, and the dates given for the present construction vary between the 5th and the 7th centuries AD. For much of Florence's history it was the place where all Florentines were baptized and, inside, it is quite clear where the font stood until its removal in 1576.

Rich ornament The entire outer surface is covered with a beautiful design of white and green marble, added between the 11th and 13th centuries. Inside, the ceiling is encrusted with stunning mosaics: above the altar, designs show the Virgin and St. John the Baptist; the main design shows the Last Judgment, with the sinful being devoured by diabolical creatures, while the virtuous ascend to heaven. Do not miss the tessellated floor, almost Islamic in its intricate geometry.

Bronze doors The Baptistery is renowned, above all, for its bronze doors: the south doors, by Pisano (1336), and Ghiberti's north and east doors (1403–24 and 1425–52). The east doors, referred to by Michelangelo as the "Gates of Paradise," are divided into 10 panels depicting Old Testament scenes, using Renaissance techniques such as linear perspective. The originals are in the Museo dell'Opera del Duomo (► 36); the copies were funded by Japanese patronage.

HIGHLIGHTS

- 13th-century mosaics showing the Last Judgment
- Ghiberti's *Gates of Paradise*
- Pisano's south doors
- Zodiac pavement
- Romanesque marble exterior

Exterior of the Battistero

INFORMATION

- ✚ bIII
- ✉ Piazza San Giovanni
- 🕐 Mon–Sat 1:30–6:30; Sun and religious hols 9–1
- 🚌 1, 6, 7, 11, 14, 23 (in the pedestrian zone)
- ♿ Good
- 💶 Inexpensive
- ↔ Duomo (► 35), Campanile (► 34)

CAMPANILE

Tall, graceful, and beautifully proportioned, the bell tower of the Duomo is one of the loveliest in Italy and adds a calm and graceful note to the otherwise busy cathedral complex.

HIGHLIGHTS

- Views from the top
- Reliefs by Pisano and della Robbia

INFORMATION

- ✚ bIII
- ✉ Piazza del Duomo
- ☎ 055 271071
- 🕓 Apr–Sep: daily 9–7:30.
  Oct–Mar: daily 9–5:30
  (last admission 40 minutes before closing)
- 🚶 In the pedestrian zone
- ♿ Impossible
- 💲 Moderate
- ↔ Duomo (➤ 35), Battistero (➤ 33)

It's a 414-step climb to the top of the Campanile —a real test of stamina

Multiple effort   The Campanile, or bell tower, of the Duomo stands 279 feet, just 19 feet lower than the Duomo. It was begun in 1334 and completed in 1359. Giotto was involved in its design, but by the time of his death in 1337 only the base had been completed. Andrea Pisano completed the second story, and the tower was finished by Francesco Talenti.

Relief sculpture   The outer surface is decorated in the same polychrome marble as the Duomo: white marble from Carrara, green marble from Prato, and pink marble from the Maremma—the flat marshland area along the coast of southern Tuscany. Around the bottom are two sets of relief sculptures: the lower tier are in hexagonal panels, the upper tier in diamonds. What you see are in fact copies; the originals have been moved to the Museo dell'Opera del Duomo (➤ 36) to prevent further atmospheric damage. The reliefs in the hexagonal panels, which were executed by Pisano (although some are believed to have been designed by Giotto), show the Creation of Man, the Arts and the Industries, including weaving, hunting, and navigation. On the north face the five Liberal Arts (grammar, philosophy, music, arithmetic, and astrology) were executed by Luca della Robbia. The upper tier of reliefs, also the work of Pisano, illustrate the Seven Planets, the Seven Virtues, and the Liberal Arts; while the Seven Sacraments have been attributed to Alberto Arnoldi.

DUOMO

The famous dome of this cathedral dominates the Florence skyline, with its eight white ribs against a terra-cotta tiles background. From close up, the sheer size of the building is overwhelming.

Origins The cathedral of Santa Maria del Fiori, the Florence Duomo, is a vast Gothic structure built on the site of the 7th-century church of Santa Reparata, whose remains can be seen in the crypt. It was built at the end of the 13th century, although the colossal dome, which dominates the exterior, was not added until the 15th century, and the facade was not finished until the 19th century. The exterior is a decorative riot of pink, white, and green marble; the interior is stark and plain. The clock above the entrance on the west wall inside was designed in 1443 by Paolo Uccello in accordance with the *ora italica*, according to which the 24th hour of the day ends at sunset.

The dome Built by Filippo Brunelleschi, who won the competition for its commission in 1418, the dome is egg-shaped and was made without scaffolding. Its herringbone brickwork was copied from the Pantheon in Rome. The best way to see the dome is to climb its 463 steps: the route takes you through the interior, where you can see Vasari's much-reviled frescoes of the Last Judgment (1572–9), and toward the lantern, from which the views are fantastic.

Explosion of the cart At Easter the *Scoppio del Carro*, a Mass-cum-theatrical pageant, culminates in a mechanical dove being launched from the altar along a wire to the entrance, so that at noon its beak ignites a cart full of fireworks outside the Duomo doors.

HIGHLIGHTS

- Brunelleschi's dome
- Remains of Santa Reparata
- Uccello's mural to a 14th-century Captain-General

Detail from one of the Duomo's doors

INFORMATION

- ✛ bIII
- ✉ Piazza del Duomo
- ☎ 055 271071
- 🕓 Cathedral Mon–Sat 10–5, Sun 1–5; 1st Sat of the month 10–3:30. Dome (access to staircase) Mon–Sat 9:30–5:30
- 🚌 1, 6, 7, 11, 14 (in the pedestrian zone)
- ♿ Good (access via the entrance for the dome)
- 🎟 Free. Dome moderate
- ↔ Campanile (➤ 34), Battistero (➤ 33)

13

MUSEO DELL'OPERA DEL DUOMO

There is something very pleasing about the idea of visiting the Cathedral Workshop, the maintenance section of the huge artistic undertaking that the cathedral complex represents.

Refuge from pollution This workshop-museum was founded when the Duomo was built, to maintain the art of the cathedral. Its location was chosen in the 15th century, and it was in its courtyard that Michelangelo sculpted his *David*. Since 1891, it has housed works removed from the cathedral complex: indeed, one reason why the Duomo seems so empty is that so much is now exhibited in the Museo dell'Opera del Duomo. It is also a refuge for outdoor sculptures.

Michelangelo's *Pietà* The second room you enter shows the construction materials and instruments used for Brunelleschi's dome, such as pulleys, buckets, and brick molds. On the landing is the *Pietà* (begun *c*1550) by Michelangelo, which used to be in the Duomo. It is believed that he intended it for his own tomb; the hooded figure of Nicodemus is often interpreted as a self-portrait. The damage to Christ's left leg and arm is believed to have been inflicted by Michelangelo in frustration at his failing skills.

Artists compared The main room on the second floor contains two choir lofts that once stood in the Duomo: one by Luca della Robbia (1431–8), the other by Donatello (1433–9). This is an opportunity to compare two great Renaissance artists: della Robbia's infants are smooth, their movements lyrical; Donatello's convey a more immediate vigor. In the room on the left are reliefs by Pisano from the Campanile (➤ 34); in the room on the right Ghiberti's original "Gates of Paradise" are displayed as their restoration is completed.

Detail from della Robbia's choir loft

ORSANMICHELE

In Orsanmichele, perhaps more than anywhere else in Florence, you are made aware of the guilds that were so influential in the history of the city. It is their emblems and patron saints that adorn this building.

Vegetable garden   Orsanmichele gets its name from the fact that it was surrounded by the *orto* (vegetable garden) of a Benedictine monastery when it was first built around AD 750, as the oratory of St. Michael. The present building was constructed in 1336 as a market and grain store; by 1380 the first floor had become a church.

Saintly sculptures   In 1339 it was decided that each of the major tradesmen's guilds should provide a statue of their respective patron saint to stand outside. By happy accident, nothing was completed until the Renaissance was in full swing in the 15th century, so the commissions were executed by artists of the caliber of Verrocchio, Ghiberti, Donatello, and Luca della Robbia. Most of the niches for the saints are now empty or filled with copies. Many of the sculptures are in the Museo di Orsanmichele, in the upper two stories of this building.

Interior   Inside Orsanmichele is gloomy. The walls reveal patchy traces of frescoes; these, too, depict the various guild patron saints. The central feature, however, is the tabernacle (1348–59) by Orcagna, which frames the exquisite *Madonna and Child* (1347) by Bernardo Daddi. To properly appreciate the architecture of Orsanmichele visit the museum, where you can admire the superb vaulting and brickwork and get a true impression of the immense size of the building. The views are spectacular (▶ 55).

HIGHLIGHTS

- ● Bernardo Daddi's *Madonna and Child*
- ● Orcagna's tabernacle
- ● della Robbia roundels
- ● Museo di Orsanmichele

INFORMATION

- ✚ bIII
- ✉ Via dei Calzaiuoli; museum entrance at the Palazzo dell'Arte di Lana, opposite the entrance to Orsanmichele on Via dell'Arte di Lana
- ☎ 055 284715
- ◉ Daily 9–noon, 4–6. Museum Mon–Sat 9–2; Sun 9–12:30
- ▣ In the pedestrian zone
- ♿ Good (except museum)
- ▣ Free
- ↔ Piazza della Signoria (▶ 40), Palazzo Vecchio (▶ 41)

Bernardo Daddi's Madonna and Child

37

15

GALLERIA DEGLI UFFIZI

The Uffizi encompasses the artistic developments of the Renaissance and beyond. It is a powerful expression of Florence's extraordinary role in the history of art.

The gallery The Uffizi Gallery contains part of the Medicis' art collection, bequeathed in 1737 by Anna Maria Luisa. The building was designed by Vasari, in the 1560s, as the administrative offices (*uffizi*) of the Grand Duchy. Parts of the building and collection that were damaged by the 1993 bomb were restored and reopened in 1998.

Art collection Today people come for the paintings, but until the 19th century the attraction was sculpture (mostly now in the Bargello, ▶ 42). The collection is displayed in broadly chronological order, starting with the first stirrings of the Renaissance in the 13th century and ending with works by Caravaggio, Rembrandt, and Canaletto from the 17th and 18th centuries. Uccello's *Battle of San Romano* (1456) exemplifies the technical advances of the Renaissance, such as the mastery of linear perspective, while Filippo Lippi's *Madonna and Child with Two Angels* (c1465) reveals the emotional focus typical of the period.

The Tribune Perhaps most fascinating is the Tribune, an octagonal chamber with a mother-of-pearl ceiling, containing favorite Medici pieces. In the center is the Medici *Venus* (a copy of Praxiteles' Aphrodite of Cnidos, c350 BC), whose sensuous derrière earned her the reputation of the sexiest sculpture of the ancient world. On the walls, portraits of the Medicis include Bronzino's enchanting *Giovanni de Medici* (c1545), a smiling little boy in crimson satin holding a goldfinch.

Early birds Go to the Uffizi early in the morning or in the late afternoon to avoid the lines. The café has superb views of Piazza della Signoria.

Above: Botticelli's Birth of Venus *(1485)*

Museo di Storia della Scienza

The Museo di Storia della Scienza has a fascinating and well-organized collection of scientific instruments, a reminder that the Florentine Renaissance was not merely an artistic movement, but also fostered the origins of modern science.

Origins Located in the 14th-century Palazzo Castellani, the Museum of the History of Science houses a collection of which in large part belonged to the Medici Grand Dukes. In 1775 the Museum of Physics and Natural Sciences was opened and in 1929 the collection was moved to its current location. The galleries are on the second and third floors; the first floor is the library of the Istituto di Storia della Scienza.

Galileo Galilei There is a sizable exhibition devoted to Galileo (1564–1642), Pisa-born but adopted by the Medici as the court mathematician. Some exhibits border on the hagiographic: not only is his telescope displayed, but also the middle finger of his right hand, preserved in a reliquary.

Maps and planets The map room has a 16th-century map of the world by the Portuguese cartographer Lopo Homem, revealing the limit of European geographical knowledge at that time: Australasia is nowhere to be found and the tip of South America fades into blankness. It also has a collection of armillary spheres, used to divine the movements of the planets.

Obstetric models On the third floor is a series of 18th-century wax and ceramic models of birth deformities, complete with helpful hints for the doctor, such as where to insert the forceps.

HIGHLIGHTS

- Galileo's telescope
- Lopo Homem's map of the world
- Antonio Santucci's armillary sphere (1573)
- Copy of Lorenzo della Volpaia's clock of the planets (1593)
- 18th-century models of birth deformities

INFORMATION

- ✚ blV
- ✉ Piazza dei Guidici 1
- ☎ 055 239 8876
- ◉ Tue, Thu, Sat 9:30–1; Mon, Wed, Fri 9:30–1, 2–5. Closed Sun and hols
- ▭ 23
- ♿ Excellent
- ▣ Moderate
- ⟷ Galleria degli Uffizi (➤ 38), Ponte Vecchio (➤ 28)
- ❓ Excellent guide book

Above: a sketch of Galileo's telescope
Top: 16th-century sundials

17

PIAZZA DELLA SIGNORIA

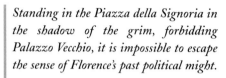

INFORMATION

- ✚ bIII
- ✉ Piazza della Signoria
- ▣ In the pedestrian zone
- ♿ Good
- 🎟 No entrance charge
- ↔ Palazzo Vecchio (➤ 41), Galleria degli Uffizi (➤ 38)

Sculpture of Neptune by Ammannati

Standing in the Piazza della Signoria in the shadow of the grim, forbidding Palazzo Vecchio, it is impossible to escape the sense of Florence's past political might.

Political piazza   The Piazza della Signoria has been the center of political life in Florence since the 14th century. It was the scene of great triumphs, such as the return of the Medici in 1530, but also of the Bonfire of the Vanities instigated by Savonarola (➤ 12), who was himself burned at the stake here in 1498, denounced as a heretic by the Inquisition.

Significant sculptures   The sculptures in Piazza della Signoria bristle with political connotations, many of them fiercely contradictory. Michelangelo's *David* (the original is in the Accademia) was placed outside the Palazzo Vecchio as a symbol of the Republic's defiance of the tyrannical Medici. The *Neptune* (1575), by Ammannati, celebrates the Medici's maritime ambitions, and Giambologna's equestrian statue of Duke *Cosimo I* (1595) is an elegant portrait of the man who brought all of Tuscany under Medici military rule. The statue of *Perseus* holding Medusa's head, by Cellini (1554), is a stark reminder of what happened to those who crossed the Medici.

Loggia dei Lanzi   The graceful Loggia dei Lanzi, which functions as an open-air sculpture gallery, was designed by Orcagna in 1376; its curved arches foretell Renaissance classicism.

Postcard paradise   Sorbi (➤ 76), the newspaper kiosk, has an unrivaled collection of postcards and newspapers which you could enjoy over a cappuccino in the Rivoire café (➤ 68).

PALAZZO VECCHIO

With its fortress-like castellations and its 311 foot bell tower, the Palazzo Vecchio conveys a message of political power supported by military strength.

Town Hall The Palazzo Vecchio is still Florence's town hall, as it has been since its completion by Arnolfo di Cambio in 1302. It was substantially remodeled for Duke Cosimo I, who made it his palace in 1540. It became known as the Palazzo Vecchio (Old Palace), when Cosimo transferred his court to the Palazzo Pitti. During the brief period when Florence was the capital of Italy (1865–71), it housed the Parliament and Foreign Ministry.

Assembly room The vast Salone dei Cinquecento (175 by 72 feet; 59 feet high) was designed in the 1490s, during the era of the Florentine Republic, as the meeting place of the 500-strong ruling assembly. Vasari painted the military scenes of Florence's victory over Siena and Pisa (1563–5). The theme of Florence's might is further underscored by the presence of Michelangelo's *Victory* (1533–4) as well as sculptures of the *Labors of Hercules* by Vincenzo dei Rossi. The ceiling is painted with the *Apotheosis of Cosimo I* (also by Vasari), lest we miss the point.

Loggia views On the third floor the Terrazza di Saturno is an open loggia with views towards the hills. The Sala dei Gigli is decorated with gold fleurs-de-lys (the symbol of Florence) against a blue background and houses Donatello's *Judith and Holofernes* (1456–60). The most interesting room is last: the Sala delle Carte (Map Room), with its wonderful collection of globes and 57 maps painted on leather, showing the world as it was known in 1563.

HIGHLIGHTS

- Sala delle Carte
- Sala dei Gigli
- Michelangelo's *Victory*
- Donatello's *Judith and Holofernes*
- View from the Terrazza di Saturno
- Salone dei Cinquecento

INFORMATION

- ✚ bIV
- ✉ Piazza della Signoria
- ☎ 055 276 8465
- ◷ Mon–Wed, Fri, Sat 9–7; Sun 8–1. Closed May 1, Aug 15
- ▣ 19, 23, 31, 32
- ♿ Good
- 🖱 Expensive
- ↔ Piazza della Signoria (► 40), Gallerie degli Uffizi (► 38)
- ❷ In summer, walks along the parapets and other parts of the Palazzo Vecchio not normally open to the public are organized. Details from the tourist information center

19

BARGELLO

INFORMATION

- ✚ bIII
- ✉ Via del Proconsolo 4
- ☎ 055 238 8606
- 🕐 Daily 8:30–2. Closed 1st, 3rd, and 5th Sun, 2nd and 4th Mon of every month; Apr 25, May 1
- 🚌 19
- ♿ Good
- 💰 Moderate
- ↔ Piazza della Signoria (► 40)

The Bargello, with its airy courtyard, is so pleasant that you would want to visit it even if it were not home to what is arguably the finest collection of Renaissance sculpture in the world.

Origins   Built in 1255, the Bargello was the first seat of Florence's city government and served as the city's main law court before being passed to the *Bargello* (Chief of Police) in 1574; it was used as a prison until 1859. In 1865 it opened as a museum, with an unrivaled collection of Renaissance sculpture and decorative arts.

The courtyard   The walls of the courtyard, once the site of executions, are decorated with the coats-of-arms of the Podestà (chief magistrates), whose headquarters were here, and 16th-century sculpture, including Giambologna's *Oceanus* from the Boboli Gardens (► 27). The first floor has works by Michelangelo (► 54), Cellini and Giambologna, including his *Mercury* (1564).

The second floor   In the Salone del Consiglio Generale, a vaulted hall on the second floor that was once the courtroom, works by Donatello include his decidedly camp bronze *David* (*c*1430–40), dressed in long boots and a jaunty hat (the first freestanding nude since the Roman period), and his *St. George* (1416), sculpted for the exterior of Orsanmichele (► 37).

The Salone del Consiglio Generale, which once served as a courtroom

The third floor   Enameled terra-cottas by the della Robbia family include the bust of a boy by Andrea della Robbia. There is also a display of Italian medals and a superb collection of small Renaissance bronzes. The arms room has ivory-inlay saddles as well as guns and armor.

GALLERIA DELL'ACCADEMIA

Michelangelo's David, *exhibited in the Accademia, always has a powerful impact: the intensity of his gaze, the assured posture, those huge hands, the anatomical precision of the veins and the muscles.*

Origins The Accademia was founded in 1784 to teach techniques of painting, drawing, and sculpture. Since 1873 it has housed the world's single most important collection of sculptures by Michelangelo. There are, however, sculptures by other artists as well as many paintings, mostly from the Renaissance period.

Michelangelo's masterpiece The principal attraction is the *David* by Michelangelo, sculpted in 1504 and exhibited outside the Palazzo Vecchio until 1873, when it was transferred to the Accademia to protect it from environmental damage. It captures the moment at which the young David contemplates defying the giant Goliath. The pose is classical, determined by the thin dimensions of Carrara marble slab.

Freedom from stone The *Prisoners* (1505) were made for the tomb of Pope Julius II. The title refers to Michelangelo's belief that when he sculpted a statue, he was freeing the figure from the marble, and the style, particularly favored by Michelangelo, was called the *non finito* (unfinished). After his death, the *Prisoners* were moved to the Grotta Grande in the Boboli Gardens (► 27), where the originals were replaced with casts in 1908. Among the other sculptures is the original plaster model for *The Rape of the Sabine Women* (1583), Giambologna's last work; the marble version is in the Loggia dei Lanzi in Piazza della Signoria (► 40).

HIGHLIGHTS

- Michelangelo's *David*
- Michelangelo's *Prisoners*
- Giambologna's *Rape of the Sabine Women*
- Buonaguida's *Tree of Life*

INFORMATION

✚ bll
✉ Via Ricasoli 60
☎ 055 238 8609
🕐 Tue–Sat 8:30AM–10PM; Sun 8:30–2. Closed May 1
🚇 San Marco
♿ Good
💲 Expensive
↔ San Marco (► 44), Santissima Annunziata (► 45)

Michelangelo's David

SAN MARCO

HIGHLIGHTS

- Fra Angelico's cell paintings
- Fra Angelico's *Annunciation*
- Savonarola's cells
- Cosimo il Vecchio's cells

INFORMATION

- ✚ bII
- ✉ Piazza San Marco
- ☎ 055 238 8608
- ◷ Wed, Sat–Mon 8:30–2; Tue, Thu, Fri 8:30–4 (last admission 30 minutes before closing). Closed 1st, 3rd, and 5th Sun; 2nd and 4th Mon of every month
- 🚌 1, 6, 7, 10, 11, 17, 20, 25, 31, 32, 33
- ♿ Good
- 🎫 Moderate
- ↔ Accademia (➤ 43), Santissima Annunziata (➤ 45)

The Annunciation *(1442), Fra Angelico*

Dominated by the lovely paintings of Fra Angelico, the soothing convent of San Marco has an aura of monastic calm that is conducive to appreciating the religious themes depicted.

Medici motives   San Marco was founded in the 13th century by Silvestrine monks. In 1437 Cosimo il Vecchio invited the Dominican monks of Fiesole to move into the convent and had it rebuilt by Michelozzo, a gesture motivated by his guilt for having made so much money from banking (which was not theologically correct) and also by the fact that the Dominicans were useful allies. Ironically, Savonarola (➤ 12), who denounced the decadence of the Medici at the end of the 15th century, came to prominence as the Dominican prior of San Marco.

A feast for the eyes   The Chiostro di Sant' Antonino, the cloister through which you enter, is decorated with faded frescoes by Fra Angelico and other Florentine artists. In the Ospizio dei Pellegrini, where pilgrims were cared for, there is a superb collection of freestanding paintings by Fra Angelico and his followers. At the top of the staircase on the way to the dormitory is Fra Angelico's *Annunciation* (1440), an image of great tenderness and grace. Each of the 44 monks' cells is adorned with a small fresco by Fra Angelico or one of his assistants. The themes include the *Entombment* (cell 2) and the *Mocking of Christ* (cell 7). Savonarola's rooms house an exhibition about him. Cells 38 and 39 were reserved for Cosimo il Vecchio, who periodically spent time in the monastery.

Public library   The library, also on the second floor, built in 1441 by Michelozzo, was the first public library in Europe.

SANTISSIMA ANNUNZIATA

Make time for Piazza della Santissima Annunziata, which is central but off the beaten tourist track. Its intimacy and delicate architecture contrast with the grandeur of much of Florence, and the roundels of babies on the Spedale degli Innocenti's facade are quite enchanting.

Old New Year The Feast of the Annunciation on March 25 used to be New Year in the old Florentine calendar, and for that reason the church and the square have always played a special role in the life of the city. Every year, on March 25, a fair is still held in the square and special biscuits called *brigidini* are sold.

Wedding flowers The church of Santissima Annunziata was built by Michelozzo in 1444–81 on the site of a Servite oratory. Entry is through an atrium known as the Chiostrino dei Voti (1447), which has the air of a rickety greenhouse though the frescoes inside are superb. They include Rosso Fiorentino's *Assumption*, Pontormo's *Visitation* and Andrea del Sarto's *Birth of the Virgin*. For some Florentines, the star attraction is a fresco of the Virgin Mary (said to have been started by a monk in 1252 and finished by an angel), to which newlyweds present the wedding bouquet to ensure a happy marriage.

Early orphanage The Spedale degli Innocenti, on the east side of the piazza, was the first orphanage in Europe; part of the building is still used for the purpose, and UNICEF has offices here. Designed by Filippo Brunelleschi in 1419, it is decorated with enameled terra-cotta roundels by della Robbia showing babies in swaddling clothes (1498).

HIGHLIGHTS

- Andrea della Robbia's roundels
- Facade of the Spedale degli Innocenti
- Rosso Fiorentino's *Assumption*
- Pontormo's *Visitation*
- Andrea del Sarto's *Birth of the Virgin*

INFORMATION

- ✚ cll
- ✉ Piazza della Santissima Annunziata
- ☎ 055 239 8034. Spedale degli Innocenti 055 234 9317
- 🕓 Mon–Sat 7–12:30, 4–6:30; Sun 4–6:30. Spedale Mon, Tue, Thu–Sat 8:30–2; Sun 8–1
- 🚌 6, 31, 32
- ♿ Good
- 💶 Inexpensive to Spedale
- 🔗 Accademia (➤ 43), San Marco (➤ 44)

Andrea del Sarto's work in the Chiostrino

45

23

CAPPELLA DEI PAZZI

INFORMATION

✠ cIV

✉ Piazza Santa Croce

☎ 055 244619

⊙ Apr–Oct: Thu–Tue
10–12:30, 2:30–6:30.
Nov–Mar: Thu–Tue
10–12:30, 3–5

🚌 23, 13, B

♿ Good

💰 Inexpensive

↔ Santa Croce (➤ 47)

In contrast to the adjacent church of Santa Croce, a key stop on the tourist circuit, the cloisters are not much visited. The solitude you find is perfect for appreciating their grace and harmony.

Convent building On the south side of Santa Croce are the buildings of a former convent. These include the Cappella dei Pazzi, one of the great architectural masterpieces of the early Renaissance, and a 14th-century refectory, which houses the Museo dell'Opera di Santa Croce. This is one of the lowest areas in Florence, and to the left of the Cappella dei Pazzi a plaque almost 20 feet up shows the high point of the November 1966 floodwaters. The second cloister, a haven of calm, was designed by Filippo Brunelleschi.

The Pazzi Chapel The Cappella dei Pazzi, which was commissioned as a chapter house by Andrea dei Pazzi and designed by Brunelleschi (*c*1430), is incorporated into the cloisters. Inside, this graceful domed chapel is done in gray *pietra serena* against a plain white plaster background, embellished only by enameled terra-cotta roundels: 12 roundels by Luca della Robbia show the Apostles, with four more of the evangelists, attributed to Brunelleschi or Donatello, around the dome.

Museum The museum is small but contains many important works, including a restored crucifix by Giovanni Cimabue, almost destroyed in the 1966 floods. On the walls a huge fresco by Taddeo Gaddi shows the Last Supper, the Tree of Life, St. Louis of Toulouse, St. Francis, St. Benedict and Mary Magdalene washing Christ's feet. It is hard to miss the gilded bronze statue of *St. Louis of Toulouse* (1424), sculpted by Donatello for the Orsanmichele (➤ 37).

Roundel of St. Luke, one of the four evangelists

SANTA CROCE

Despite its vast size and swarms of tourists, the Franciscan church of Santa Croce is touchingly intimate, perhaps because of the sense that one somehow knows the people buried here.

Florentine favorite Santa Croce, rebuilt for the Franciscan order in 1294 by Arnolfo di Cambio, is the burial place of the great and the good in Florence.

Civic pantheon Michelangelo is buried in Santa Croce, as are Rossini, Machiavelli, and the Pisa-born Galileo Galilei, who was excommunicated during the Inquisition and was not allowed a Christian burial until 1737—95 years after his death. There is also a memorial to Dante, whose sarcophagus is empty (▶ 17).

Exterior The church exterior is covered with a polychrome marble facade added in 1863 and paid for by the English benefactor, Sir Francis Sloane. It looks over the Piazza Santa Croce, site of an annual soccer game in medieval costume (▶ 83).

Artistic riches The artistic wealth in Santa Croce is stunning; frescoes by Gaddi (1380) in the Cappella Maggiore tell the story of the holy cross ("Santa Croce") and beautiful frescoes by Giotto in the Bardi and Peruzzi chapels show scenes from the lives of St. Francis and St. John the Evangelist. An unusual relief *Annunciation* in gilded limestone by Donatello decorates the south nave's wall. Don't miss the memorial to 19th-century playwright Giovanni Battista Nicolini, left of the entrance facing the altar, said to have inspired the *Statue of Liberty*. Santa Croce was severely hit by flooding in 1966, and a tide mark shows far up on the pillars and walls.

HIGHLIGHTS

- Giotto frescoes
- Tomb of Michelangelo
- Tomb of Machiavelli
- Painted wooden ceiling
- Tomb of Galileo
- Donatello's *Annunciation*
- Polychrome marble facade

INFORMATION

- ✚ clV
- ✉ Piazza Santa Croce
- ☎ 055 244619
- ◷ Daily 8–12:30, 3–6:30
- ▤ 23, 13, B
- ♿ Acceptable
- ▨ Free
- ⟷ Cappella dei Pazzi (▶ 46)

The vast interior of Santa Croce

25

SAN MINIATO AL MONTE

INFORMATION

- ✚ J8
- ✉ Off Viale Galileo Galilei
- ☎ 055 234 2768
- ⏱ Mon–Sat 8–12:30, 2–6; Sun 8–6
- 🚌 12, 13
- ♿ Good
- ✋ Free

San Miniato is a wonderful sight on the hill above Florence, its marble facade glistening in the sunlight. Close up it is even more appealing, a jewel of the Romanesque inside as well as outside.

Christian martyr San Miniato (St. Minias) was an early Christian martyr who came to Florence from the Levant in the 3rd century and was martyred in the Roman amphitheater that stood on the site of today's Piazza della Signoria, by order of the Emperor Decius. It is said that his decapitated body picked up his head and walked into the hills. His shrine, the site of the present church, was built where he finally collapsed. The church was initially run by Benedictine monks, then by Cluniacs, and finally, from 1373 to the present day, by the Olivetans. In the Benedictine shop on the right as you exit, monks sell honey and herbal potions as well as Coca-Cola.

The exterior The church was built in 1018, with a green-and-white marble facade, typical of the Tuscan Romanesque added at the end of the 11th century and mosaics in the 13th century. On the pinnacle of the church a gilded copper statue of an eagle carries a bale of cloth (1410): this is the symbol of the Arte di Calimala, the wool importers' guild, which supported the church in the Middle Ages.

The interior Inside, a lovely inlaid floor (*c*1207) incorporates zodiac and animal themes. The capitals of the columns are Roman and Byzantine, and the wooden ceiling, restored in the 19th century, dates from 1322. The mosaics in the apse (1297) show the Virgin and St. Minias. In the nave is a chapel (1448) by Michelozzo, built to house a miraculous crucifix that is now in Santa Trinita (▶ 53).

Michelozzo's free-standing chapel

FLORENCE's *best*

MUSEUMS & GALLERIES

Joint ticket

If you are on a serious culture trip, buy a joint ticket for the museums run by the *comune* (town hall)—the Museo Bardini, the Museo di Santa Maria Novella (► 25), the Palazzo Vecchio (► 41), and the Museo di "Firenze Com'era." This ticket gets you to several sights for much less than you'd pay buying individual tickets. Valid for six months, it can be bought from any of the participating museums.

Museo Archeologico

> **See Top 25 Sights for**
> **ACCADEMIA (► 43)**
> **BARGELLO (► 42)**
> **GALLERIA DEGLI UFFIZI (► 38)**
> **MUSEO DELLA CASA FIORENTINA ANTICA (► 29)**
> **MUSEO DELL'OPERA DEL DUOMO (► 36)**
> **MUSEO DELL'OPERA DI SANTA CROCE (► 46)**
> **MUSEO DI SAN MARCO (► 44)**
> **MUSEO DI SANTA MARIA NOVELLA (► 25)**
> **MUSEO DI STORIA DELLA SCIENZA (► 39)**
> **PALAZZO PITTI: GALLERIA PALATINA, GALLERIA D'ARTE MODERNA, MUSEO DEGLI ARGENTI, MUSEO DEL COSTUME (► 26)**

MUSEO ARCHEOLOGICO

One of the best places to see Etruscan art. There are also Roman, Greek, and Egyptian exhibits.

✚ cII ✉ Palazzo della Crocetta, Via della Colonna 36 ☎ 055 23575 🕐 Mon–Sat 8:30–2; Sun 8:30–1. Closed alternate Sun and Mon 🚌 6 ♿ Good 💰 Moderate

MUSEO BARDINI

Stefano Bardini was a 19th-century art dealer with a knack of acquiring choice pieces at knock-down prices. He made some particularly judicious purchases in the field of church architecture, some of which are worked into the fabric of the palazzo, such as door frames and the wooden ceiling in room 20. There are also ceramics, medieval weapons, Renaissance paintings, and sculptures.

✚ J7 ✉ Piazza de' Mozzi 1 ☎ 055 234 2427 🕐 Mon, Tue, Thu–Sat 9–2; Sun 8–1. Closed hols 🚌 B, C ♿ Good 💰 Moderate

MUSEO MARINO MARINI

One of Florence's oldest churches (9th century, with a 15th-century facade and porch) is now a museum dedicated to the sculptor Marino Marini (1901–80) who studied in Florence. An excellent reminder that Italian art didn't grind to a halt in the 17th century.

✚ aIII ✉ Piazza San Pancrazio (Via della Spada) ☎ 055 219432 🕐 Mon, Wed–Sat 10–5; Sun 10–1 🚌 6, 11, 36, 37 ♿ Good 💰 Moderate

"LA SPECOLA": MUSEO ZOOLOGICO

La Specola is so called after the observatory that used to be here. Highlights are the *Cere Anatomiche*, a gruesome set of 18th-century wax models of bits of human bodies. Four vignettes of the plague in Florence show rats eating the intestines of decaying bodies.

✚ H7 ✉ Via Romana 17 ☎ 055 222451 🕐 Mon, Tue, Thu–Sat 9–noon; Sun 9–1. Closed hols 🚌 11, 36, 37 ♿ Few 💰 Moderate

MUSEO DI "FIRENZE COM'ERA"
This museum houses paintings and maps showing what Florence used to look like from the late 15th until the early 20th centuries. You'll also find delightful 16th-century lunettes of the Medici villas, and the *Pianta della Catena*, an 1887 copy of a 1470 view of Florence.
➕ bIII ✉ Via dell'Oriuolo 24 ☎ 055 239 8483 🕐 Mon–Wed, Fri, Sat 9–2; Sun 8–1 🚌 14, 23, B ♿ Acceptable 💷 Inexpensive

Museo di "Firenze com'era"

MUSEO FRATELLI ALINARI
A collection of black-and-white photographs of the Fratelli Alinari company, which was founded in 1852. Temporary photographic exhibitions are also held. It is housed in the 15th-century Palazzo Rucellai.
➕ aIII ✉ Via della Vigna Nuova 16 ☎ 055 213370 🕐 Mon, Tue, Thu, Sun 10–7:30; Fri, Sat 10AM–11:30PM 🚌 6, 11, 36, 37 ♿ Good 💷 Moderate

MUSEO NAZIONALE DI ANTROPOLOGIA E L'ETNOGRAFIA
Founded in 1869, this museum offers something more than art and history. Exhibits relating to the Kafiri people of Pakistan are academically interesting; the peoples of the areas of Africa that came under Italian colonial rule are well represented.
➕ bIII ✉ Palazzo Nonfinito, Via del Proconsolo 12 ☎ 055 239 6449 🕐 Thu–Sat, 3rd Sun of the month (except Jul–Sep) 9–1 🚌 14, 23 ♿ Good 💷 Free

MUSEO STIBBERT
A quirky museum of 50,000 pieces gathered by the Italian-Scottish eccentric Frederick Stibbert. It houses one of the world's finest collections of armor, and all manner of curiosities, including Murano glass chandeliers and Stibbert's dress kilt.
➕ H4 ✉ Via Federico Stibbert 26 ☎ 055 486049 🕐 Fri–Wed 9–1 🚌 31, 32 ❓ Guided tours only (on the hour) except Sun when visitors are free to wander

OPIFICIO E MUSEO DELLE PIETRE DURE
This small museum is a workshop showing the techniques of working semi-precious stones.
➕ bII ✉ Via degli Alfani 78 ☎ 055 294145 🕐 Mon–Sat 9–2 🚌 6, 31, 32 ♿ Good 💷 Inexpensive

SALVATORE FERRAGAMO SHOE MUSEUM
Founded in 1995, this collection of 10,000 pairs of shoes by Ferragamo only, date from his return from Hollywood to Florence in 1927 until his death in the 1960s.
➕ aIV ✉ Palazzo Spini Feroni, Via de' Tornabuoni 14 ☎ 055 336 0456 🕐 Visits by appointment only 🚌 6, 11, 31, 32, 36, 37 ♿ Good 💷 Free

Art exhibitions
A number of galleries in addition to the museums listed here have changing exhibitions. These include the Spedale degli Innocenti (► 45), the Palazzo Medici (► 32), and Casa Buonarroti (► 54).

19th-century collectors' museums
Florence has three museums that evolved out of somewhat eccentric private collections of the 19th century—the Museo Stibbert, the Museo Bardini, and the better known but less interesting Museo Horne: ➕ J7 ✉ Via dei Benci 6 ☎ 055 244661 🕐 Mon–Sat 9–1. Closed hols 🚌 B, C ♿ None 💷 Moderate 🔗 Santa Croce (► 47).

Exhibits in the Museo Bardini

51

CHURCHES

Passport to heaven?

For centuries the focus of Florence's life, churches contain some of the city's best art. In the Middle Ages, many of Florence's bankers attempted to assuage their guilt for being so rich by paying for a chapel to be decorated with frescoes of uplifting spiritual themes (often featuring the patrons). The chapels are invariably named after them—the Bardi Chapel in Santa Croce, for example and the Strozzi and Tornabuoni chapels in Santa Maria Novella.

BADIA FIORENTINA

The Badia Fiorentina, the oldest monastery in Florence, was founded in AD 978 by Willa, widow of Umberto, Margrave of Tuscany. It is best known in connection with Dante, who used to meet Beatrice here. Its magnificent bell tower, which is Romanesque at the base and Gothic at the top, is one of the most characteristic features of the Florentine skyline. Inside are two fine works of art, namely Filippino Lippi's *The Madonna Appearing to St. Bernard*, to the left of the entrance, and the tomb of Count Ugo, son of Willa and Umberto, which is nearby. The two-story *Chiostro degli Aranci* (orange tree cloister) has charming frescoes of the life of St. Bernard, by an unknown artist (c1440).
✚ bIII ✉ Via del Proconsolo/Piazza San Firenze ☎ 055 287389 🕐 Thu–Tue 5AM–7PM; Sun 7:30–11:30 🚇 In the pedestrian zone 🚻 Poor 🎫 Free

Fresco from the Badia Fiorentina

OGNISSANTI

This was the parish church of the Vespucci family, one of whose members, Amerigo, named the continent of America after himself. In the second chapel on the right facing the altar is a fresco by Ghirlandaio which is said to include Amerigo's portrait (the boy standing behind the Virgin, with a man in a red cloak to his right). It was also the church of Botticelli's family, and he was buried here. In the *cenacolo* (refectory) there are more Ghirlandaio pieces—a *Last Supper* and *St. Jerome in his Study*—and Botticelli's *St. Augustine in his Study*.
✚ H6 ✉ Borgo Ognissanti 42 ☎ 055 239 6802 🕐 Daily 8–noon, 4–6:30 🚇 At the station 🚻 Acceptable 🎫 Free

SANTA MARIA MADDALENA DEI PAZZI

Although the original church dates from the 13th century, most of the present building is a Renaissance rebuild designed by Guiliano da

Sangallo at the end of the 15th century. The spectacular interior decoration with its colored marble and trompe l'oeil dates from the baroque. The highlight here, however, is in the chapter house (reached via the crypt) where there is a fresco of the Crucifixion and saints done by Perugino in the 1490s. The lovingly detailed background of a Tuscan landscape is typical of his works.

✚ cIII 🖂 Borgo Pinti 🕐 Daily 9–noon, 5–7 🚌 6 ♿ Poor 💶 Inexpensive

Ghirlandaio's Miracle of the Boy brought back to Life *in Santa Trinita*

SANTA FELICITA

This is the second church oldest in Florence, dating to the 2nd century AD when Syrian and Greek merchants settled here. The highlight is to see the Mannerist *Deposition* (1525–8) by Pontormo, which is in the Cappella Caponi, immediately on your right as you enter. It is a quite stunning vortex of improbable forms and colors: lime green, bubblegum pink, acid yellow. On the wall a charming *Annunciation*, also by Pontormo.

✚ aIV 🖂 Piazza Santa Felicita ☎ 055 213018 🕐 Daily 8–noon, 3:30–6:30 🚌 B, C ♿ Poor 💶 Free

SANTA TRINITA

The baroque facade of Santa Trinita gives no indication of its austere and tranquil interior. The church dates from 1092 and was rebuilt between 1258 and 1280 in a sparse version of the Gothic. To the far right of the high altar as you face it, the Sassetti Chapel is decorated with frescoes showing scenes from the life of St. Francis by Ghirlandaio (1483) and including portraits of Francesco Sassetti, the patron of the chapel, and his wife, who are shown on either side of the altar.

✚ aIII 🖂 Piazza Santa Trinita ☎ 055 216912 🕐 Daily 7:30–noon, 4–6 🚌 6, 11, 31, 32, 36, 37 ♿ Good 💶 Free

SANTO SPIRITO

Designed by Filippo Brunelleschi in 1435, this church acquired a baroque facade in the 18th century. The interior is gloomy, but Filippino Lippi's excellent *Madonna and Child* (1466) is in the Nerli Chapel in the south transept. The *cenacolo* (refectory) houses an 11th-century sculpture and a beautiful Gothic *Crucifixion*, believed to be by the followers of Andrea Orcagna.

✚ aIV 🖂 Piazza Santo Spirito ☎ 055 210030 🕐 Thu–Tue 8:30–noon, 4–5:30 🚌 C, 6 ♿ Poor 💶 Free
Refectory ☎ 055 287043 🕐 Tue–Sun 10–1. Closed hols ♿ Good 💶 Moderate

SANTO STEFANO AL PONTE

This little church, which dates from AD 969, is tucked into a courtyard just behind the Ponte Vecchio. The exterior is a Romanesque delight added in the 1230s.

✚ bIV 🖂 Piazza Santo Stefano al Ponte 🕐 Closed for restoration 🚌 In the pedestrian zone

Dress code

Florence's churches may contain some of the most important works of art in the world but try not forget that they are also (and indeed, primarily) places of worship and spiritual, rather than purely artistic, contemplation. All visitors are expected to be appropriately dressed; shoulders and upper arms should be covered and shorts or very short skirts aren't welcome. Try to avoid visiting during services or disturbing those who come in to pray.

An altarpiece within Santo Spirito

MICHELANGELO IN FLORENCE

Life of genius

Michelangelo Buonarroti (1475–1564) was born in Caprese, about 60 miles east of Florence, but his family came to the city very soon after his birth. When he began his apprenticeship at the age of 13, his teacher, Ghirlandaio, was astounded by his skill, and within a year Michelangelo had left his studies. Initially his patron was Lorenzo the Magnificent but with the political turbulence of the times, he was exiled in 1494. He returned to Florence in 1501 and sculpted David. He next returned from Rome to Florence in 1516 to sculpt the Medici tombs in San Lorenzo. In 1534 he left Florence for good; he died in Rome but is buried in Santa Croce in Florence. Although Michelangelo painted, made frescoes, designed buildings and wrote poetry, he regarded himself primarily as a sculptor.

CASA BUONARROTI

This house, which Michelangelo bought in 1508, is now a fascinating museum and gallery. Exhibits include the artist's earliest known work, the *Madonna della Scala* (c1491), a wood and wax model (the only one of its type) of a river god, and a model of the facade for San Lorenzo that was never executed.
🔲 cIII ✉ Via Ghibellina 70 ☎ 055 241752 🚌 14 🕐 Wed–Mon 9:30–1:30 ♿ Good 💶 Expensive

BARGELLO SCULPTURES

The Bargello houses (► 42) three sculptures by Michelangelo: *Bacchus Drunk* (1497), his earliest freestanding work; *Brutus* (1539–40), his only bust, sculpted after the murder of Duke Alessandro de' Medici as a statement against tyranny; and the tondo of the *Madonna and Child with the infant St. John* (1503–5), a fine example of his low relief style.
🔲 bIII ✉ Via del Proconsolo 4 ☎ 055 238 8606 🕐 Tue–Sun 8:30–2. Closed alternate Sun and Mon, Apr 25, May 1 🚌 19 ♿ Good 💶 Moderate

THE *DONI TONDO* IN THE UFFIZI

The *Doni Tondo* (1504–5), the only easel painting that Michelangelo came near to finishing, breaks new ground by showing the infant Jesus above Mary's shoulder, rather than in her lap. The figures' contorted postures were much copied by Mannerists.
🔲 bIV ✉ Loggiato degli Uffizi 6 ☎ 055 238 8651 🕐 Tue–Sat 8:30–7; Sun 8:30–2 (last admission 30 minutes before closing). Closed May 1 🚌 In the pedestrian zone ♿ Good 💶 Expensive

THE *VICTORY*, PALAZZO VECCHIO

Michelangelo began painting frescoes for the Sala dei Cinquecento in the Palazzo Vecchio, but these came to nothing. There is a sculpture by Michelangelo: the *Victory*, opposite the entrance of the Sala dei Cinquecento, which shows a young man holding down the figure of adversity.
🔲 bIV ✉ Piazza della Signoria ☎ 055 276 8465 🕐 Mon–Wed, Fri, Sat 9–7; Sun 8–1. Closed Easter Sun, May 1, Aug 15 🚌 19, 23, 31, 32 ♿ Good 💶 Expensive

One of the Prisoners now in the Accademia

VIEWS

See Top 25 Sights for
GIARDINO DI BOBOLI (► 27)
CAMPANILE (► 34)
DUOMO (► 35)
PALAZZO VECCHIO (► 41)
SAN MINIATO AL MONTE (► 48)

FORTE DI BELVEDERE

This fortress was built by the Medici in 1590, ostensibly to protect Florence from attackers, but actually as a refuge for the Medici Grand Dukes in their struggle against the Florentine Republic and as a reminder of Medici military might. There are fabulous views and this is a lovely place to come and sunbathe or have a picnic. In the middle of the fortress there is a three-story Palazzetto in the manner of a Medici villa, used to house exhibitions. For these an entrance fee is charged, otherwise the fortress is free.

➕ H7 ✉ Costa di San Giorgio and Via di Belvedere 🕐 Daily 9–6 (later in summer and when there is an exhibition) 🚌 No bus ♿ Impossible 🎫 Free

MUSEO DI ORSANMICHELE

Behind Orsanmichele on the Via dell'Arte di Lana is the Palazzo dell'Arte di Lana, which is the entrance for the Museum of Orsanmichele, actually the two upper stories of the church. Climb up for fantastic views of the rooftops of central Florence.

➕ aIII ✉ Palazzo dell'Arte di Lana, Via dell'Arte di Lana 🕐 Daily 9–1:30 🚌 In the pedestrian zone ♿ Impossible 🎫 Free

PIAZZALE MICHELANGELO

Despite the fact that Piazzale Michelangelo is frequented by bus loads of tourists, this stupendous vantage point is still very much worth the trip, either by bus or by foot. Ignore the poor green copy of Michel-angelo's *David* and the rapidly mushrooming crop of souvenir stands, beware of pickpockets, and soak up the wonderful view.

➕ J7 ✉ Piazzale Michelangelo, off Viale Galileo Galilei 🚌 12, 13 ♿ Good 🎫 Free

PONTE SANTA TRINITA

One of the best places to view the Ponte Vecchio.

➕ aIV ✉ Ponte Santa Trinita 🚌 6, 11, 36, 37, C ♿ Good 🎫 Free

Hilltop vistas

E M Forster put the idea of a "room with a view" in Florence on the map. There are wonderful views from hotel rooms across terra-cotta roofs, but perhaps the most breathtaking vistas are from the hills that surround the city, both close up—for example from the Forte di Belvedere, integrated into the medieval walls—and from a distance, typically from Fiesole (► 20), where people go to see the lights by night.

Looking across the rooftops to the Bargello

PARKS, GARDENS & OPEN SPACES

See Top 25 Sights for
GIARDINO DI BOBOLI (➤ 27)
PIAZZA DELLA SIGNORIA (➤ 40)

Rare commodity

Given the Renaissance artists' veneration for nature, it is ironic that Florence is so bereft of greenery. So make the most of such green spaces as there are, including Forte di Belvedere (➤ 55) and the Villa Medicea di Poggio a Caiano, with its English-style gardens (➤ 21).

LE CASCINE

Florence's largest park is a long way from the town center, and is tacky (badly kept and given to seediness at night) when you eventually get there. Long (2 miles) and thin (sometimes as narrow as 110 yards), it was laid out as a public park by Napoleon's sister Elisa Baciocchi Bonaparte in 1811, on the site of the Medici dairy pastures (*cascine*). There is a lively market on Tuesday and one of Florence's open-air swimming pools is also in the park.

➕ G6 ✉ Ponte della Vittoria 🚌 17c ♿ Good 🎫 Free

GARDEN TOURS

From May to October you can visit some of Florence's grandest villas and their gardens, not normally open to the public because they are privately owned. Contact the tourist office for details
☎ 055 288049 (➤ 19).

GIARDINO DEI SEMPLICI

This oasis of neat greenery, the botanical garden of Florence University, is on the site of a garden laid out in 1545–6 for Cosimo I, who wanted to keep up with the Pisans and Genoans. It is named after the medicinal plants (*semplici*) grown here in addition to water plants, Tuscan flora, irises, and shrubs. There are also greenhouses with tropical palms, ferns, orchids, and citrus fruits.

➕ cII ✉ Via Micheli 3 🕐 Mon, Fri 9–noon, 2:30–5; Wed, Sat 9–noon 🚌 10, 11, 17, 20 ♿ Good 🎫 Free

Giardino dei Semplici

PIAZZA DELLA REPUBBLICA

This grandiose square in the middle of Florence, on the site of the old market, was built in the 1870s, when Florence briefly was the capital of Italy. Florentines are not fond of the square's architecture nor its crass neoclassical triumphal arch, but it is an unusually large open space, where you can breathe a little and let a child run free. All around are grand cafés, and in the center old men gather to discuss the day's affairs.

➕ bIII ♿ Good

FLORENCE FOR FREE

Strolling the streets

Half the appeal of Florence is the fact that it is eminently walkable—just to wander its streets and bridges is enormously pleasurable. Much of the best art in Florence is to be found in churches (➤ 52–3), where, in most instances, there is no entrance charge.

MUSEUMS WITHOUT ENTRANCE FEES

The Florentine aptitude for making money is alive and thriving now just as it was in the time of the Medici. In short, there is not a great deal to be had for free in Florence! However, exceptions include the Anthropological Museum (➤ 51), La Specola (➤ 50), and Salvatore Ferragamo Shoe Museum (➤ 51).

PARKS WITHOUT ENTRANCE FEES

The Giardino di Boboli entry fee, imposed in 1992, was extremely unpopular with Florentines, who had relied upon it for fresh air and greenery. Now, all that remain free are the small Giardino dei Semplici and the less-than-lovely Cascine.

Giardino dei Semplici ➕ cII ✉ Via Micheli 3 ⏰ Mon, Fri 9–noon, 2:30–5; Wed 2:30–5 🚍 10, 11, 17
Cascine ➕ G6 ✉ Ponte della Vittoria 🚍 17c

WALKS AND VIEWS

Take a walk along the medieval city walls, passing through the Forte di Belvedere and Piazzale Michelangelo (➤ 16 and 55).

TICKET TO RIDE

When you have had enough of walking you can take a wonderful tour of suburban Florence for the price of a single bus ticket. The No. 12 and No. 13 buses do a loop around Florence (clockwise and counter-clockwise respectively) that lasts about one hour, starting and finishing at the train station. You do grind through some of the less picturesque suburbs, but the buses also wind along the leafy boulevards, such as Viale Machiavelli in the hills south of Florence, where you can ogle the fabulous villas of the rich and famous. If you want to go a little farther out into the countryside take bus No. 7 to Fiesole ➕ M2 or No. 13 to the pretty little town of Settignano east of Florence. Both buses leave from the train station.

Crossing the Arno

FLORENCE FOR CHILDREN

Limited viewing

Florence is very much an adults' city. However, it would be very sad to take children to Florence and not show them some great art. The trick is to choose the right amount of the right kind of art at the right time. It pays to limit your ambitions to a very few, well-chosen works of art. Remember, too, that people in Italian restaurants and shops are more welcoming to children than they are in many other parts of the world: waiters and hotel staff will lavish attention on them.

Il Porcellino, in the Mercato Nuovo

ARMOR
For the child into medieval knights, a trip to the Museo Stibbert (► 51), which has one of the best collections of armor in the world, would be the highlight of Florence. The Bargello (► 42) also has a fine collection of arms and armor.

CLIMBS, WALKS, VIEWS, AND PARKS
The physical exertion and visual exhilaration of climbing towers and walking along city walls have a lot to recommend them. Both the bell tower and the dome of the cathedral can be climbed. The walk to San Miniato (► 48) encompasses a stretch of the medieval city walls as well as the fortress of the Belvedere, which is fascinating for a child with an interest in castles and military architecture. If yours simply need to blow off steam, head for the Boboli Gardens (► 27) or the Cascine (► 56).

MICHELANGELO'S *DAVID*
The story of David is one that some children know and many will identify with. Michelangelo's sculpture *David* has a very immediate physical impact. Furthermore, you can encourage your children to compare the original in the Galleria dell'Accademia (► 43) with the copies—one outside the Palazzo Vecchio (► 41) and one (much reviled) on the Piazzale Michelangelo (► 55).

SAN MARCO
The monks' cells in San Marco, each with a painting by Fra Angelico, provide a rare instance of art in its original context, and the cells evoke the monks' life in a way that can capture a child's imagination. Fra Angelico's *Annunciation* expresses a moment in the story of the Nativity that many children will know.

SHOPPING AND CLOTHES
Soccer shirts, a big hit with both boys and girls, can be found in sports shops such as Casa dello Sport (► 72) and much cheaper in the Mercato San Lorenzo (► 72). The markets also have cheap leather and sheepskin gloves and slippers, and the Mercato Nuovo has the brass boar, Il Porcellino (► 60). If your children are fashion mad, try the Salvatore Ferragamo Shoe Museum (► 51 and 70) and the Museum of Costume in the Palazzo Pitti (► 26).

SPORTS
If Fiorentina are playing soccer, a trip to the stadium is a real wow (► 82). Or try the swimming pool at Le Cascine (► 56), or go canoeing along the River Arno (► 82).

THE RIVER ARNO & ITS BRIDGES

> **See Top 25 Sights for**
> **PONTE VECCHIO (► 28)**

The River Arno has been crucial to the history of Florence, providing water for the textile industry on which the city's prosperity was based.

PONTE ALLA CARRAIA

The city's second oldest bridge was originally built around 1218 and reconstructed after floods in 1269 and 1333; the current bridge was rebuilt after World War II as a copy of the 16th-century bridge. The name comes from the carts (*carri*) that carried cloth between the cloth-making districts of San Freddiano on the south side and Ognissanti on the north side of the bridge.
➕ aIV

PONTE ALLE GRAZIE

First constructed in 1237, when it was known as Ponte Rubaconte (the bridge over the River Rubicon), it was rebuilt after World War II to a modern design. It takes its name from the oratory of Santa Maria delle Grazie, which once stood here.
➕ bIV

THE LUNGARNI

Along the roads that hug the banks of the Arno—you'll find the *Lungarni*—some of the finest palaces in Florence: the baroque Palazzo Corsini on Lungarno Corsini, with its private art collection, and the Palazzo Spini-Ferroni on Lungarno degli Accaiuoli, which houses the Salvatore Ferragamo Shoe Emporium (► 70).
➕ aIV–bIV

PONTE SANTA TRINITA

The finest of Florence's bridges dates as far back as 1252, although what you see today is a very well-executed replica of Ammannati's bridge built in 1567 and destroyed by the Nazis in 1944. Ammannati was commissioned by Cosimo I and probably consulted Michelangelo in his designs. Some of the loveliest views of Florence, especially of the Ponte Vecchio, are to be had from this bridge.
➕ aIV ✉ Ponte Santa Trinita 🚌 6, 11, 31, 32, 36, 37 ♿ Good
🎫 Free

Flood facts

In November 1966 the River Arno burst its banks to disastrous effect: the tide marks noted all over the city bear witness to the immense weight of water and sludge that bludgeoned through the streets, reaching as high as 20 feet. in the Santa Croce region. This was not the only flood there has ever been, however: bridges were swept away in 1269 and 1333, and the city was submerged in 1557 and 1884 but not as badly as in 1966.

Sunset over the Arno

MARKETS

Surveying the range of goods for sale in the Mercato Nuovo

To market, to market

Florence markets give you the opportunity to participate in everyday Florentine life. Planning a daily picnic lunch is an excellent excuse to go shopping.

LE CASCINE

Florence's biggest general market selling everything from fresh food to household and cooking equipment is held every Tuesday in Le Cascine (► 56).

➕ G6 ✉ Ponte della Vittoria 🚌 D

MERCATO CENTRALE

The largest of Florence's produce markets is held in the magnificent cast-iron structure of the Mercato Centrale, built in 1874, with an extra floor added in 1980. Just about every kind of fresh food is sold here.

➕ all ✉ Piazza Mercato Centrale 🕐 Mon–Fri 7–2; Sat 7–2, 4–7:30 🍽 Yes 🚌 10, 12, 25, 31, 32 ♿ Good (though crowded)

MERCATO DELLE PULCI

The Piazza dei Ciompi, traditionally the heart of the blue-collar area of Florence, is a fitting spot for the flea market. The goods generally come under the heading of "junk" but the prices cannot be said to match.

➕ cIII ✉ Piazza dei Ciompi 🚌 B ♿ Good

MERCATO DI SANT'AMBROGIO

After the Mercato Centrale, this is the second most important market for fresh produce in Florence. It is favored by Florence's working population and is very cheap as well as pleasantly noisy.

➕ dIII ✉ Piazza Sant'Ambrogio 🕐 Mon–Fri 7–2 🍽 Yes 🚌 B ♿ Good

MERCATO NUOVO

So called to distinguish it from the Mercato Vecchio, which used to be on the site of what is now the Piazza della Repubblica, this market is most famous for the engaging brass boar with a shiny, well-stroked nose, the Porcellino, which sometimes lends its name to the market. It is also known as the "straw market," a reference to the straw hats historically sold here, and still to be found.

➕ bIII ✉ Piazza Mercato Nuovo 🕐 Summer: Mon–Sat. Winter: Tue–Sun 🍽 Yes 🚌 In the pedestrian zone ♿ Good (though crowded)

MERCATO SAN LORENZO

The Mercato San Lorenzo is fun, touristy, and very centrally located, in the shadow of the church of San Lorenzo. There are lots of stands selling leather goods, many of which are genuinely good value, but go armed with a healthy skepticism (► 70). In the souvenir category you will find T-shirts with lewd designs and artistic clichés, aprons, soccer shirts, and paper goods (► 76) including delightful calendars.

➕ bII ✉ Piazza San Lorenzo 🕐 Summer: Mon–Sat 8–7. Winter: Tue–Sun 8–7 🍽 Yes 🚌 In the pedestrian zone ♿ Good

FLORENCE
where to...

ELEGANT RESTAURANTS

Prices

Expect to pay per person for a meal, excluding drink

$	up to L25,000
$$	up to L50,000
$$$	over L50,000

It is standard practice for Italian restaurants to add a cover charge (*coperto*), usually L2,000 –L5,000. This is said to cover the bread and the table linen and is separate from the service charge (*servizio*), which is about 10 percent. Sometimes the *coperto*, the service charge or both is included. Take a look at your check.

Restaurant etiquette

Italians have a strongly developed sense of how to behave, which applies in restaurants as much as anywhere else. It is bad form to order only one course in any restaurant (if that is what you want, go to a *pizzeria*). And the concept of a doggy bag could not be more at odds with Italian ideas of eating out. You might succeed in getting one if you want, but you will pay a very high price in the loss of your dignity. Italians do not get drunk in public; to do so is to make a *brutissima figura*, an appalling impression.

ALLE MURATE ($$$)

This is one of those places where traditional Tuscan favorites are given a twist. Choose from one of two menus—the Tuscan and the innovative. There's also a good range of fish, game and offal-based dishes.

♥ dIV ✉ Via Ghibellina 52r
☎ 055 240618 🕒 Closed lunch and Mon 🚌 6, 14

CANTINETTA ANTINORI ($$)

A refined setting for the chic Florentine elite. The food comes from the farm of the Antinori family, whose wines are world renowned. Dress up or you are likely to feel completely out of place.

♥ alII ✉ Piazza Antinori 3
☎ 055 292234 🕒 Closed Sat, Sun 🚌 6, 11, 31, 37

CARPE DIEM ($$)

It's worth making the trek out to Fiesole at lunch or dinner for the fine, innovative dishes that are served on a spectacular summer terrace with views over the city.

♥ M3 ✉ Via Giuseppe Mantellini 2b, Fiesole ☎ 055 599595 🕒 Closed Mon 🚌 Bus to Fiesole from station

IL CIBREO ($$)

This restaurant near the market of Sant'Ambrogio offers no pasta but instead an intriguing range of robust Florentine dishes, some made with less familiar parts of the animal such as tripe and cockscombs. In all cases the food is first class. There is also an inexpensive section (► 64).

♥ dIII ✉ Via dei Macci 118r
☎ 055 234 1100 🕒 Closed Sun, Mon 🚌 14, B

DINO ($$)

The unprepossessing exterior hides a cool, airy dining area, with beautifully vaulted ceilings and sparse decoration. A range of sophisticated but unfussy food is prepared in the open kitchen. The wine cellar is exceptionally good. During peak season there are sometimes groups in the early evenings; arrive after 8PM to avoid them.

♥ dIV ✉ Via Ghibellina 51r
☎ 055 241452 🕒 Closed Sun evening, Mon 🚌 14

ENOTECA PINCHIORRI ($$$)

The city's most fashionable and priciest eatery is somewhat serious. For wine connoisseurs it is a must, possessing one of Europe's very finest wine cellars. The *menù degustazione* includes wines appropriate to each course.

♥ cIV ✉ Via Ghibellina 87
☎ 055 242777 🕒 Closed Sun, Mon and Wed lunch 🚌 14

SABATINI ($$$)

One of Italy's best tables, Sabatini is still chic, if no longer quite what it once was. However, it remains both extremely good and pleasantly old-fashioned.

♥ alII ✉ Via dei Panzani 9a
☎ 055 211559 🕒 Closed Mon 🚌 6, 9, 11

TUSCAN & FLORENTINE CUISINE

ANTICA TRATTORIA ORESTE ($$)
A delightful trattoria with outdoor seating, a menu of robust main courses, and pasta dishes such as penne with lemon and arugula.
🏢 aIV ✉ Piazza Santo Spirito 16r ☎ 055 238 2383 🕐 Closed Tue 🚌 B

BALDINI ($$)
Garibaldi ate here, and it's a popular Florentine lunch spot between Santa Maria Novella and the park of the Cascine. Try the home-made gnocchi (potato dumplings) with tomatoes and mushrooms.
🏢 G6 ✉ Via Il Prato 96r ☎ 055 287663 🕐 Closed Sat and Sun evening 🚌 1, 9, 12, 26, 27, 35

LA BARAONDA ($$)
Baraonda means chaos but there is nothing chaotic about the carefully prepared traditional dishes it serves in a bustling informal atmosphere. Popular with the locals.
🏢 dIV ✉ Via Ghibellina 67r ☎ 055 234 1171 🕐 Closed Sun, Mon, lunch in winter 🚌 14

IL CINGHIALE BIANCO ($$)
The "White Boar," is named after one of Tuscany's greatest culinary specialties.
🏢 aIV ✉ Borgo San Jacopo 43 ☎ 055 215706 🕐 Closed Tue and Wed 🚌 3, 13, 32

COCO LEZZONE ($$$)
White-tiled rooms make an informal setting for this Florentine favorite. The short menu offers all the Tuscan classics.
🏢 aIII ✉ Via del Parioncino 26r ☎ 055 287178 🕐 Closed Sun and Tue evening 🚌 C

GARGA ($$)
A lively, arty bistro with a fashionable clientele.
🏢 aIII ✉ Via del Moro 48r ☎ 055 239 8898 🕐 Closed Mon 🚌 6, 11

IL LATINI ($)
Boisterous restaurant offering Tuscan classics such as *pappardelle con la lepre* (wide strips of pasta with hare sauce). Seating is at communal tables.
🏢 aIII ✉ Via Palchetti 6r ☎ 055 210916 🕐 Closed Mon 🚌 6, 11

OSTERIA DE' BENCI ($)
A genuine Florentine *osteria*. Start with *crostini* (a Tuscan version of *bruschetta*, toasted bread served with spreads, cheeses and cold meats) then choose from the day's menu that often includes spaghetti in red wine and/or a delicious vegetable soup. The meat is particularly good.
🏢 cIV ✉ Via de' Benci ☎ 055 234 4923 🕐 Closed Sun and Aug 🚌 14

PONTE VECCHIO ($$)
Good eatery specializing in mushroom dishes. Popular with tourists.
🏢 bIV ✉ Lungarno Archibusieri 8r ☎ 055 292289 🕐 Closed Mon 🚌 In the pedestrian zone

QUATTRO LEONI ($$)
An attractive atmosphere with outdoor seating and excellent food.
🏢 aIV ✉ Via Vellutini 1r ☎ 055 218562 🕐 Closed Sun 🚌 11, 36, 37, 68

Naturally robust

The classic Florentine dish is *bistecca alla fiorentina* (T-bone steak sold by the weight, usually 100g). Grilled and served rare with lemon, it can be found in the few remaining authentic Florentine trattorias such as:
Sostanza 🏢 aIII ✉ Via Porcellana 25r 🕐 Closed Sat, Sun ☎ 055 212691 🚌 B, C

Other specialties include *trippa alla fiorentina* (tripe stewed with tomatoes and served with parmesan), *crostini* (toasted bread and a pâté of roughly chopped chicken livers), *panzanella* (a salad of crumbled bread tossed with tomatoes with olive oil, onions, basil, and parsley), and *pappa con pomodoro* (a thick cold soup of bread and tomatoes). The classic Tuscan dessert is *biscotti di Prato*—hard and dry almond biscuits dunked in *vin santo* (fortified wine). *Zucotto* is a dome-shaped confection of alcohol-soaked madeira cake, whipped cream, nuts, and chopped chocolate.

BUDGET, ETHNIC & VEGETARIAN FARE

Something Italian

In Italy you will probably find the same dishes in a budget trattoria as in the most expensive restaurants. The difference is primarily one of ambience and decor—and frequently—the wine list.

Bread

Almost all bread in Tuscany is made without salt. This takes some getting used to, but the blandness makes a good background to highly flavored foods such as Florentine salami *Finocchiona*, which is scented with fennel and garlic. And the bread's texture—firm, almost coarse, and very substantial—is wonderful. Strict laws govern what goes into Italian bread: it is free of chemical preservatives.

ACQUACOTTA ($)
A reliable trattoria named after a Tuscan soup (literally "cooked water"). The menu covers other dishes, however, including *bollito*, mixed boiled meats with herb sauce.
🔳 cIII ⬛ Via dei Pilastri 51r ☎ 055 242907 🅾 Closed Tue evening, Wed, Aug 🚌 B

AMON ($)
An Egyptian snack bar, not far from the station, serving bread filled with tasty delicacies, including falafel.
🔳 aIII ⬛ Via Palazzuolo 26–28r ☎ 055 293146 🅾 Closed Sun 🚌 36, 37

LA BARRIQUE ($)
A wine bar where the menu of main vegetable-based pasta dishes, cheeses and salads changes daily. Seating is at a big communal table near the entrance, but ask for one of the smaller tables inside if you want more intimacy.
🔳 G7 ⬛ Via del Leone 40 ☎ 055 224292 🅾 Evenings (from 5PM) only. Closed Mon 🚌 6

BELLE DONNE ($)
A cheap option in an expensive part of town. It's small and modest and you can barely see inside because of the cascades of potted plants. The menu includes some interestingly prepared vegetables.
🔳 aIII ⬛ Via delle Belle Donne 16r ☎ 055 238 2609 🅾 Closed Sat evening and Sun 🚌 6, 9, 11

IL CARMINE ($)
Small, friendly trattoria in the delightful Piazza del Carmine. Lengthy (difficult) menu of traditional dishes.
🔳 H7 ⬛ Piazza del Carmine 18r ☎ 055 218601 🅾 Closed Sun 🚌 B

LA CASALINGA ($)
This busy family-run establishment is a good place to try *ribollita*, the thick Florentine soup made with bread and vegetables.
🔳 aIV ⬛ Via dei Michelozzi 9r 🅾 Closed Sun 🚌 6, 11, 31, 32, 36, 37

IL CIBREO ($–$$)
At the back of this mid-range restaurant you can eat the same food for a fraction of the price—but you won't be encouraged (or indeed, welcome) to loiter. A steal.
🔳 dIII ⬛ Via dei Macci 118 ☎ 055 234 1100 🅾 Closed Sun and Mon 🚌 14

CIKUTEI ($$$)
Japanese cuisine near the Duomo.
🔳 bIII ⬛ Piazza dell'Olio 10r ☎ 055 211466 🅾 Closed Sun, Aug 🚌 In the pedestrian zone

DA SERGIO ($)
A basic but very good trattoria with a different menu every day. Hidden behind the Mercato San Lorenzo, it is not the easiest place to find and it's open only for lunch, but it's worth a detour.
🔳 bII ⬛ Piazza San Lorenzo 8r ☎ 055 281941 🅾 Closed evenings, Sun and Aug 🚌 In the pedestrian zone

FUORIPORTA ($$)
The wine bar of the moment is near San

Miniato al Monte. In the evening, cheeses, cold meats, and *crostini* are served; at lunchtime, pasta dishes and desserts. The wine list is vast (more than 600) and there are also whiskies and *eaux de vie* for serious tasters.

✚ J8 ✉ Via Monte alle Croci 10r ☎ 055 234 2483 🕐 Closed Mon 🚌 12, 13, 38

GANESH ($$)

An Indian restaurant serving North Indian specialties.

✚ alll ✉ Via del Giglio 26–28r ☎ 055 289694 🕐 Closed Mon 🚌 In the pedestrian zone

GAUGUIN ($$)

This vegetarian restaurant near the university has an imaginative menu with quirky dishes such as eggplant baked with mozzarella and cocoa.

✚ cll ✉ Via degli Alfani 24r ☎ 055 234 0616 🚌 6

IL MANDARINO ($$–$$$)

A centrally located Chinese restaurant.

✚ blll ✉ Via della Condotta 17r ☎ 055 239 6130 🕐 Closed Mon 🚌 In the pedestrian zone

LE MOSSACCE ($–$$)

Bustling eatery between the Duomo and the Bargello; excellent Tuscan food including rich soups.

✚ blll ✉ Via del Proconsolo 55r ☎ 055 294361 🕐 Closed Sat, Sun, Mon evenings and Aug 🚌 14, 23

MISTER HANG ($$–$$$)

This popular Chinese

restaurant has air-conditioning. Reservations are a good idea.

✚ clll ✉ Via Ghibellina 134r ☎ 055 234 4810 🕐 Closed Mon 🚌 14

PALLE D'ORO ($)

Spotless, spartan surroundings and good food—which you can take away to eat outside.

✚ all ✉ Via Sant'Antonino 43r ☎ 055 288383 🕐 Closed Sun and Aug 🚌 Short walk from the railroad station

AL TRANVAI ($)

Diners are packed into this lively trattoria in the heart of Florence on the same square as the weekly market. The specialty is *frattaglie* (a mind-boggling range of offal) but the menu changes every day with a range of pastas and soups followed by filling vegetable *contorni*.

✚ G7 ✉ Piazza Torquato Tasso 14 ☎ 055 225197 🕐 Closed Sat, Sun 🚌 12, 13

TRATTORIA MARIONE ($)

Good home cooking based on simple ingredients. Well-prepared dishes include *bollito* (boiled beef), soups, and tripe.

✚ alll ✉ Via della Spada 27r ☎ 055 214756 🚌 In the pedestrian zone

RUTH'S ($)

A bright, modern eatery next to the synagogue serving an interesting mix of vegetarian (although fish is also served), Middle Eastern and kosher.

✚ clll ✉ Via Farini 2a ☎ 055 248 0888 🕐 Closed Fri evening and Sat lunch 🚌 6

Contradiction

The concept of vegetarianism is not one that sits easily with Italian ideas about food, and there are very few vegetarian restaurants in Italy. However, there are few better countries for those who do not eat meat (or fish). Many pasta dishes contain no meat—pesto, tomato sauce, or ravioli stuffed with spinach and ricotta, to name but a few. For a main course, try *grigliata di verdura* (grilled vegetables) or else restaurant stalwarts such as *parmigiana di melanzane* (eggplant layered with tomato and mozzarella, and baked with a parmesan crust), *mozzarella in carrozza* (fried mozzarella), and *fritate* (omelettes). In Tuscany there are also wonderful bean dishes, such as *fagioli all'uccelletto* (white beans with a sage-flavored tomato sauce). *Pizza margherita* is made with just cheese and tomato (▶ 66). *Ribollita* is a thick Tuscan soup made with cabbage, beans, and other vegetables; to be sure that it is meat-free, be sure to ask.

PIZZAS & SNACKS

Vinaii and fiaschetterie

These traditional little wine and snack bars are becoming increasingly rare. They are wonderful places to drop into for a glass of wine and a slice of salami or cheese and a wedge of rustic bread—and just the thing after a hard day of sightseeing:

Quasigratis ✉ Via de' Castellani 2 (near Palazzo Vecchio 5)

Zanobi ✉ Via Sant'Antonino 47 (between the station and San Lorenzo)

Balducci ✉ Via de' Nevi 2 (near Santa Croce)

As in just about every Italian town, pizzas are all over and many stores sell *pizza a taglio* (cut pizza). One of the best options for a quick snack is a slice. In addition to the standard *margherita* pizza (tomato and mozzarella), you will find all kinds of other delicious toppings, such as zucchini flowers and eggplant. Go when they're busy and the turnover is high to avoid eating cold pizza that's been sitting around for a while. If you do not want a multi-course meal, opt for a pizzeria, where no one will be offended if you have just one course.

BORGO ANTICO ($$)

A popular trendy restaurant and pizzeria in the Piazza Santo Spirito. The excellent pizzas as well as the full range of salads, pastas and main courses are served on huge, colorful plates. Reserve ahead.
➕ aIV ✉ Piazza Santo Spirito 6r ☎ 055 210437 🕐 Closed Mon 🚌 B

CANTINETTA DEI VERRAZZANO ($$)

An absolutely stunning wine bar-cum-store selling breads baked on the premises and wines from the Castello di Verrazzano estates near Greve in Chianti Classico. The marble-topped tables are both rustic and sophisticated, like the wines and food. Don't miss the *focaccia* (flat loaf), baked in the wood-burning ovens out back.
➕ bIII ✉ Via dei Tavolini

18–20r ☎ 055 239 8132 🕐 Closed Sun 🚌 In the pedestrian zone

LA MESCITA ($)

An unassuming but excellent wine bar in the student area, where hearty wines accompany *crostini* and other delicious snacks.
➕ bII ✉ Via degli Alfani 70r 🚌 6

PROCACCI ($$$)

This delightful bar is something of a legend because of its *panini tartufati*, sandwiches made with a white truffle puree. Just the thing with a glass of Tuscan wine at 11AM, as celebrated cookbook author Elizabeth David noted in *Italian Food*.
➕ aIII ✉ Via de' Tornabuoni 64r ☎ 055 211656 🚌 6, 11, 36, 37

LE SCUDERIE ($$)

This bistro in the former *scuderie* (stables) of the convent of Santo Spirito serves pizzas as well as Italian and international fare. Extensive salad bar.
➕ aIV ✉ Via Maffia 31–33r ☎ 055 287198 🕐 Closed Mon 🚌 B

LE VOLPIE L'UVA ($$)

A fabulous wine bar behind the Ponte Vecchio where you can wash down pungent Italian salamis and cheeses with robust Tuscan wines.
➕ aIV ✉ Piazza dei Rossi ☎ 055 239 8132 🕐 Closed Sun 🚌 B, C

ICE CREAM PARLORS

GELATERIA CARABÉ ($$)

A top-quality Sicilian ice cream parlor run with tremendous pride by Antonio and Loredana Lisciandro. Gelateria Carabé is the place to have a *granita* in Florence—choose from lemon, coffee, fig, watermelon, or even prickly pear. The pistachio *gelato* is outstanding, made with super-flavorful pistachio nuts, grown on the volcanic slopes of Bronte in Sicily, which cost twice as much as other pistachios. Near the Accademia, it's a rare treat not to be missed.

🚻 bII ✉ Via Ricasoli 60r ☎ 055 289476 🚏 In the pedestrian zone

PERCHÈ NO! ($$)

"Why not!" has to be a good name for an ice cream parlor. Founded in 1939, this store was such a hit with the G.I.s when they liberated Florence that they made sure this was the first building in the city to have the electricity reconnected! It is renowned for its *semifreddi*, which come in creamy flavors such as hazelnut mousse and *zuppa inglese* (trifle). The *sorbetti* are also first rate. Particularly favored by the Florentines, Perché No! is close to Piazza della Signoria.

🚻 bIII ✉ Via dei Tavolini 19r ☎ 055 239 8969 🕐 Closed Tue 🚏 In the pedestrian zone

PERSEO ($$)

Not exactly off the beaten tourist track but it's excellently placed if you want to get your blood sugar levels up after a hard morning in the Uffizi.

🚻 bIII–bIV ✉ Piazza della Signoria 16r ☎ 055 239 8316 🕐 Closed evenings 🚏 3, 23, 31, 32

VIVOLI ($$)

Vivoli is legendary among foreign visitors. It is not so much the range of *gelati* that is exceptional as the quality. Among the more unusual flavors, you will find frozen rice pudding, studded with little nuggets of rice. The fruit flavors include a wonderful green apple, complete with little bits of peel. Close to Piazza Santa Croce, it's a little hard to find—but definitely worth the trouble.

🚻 cIII ✉ Via Isola delle Stinche 7r ☎ 055 292334 🕐 Closed Mon 🚏 Short walk from Piazza Santa Croce which is served by 23

Shockingly clear flavors

Italian ice cream—*gelato*—is generally of very high quality. Italians would rather pay more and eat something made with fresh ingredients. So a basic ice cream is usually made with milk, cream, eggs, and sugar and the flavors are strikingly pure and direct. Italians' favorite flavor is *crema*, egg custard, good with a scoop of intense dark chocolate or pungent coffee. People usually opt for a selection of *creme* or *frutte* (creams or fruit) flavors, and don't mix the two types. *Creme* include *tiramisù* ("pick-me-up"), *zuppa inglese* (trifle), or a range of chocolates and marrons glacés. The best *gelaterie* serve fruit flavors made from whatever fruits are in season. A few establishments still make their own *granita*, a refreshing shaved ice slush that's sloppier and icier than the fruit *sorbetti* (sorbets), made from just fruit and sugar—no cream or eggs. A *semifreddo* ("half cold") is "half iced": rather, it's a frozen mousse—softer and lighter in texture than a *gelato*, and less intense in flavor.

COFFEE & PASTRIES

Italian cakes & coffee

There are three main types of Italian cake. *Brioche* (pastries) are made with sweet yeast dough and often filled with a delicious, oozing custard. *Torte* ("cakes") tend to be tarts, such as the ubiquitous *torta della nonna* ("granny's cake"), a kind of cake in tart form, or *torta di ricotta*, in which ricotta is mixed with sugar and candied peel. Then there are all kinds of little cookies, most of which contain nuts and have names such as the accurately named *brutti ma buoni* ("ugly but good"). Italian coffee, now widely available around the world, is no longer a novelty. Italians start the day with a *brioche* and *cappuccino*—and rarely drink *cappuccino* after about 11AM and never after dinner. *Espresso* is what people have after dinner, or as a quick shot taken standing by the bar; an excuse for a chat (just ask for *caffè*). *Caffè corretto* is "corrected" with a dash of grappa or other spirit; *caffè macchiato* is "stained" with milk and *caffè latte* is a milkier version of a *cappuccino*. *Latte macchiato* is hot milk with a dash of coffee.

BAR MAJA ($)

To all appearances this station area bar is unexceptional. However, if you go there in the morning, the barman will happily create delightful *cappuccini* with frothy white milk worked into the shape of a heart or a Florentine lily. The pastries are delicious.

🗺 all ✉ Via Luigi Alamanni 9r ☎ 055 218929 🕐 Closed Sat, Sun 🚇 By the station

BAR MANARESI ($)

Rumor has it that this is the best cup of coffee in Florence. It's roasted and ground on the premises so you are guaranteed an enticing aroma while you sip.

🗺 bIII ✉ Via de Lamberti 🕐 Early morning—8PM. Closed Sun 🚇 In the pedestrian zone

CENNINI ($)

This has the best *torte della nonna* in Florence.

🗺 aIV ✉ Borgo San Jacopo 51r ☎ 055 294930 🚇 3, 31, 32

GIACOSA ($$$)

An elegant café with a very stylish clientele. Renowned as the place where the Negroni cocktail was invented. Convenient for Gucci.

🗺 alII ✉ Via de' Tornabuoni 83r ☎ 055 239 6226 🕐 Closed Sun 🚇 6, 11, 36, 37

GILLI ($$$)

A chic, opulent café in the Piazza della Repubblica; the pastries are renowned (but pricey). Sit outside and indulge in say, a lavish ice cream sundae.

🗺 bIII ✉ Via Roma 1r ☎ 055 239 6310 🕐 Closed Tue 🚇 In the pedestrian zone

KAFFEEHAUS ($$$)

Go to this café in the Boboli Gardens not so much for the quality of the coffee and pastries as the superb view. The building is a folly dating from 1776.

🗺 H7 ✉ In the Boboli Gardens (► 27) 🕐 11–dusk 🚇 B, C

PASZKOWSKI ($$$)

Located on the grandiose Piazza della Repubblica, this is a lovely, if expensive, old-world café and tea room where a piano bar adds a note of refinement to an already delightful interior.

🗺 bIII ✉ Piazza della Repubblica 6r ☎ 055 210236 🚇 In the pedestrian zone

RIVOIRE ($$$)

At Rivoire you pay for the view, but it's worth it. Looking out towards the Palazzo Vecchio, this is the ideal place to relax after a visit to the Uffizi.

🗺 bIII ✉ Piazza della Signoria 5r ☎ 055 214412 🕐 Closed Mon 🚇 In the pedestrian zone

ROBIGLIO ($$)

The old-fashioned Florentine bar/*pasticceria* par excellence, it opened in 1928. The pastries are to die for. 🕐 Mon–Sat 7:30–1:30, 3–8 at:

🗺 bIII ✉ Via Tosinghi 11r ☎ 055 215013 🚇 In the pedestrian zone
🗺 cII ✉ Via dei Servi 112 ☎ 055 214501 🚇 12, 14, 23
🗺 bI ✉ Viale S Lavagnini 18r ☎ 055 490886 🚇 8

WINE & FOOD

LA BOLOGNESE
For those who want to take a real bit of Italian cuisine home with them, the fresh pasta made and sold here includes tortellini, ravioli and gnocchi.
✚ H7 ⊠ Via dei Serragli 24 ☎ 055 282318 🚌 6, 11, 36, 37, 68

LA FIASCHETTERIA
A heady aroma of wine pervades this marvelous store. No frills, just a real sense of pleasure in good wine.
✚ H7 ⊠ Via dei Serragli 47r ☎ 055 287420 🚌 36, 37

MERCATO CENTRALE
The place to observe the care with which Italians buy their food—note the superb fruit and vegetables, meat, poultry, cheeses, breads, salamis, and hams.
✚ all ⊠ Piazza del Mercato Centrale 🚌 In the pedestrian zone

PAOLO PERI
A no-nonsense wine and oil store selling quality products in the prestigious Via Maggio.
✚ alV ⊠ Via Maggio 5r ☎ 055 212674 🚌 36, 37

PEGNA
This lovely old-fashioned store, around since 1860, sells its delicious foods supermarket-style.
✚ blll ⊠ Via dello Studio 26r ☎ 055 282701 🚌 In the pedestrian zone

PORTA ROMANA
At the far end of the Boboli Gardens is a traditional *gastronomia* selling a mouth-watering range of cheeses, cold meats, ready prepared dishes, and other delights from several different counters.
✚ G8 ⊠ Corner of Porta Romana and Via U Foscolo 🚌 11, 12, 13, 36, 37, 68

I SAPORI DEL CHIANTI
A pretty store with an excellent range of wines, including first-class Chianti and other Tuscan specialties.
✚ blll ⊠ Via dei Servi 10r ☎ 055 238 2071 🚌 14, 23

SARTONI
A traditional baker that specializes in filled *focaccia*—great for picnics or snacks.
✚ blll ⊠ Via dei Cerchi 34 ☎ 055 212570 🚌 In the pedestrian zone

LA SORGENTE DELLE DELIZIE
Wines plus Italian candy and cookies.
✚ bll ⊠ Via Cavour 30a ☎ 055 212855 🚌 1, 7, 33

STANDA
Italy's only supermarket chain of any size. Cheap, but not always pleasant, it is worth checking out for the cultural experience. The olive oils and wines are good.
✚ clll ⊠ Via Pietrapana ☎ 055 240809 🚌 B

Holy wine & more
Trebbiano and Malvasia grapes are used to make *vin santo* ("holy wine"), which has a concentrated flavor and is about 14 percent alcohol by volume. The grapes are semi-dried and made into wine, which is aged in small barrels for a number of years before bottling. It is drunk as a dessert wine—sometimes instead of dessert, when you use it to dunk hard, dry *biscotti di Prato* (also known as *cantuccini*).
Chianti gets its name from the region in which it is made. Sangiovese grapes are harvested in October, pressed and then the juice and skins of the grapes are fermented for about 15 days, after which the juice alone is given a second fermentation. In spring the wine is matured in wooden casks. *Chianti Classico* is usually regarded as the best of the seven types of Chianti. This is produced in the eponymous region north of Siena. Wines of the Chianti Classico Consortium bear the symbol of the *Gallo Nero* (black cockerel). The most famous Tuscan reds are made with Sangiovese grapes, including *Brunello di Montalcino* and *Vino Nobile di Montepulciano*. *Sassicaia*, made from Cabernet Sauvignon grapes, is also good.

LEATHER, GLOVES & SHOES

Shoe city

The Florentines are justly famed for making superb shoes. As a testament to the historical importance of the industry in the city's economy, one of the main streets in Florence is named after the shoemakers (*Calzaiuoli*). The range of shoes available is vast, from the pinnacle of international chic to the value-for-money styles for sale in the market of San Lorenzo. The classiest leather stores are around the elegant Via de' Tornabuoni, while huge showrooms in the leather "factories" in the Santa Croce area accommodate bus loads of tourists. The San Lorenzo market also has many stands selling handbags, belts, and jackets of varying degrees of quality. There are bargains to be had, but pitfalls too. The *vero cuoio* ("genuine leather") sign refers only to the piece to which it is attached, which may be only a small proportion of the item.

LEATHER

IL BISONTE
Classic, top-class leather luggage and shoulder bags. Prices match the quality.
🔶 allI ✉ Via del Parione 11 ☎ 055 211976 🚌 C

CELLERINI
Elegant and sophisticated bags of outstanding quality. Styles tend to be fairly traditional.
🔶 allI ✉ Via del Sole ☎ 055 282533 🚌 36, 37

FURLA
Chic, handsomely designed bags and belts at prices that are less astronomic than elsewhere.
🔶 blII ✉ Via de' Tosinghi 5r ☎ 055 281416 🚌 In the pedestrian zone

LEONCINI
This is famous for classic bags and belts made in a workshop on Via Palazzuolo.
🔶 bII ✉ Via Ginori 13r (near Palazzo Medici Riccardi) ☎ 055 282533 🚌 1, 6, 7

MADOVA GLOVES
A staggering array of fine gloves lined with silk, cashmere, and fur. Family run; established in 1919.
🔶 aIV ✉ Via Guicciardini 1r ☎ 055 239 6526 🚌 B

MERCATO SAN LORENZO
Check out the San Lorenzo market glove stands for enchanting sheepskin mittens for children and more.
🔶 bII ✉ Piazza San Lorenzo 🚌 In the pedestrian zone

MISURI
One of the best Santa Croce area leather factories.
🔶 clV ✉ Piazza Santa Croce 20r ☎ 055 240995 🚌 23

PAOLO CASALINI
A tiny workshop selling beautiful small leather goods, especially boxes.
🔶 allI ✉ Via del Moro 44r ☎ 055 289100 🚌 6, 11

SHOES

B&C
It's worth the slight detour (it's near Palazzo Pitti) for this huge range of men's, women's, and children's shoes—all at good prices.
🔶 H7 ✉ Via Romana 111r ☎ 055 229 8237 🚌 12, 13

FAUSTO SANTINI
Fashionable shoes in trendy, minimalist styles.
🔶 blII ✉ Via dei Calzaiuoli 95r ☎ 055 239 8536 🚌 In the pedestrian zone

FRATELLI ROSSETTI
Beautiful shoes in classic Italian styles.
🔶 blII ✉ Piazza della Repubblica 43–45r ☎ 055 216656 🚌 In pedestrian zone

LILY OF FLORENCE
Affordable shoes in classic styles, aimed at tourists.
🔶 aIV ✉ Via Guicciardini 2r ☎ 055 294748 🚌 22, 23

SALVATORE FERRAGAMO
Designer shoes in the Palazzo Spini Feroni, which has a museum of shoes (► 51).
🔶 aIV ✉ Via de' Tornabuoni 14r ☎ 055 292123 🚌 6, 11, C

GOLD & JEWELRY

BOTTEGA ORAFA PENKO

Master goldsmith, Paolo Penco, makes jewelry to order according to techniques used in the Renaissance.

☩ aIII ✉ Via F Zannetti 14 ☎ 055 211661 🚌 22

BULGARI

Florence's branch of the world-famous fashion jeweler and watchmaker.

☩ aIII ✉ Via de' Tornabuoni 61 ☎ 055 239 6786 🚌 6, 11, 36, 37

FIORI DEL TEMPO

In this tiny store, a brother-and-sister team make exquisite reproductions of Medici jewels using semi-precious stones such as aquamarines and garnets. In place of gold, gilded brass gives a sense of antiquity and makes these lovely, unusual and very Florentine jewels decidedly affordable.

☩ bIII ✉ Via dei Pucci 3a ☎ 055 239 6443 🚌 Short walk from San Lorenzo

FREON

Quirky, stylish pieces made of unusual materials in a modern idiom that draws upon historical inspiration, notably art nouveau.

☩ aIV ✉ Via Guicciardini 118r ☎ 055 239 6504 🚌 6, C, B

THE GOLD CORNER

This frequent tour group stop in Piazza Sante Croce sells gold by weight along with typical Italian cameos and coral.

☩ cIV ✉ Piazza Santa Croce 15r ☎ 055 247 8437 🚌 23

PARSIFAL

An unusual selection of jewelry, including a small range of Renaissance styles as well as many eye-catching, affordable aluminium pieces.

☩ aIII ✉ Via della Spada 28r ☎ 055 288610 🚌 6, 11

RICCI E BARONI

Jewelry made of gold, diamonds, and other precious stones in classic styles you find on the Ponte Vecchio, but at more competitive prices. The showroom is in the same fabulous Palazzo Frescobaldi as the workshop.

☩ aIV ✉ Via Santo Spirito 11 ☎ 055 289327 🚌 6, 11

TIME OUT

Beautiful second-hand watches ranging from antique erotic pocket watches to gentlemen's dress watches. There is also a wonderful collection of gold jewelry from the 1920s and 1940s as well as second-hand Tiffany cufflinks and 1920s cigar cutters.

☩ bIV ✉ Via dei Bardi 70r ☎ 055 213111 🚌 B, C

UFFIZI GALLERY SHOP

The Uffizi Gallery store sells a small collection of jewelry modeled exactly on pieces worn in portraits in the Uffizi's collection.

☩ bIV ✉ Loggiato degli Uffizi 6 ☎ 055 238 8651 🕐 Tue–Sat 9–7; Sun 9–2 (last admission 30 minutes before closing). Closed May 1 🚌 In the pedestrian zone

Gold facts

A dazzling array of gold is for sale all over Florence. Most notably on the Ponte Vecchio: in 1593 Ferdinand I decreed that only goldsmiths and jewelers should work there and it has remained that way ever since. The gold sold in Florence is 18 carat, often expressed as a rather confusing 750 percent (with the percent sign actually referring to 1000). Gold is also found—at somewhat lower prices—in the Santa Croce area, where in accordance with tradition all gold jewelry and other items are sold by weight.

FASHION FOR ALL

Stylish city

One of Florence's many claims to fame is as the headquarters of Gucci. It was also in Florence, in 1927, that Salvatore Ferragamo established himself, after having made his reputation in Hollywood crafting shoes for the likes of Greta Garbo, Vivien Leigh, Gloria Swanson and the gladiators in Cecil B. de Mille costume epics. This family still administers a fashion empire, producing accessories and clothes as well as the trademark shoes. Ties are also for sale in Florence at remarkably good prices. The market of San Lorenzo is the cheapest place, but even on the Ponte Vecchio the prices are agreeable!

CASA DELLO SPORT
An excellent place to buy an authentic Italian soccer shirt, prized among teenagers.
🚶 bIII ✉ Via de' Tosinghi 8–10r ☎ 055 215696 🚌 In the pedestrian zone

EMILIO CAVALLINI
A wonderfully wacky collection of socks and hosiery.
🚶 alII ✉ Via della Vigna Nuova 52r ☎ 055 238 2789 🚌 C

COIN
A huge clothing and design emporium with a vast range of goods at reasonable prices on the Via dei Calzaiuoli. Open on Sunday.
🚶 bIII ✉ Via dei Calzaiuoli 56r ☎ 055 280531 🚌 In the pedestrian zone

GUCCI
The Gucci empire headquarters are predictably elegant and predictably pricey store.
🚶 alII ✉ Via de' Tornabuoni 73r ☎ 055 264011 🚌 6, 11

HERMÈS
The biggest and best-equipped branch of this Paris-based designer in Italy.
🚶 alII ✉ Piazza Antinori 6r ☎ 055 238 1004 🚌 1, 6, 12, 22

MARCELLA
A very elegant women's clothes store with an extremely well-selected collection of clothes, lingerie and accessories, suitable for women of all ages.
🚶 bIII ✉ Via dei Pecori 6r ☎ 055 213162 🚌 In the pedestrian zone

MARCELLA UOMO
Beautiful clothes for men, with a good range of styles from formal suits to well-cut casual shirts.
🚶 bIII ✉ Via Cerretani 7r ☎ 055 216352 🚌 In the pedestrian zone

MARINA LOFT
A selection of elegant but affordable Italian designer lines in a good range of sizes. The store near the Duomo is spacious and the service courteous.
🚶 bIII ✉ Via Martelli 29r ☎ 055 284097 🚌 In the pedestrian zone

MAX & CO
The trendy branch of Max Mara; sells well-designed high-fashion pieces to a mainly teenage clientele, but with a range of versatile, classic items as well.
🚶 bIII ✉ Via dei Calzaiuoli 89r ☎ 055 228 8656 🚌 In the pedestrian zone

MAX MARA
Classic elegance takes precedence over ostentation; clothes are of superb quality and beautifully tailored—yet at reasonable prices.
🚶 bIII ✉ Via dei Pecori 23 ☎ 055 287761 🚌 In the pedestrian zone

MERCATO SAN LORENZO
In the San Lorenzo market plenty of clothes fall into the value category. In addition to fun T-shirts, there is a

selection of lambswool and angora sweaters at reasonable prices. Also good for inexpensive scarves and ties.

🏠 bII ✉ Piazza San Lorenzo 🚌 In the pedestrian zone

PATTAYA DUE

This discount store offers designer clothes and accessories for men and women at up to 50 percent off. A must for designer devotees.

🏠 bII ✉ Via Cavour 51r 🕿 055 210151 🚌 In the pedestrian zone

PRADA

The world's favorite Italian fashion house of the moment. The headquarters are in Milan but there's a good range of clothes, shoes, bags and accessories in this branch.

🏠 alII ✉ Via de' Tornabuoni 67r 🚌 6, 11, 36, 37

PRINCIPE

A large store selling practical, sensible clothes for men, women, and children.

🏠 alII ✉ Via degli Strozzi 29r 🕿 055 292764 🚌 In the pedestrian zone

EMILIO PUCCI

A renowned Florentine fashion house created in 1950 by Marquis Emilio Pucci. The *haute couture* is shown in the Palazzo dei Pucci, the ready-to-wear in stores on Via della Vigna Nuova and Via Ricasoli.

🏠 alII ✉ Via della Vigna Nuova 97–99r 🕿 055 294028 🚌 In the pedestrian zone
🏠 bIII ✉ Via Ricasoli 36r 🕿 055 287622 🚌 In the pedestrian zone

QUELLE TRE

Well-tailored, original clothes that are chic and aimed at younger women.

🏠 bIII ✉ Via dei Pucci 43r 🕿 055 293284 🚌 1, 6, 7

LA RINASCENTE

This is one of the newest branches of this Italian department store. The clothes safe rather than exciting but prices are good and there's the odd find to be made. There are also perfumery, lingerie and other departments for those who like everything under one roof.

🏠 C8 ✉ Piazza della Repubblica 🚌 In the pedestrian zone

STILNUOVO

The ultimate tie store sells a wide selection of ties custom-made from a colorful selection of silks.

🏠 bIII ✉ Via Dante Alighieri 8r 🕿 055 238 1567 🚌 In the pedestrian zone

UPIM

An Italy-wide chain sells toiletries and practical items as well as inexpensive, no-nonsense clothes. A good place to look for affordable children's clothing.

🏠 bIII ✉ Piazza della Repubblica 🕿 055 280517 🚌 In the pedestrian zone

EREMENEGILDO ZEGNA

An incredibly trendy menswear shop for the seriously cool and seriously rich.

🏠 alII ✉ Piazza Rucellai 4–7r 🕿 055 283011 🚌 In the pedestrian zone

Districts for clothes shopping

Armani, Gucci, Versace, Ferragamo, Trussardi, and Valentino in the district of the Via de' Tornabuoni and the Via della Vigna Nuova. The area around Piazza della Repubblica and Via dei Calzaiuoli has a good range of expensive clothes shops, including Max Mara and Marcella. In the streets east of Via dei Calzaiuoli, in particular Via del Corso, there are many mid-range fashion boutiques. The areas around Santa Croce and San Lorenzo sell bargain fashions to the tourist market.

LINENS, FABRICS & FURNISHINGS

Hope chest

Although patterns of marriage in Italy have changed drastically in the last 20 years, with people statistically less and less likely to get married (and even less likely to have children), the idea of the *coreddo* (trousseau) persists in Italy, especially in the south, and a number of stores in Florence sell the kinds of linens that such a trousseau demands. Often the same stores sell baby clothes and women's underwear in irresistible styles.

CASA NEL CORTILE

An excellent selection of papers, fabrics and objects for the home.
✛ dIII ✉ Via Antonio Scialoia 29r ☎ 055 234 6095 🚍 6, 8

CIRRI

Beautifully finished lace handkerchiefs and embroidered pieces for men and women. There is also a large collection of extremely expensive baby clothes and layette items as well as lacy underwear for women. Italians typically expect to spend lavishly on these things and they are certainly not cheap.
✛ bIV ✉ Via Por Santa Maria 38–40r ☎ 055 239 6593
🚍 In the pedestrian zone

CONTROLUCE

The shop specializes in lighting but it also carries a good range of gift ideas and other items for the home.
✛ aIII ✉ Via della Vigna Nuova 89r ☎ 055 239 8871
🚍 6, 11

LORETTA CAPONI

Deliciously feminine linens, nightclothes and lingerie for mother and daughter. All the components of a traditional trousseau are here, including exquisite bed linen.
✛ aIII ✉ Piazza Antinori 4r ☎ 055 213668 🚍 6, 11, 36, 37

MERCATO NUOVO

This market (with the Porcellino), not the San Lorenzo market, is the best place to look for cheap tablecloths, linens and lace. You'll find an impressive variety of modern and more traditional designs.
✛ bIII ✉ Piazza Mercato Nuovo 🚍 In the pedestrian zone

PASSAMANERIA TOSCANA FIRENZE

This store sells a comprehensive range of furnishing fabrics, brocades, tassels and other trimmings as well as finished goods such as cushions and footstools. The colors and textures are rich and sensuous, bordering on the abandoned. A treat for anyone with an interest in fabric and furnishing.
✛ bII ✉ Piazza San Lorenzo 12r ☎ 055 239 6389 🚍 In the pedestrian zone

PASSAMANERIA VALMAR

A compact store that sells trims and finishings for fashion and upholstery.
✛ bIII ✉ Via Porta Rossa 53r ☎ 055 283 4493 🚍 In the pedestrian zone

TAF

This shop specializes in trousseau articles, including high-quality hand-finished table and bed linens.
✛ bIV ✉ Via Por Santa Maria 17r ☎ 055 239 6037 🚍 In the pedestrian zone

VALLI

Fine dress fabrics as used by Dormeuil, Armani, Versace, Gianfranco Ferré, and their ilk.
✛ aIII ✉ Via Strozzi 4–6r ☎ 055 282485 🚍 In the pedestrian zone

CERAMICS

CARNESECCHI

A huge emporium of Italian ceramics, particularly Deruta wares.

➕ aIV ✉ Via Guicciardini 4r ☎ 055 239 8523 🚌 B, C

CERAMICHE ND DOLFI

If you're serious about buying ceramics, head out to Montelupo Fiorentino, southeast of the city, to this family-run producer where a whole range of house and garden objects are made and decorated by hand. Signor Dolfi will advise you himself.

➕ Off map ✉ Via Toscoromagnola nord 1, Località Antinoro, Montelupo Fiorentino ☎ 0571 51264

COSE DEL PASSATO

An antique store specializing in vintage ceramics from Montelupo.

➕ aIII ✉ Via dei Fossi 3–5r ☎ 055 294689 🚌 In the pedestrian zone

DISS

A charming, unpretentious selection of rustic ceramics, including spotted peasant pots. There is also a selection of glass from Empoli.

➕ H7 ✉ Piazza del Carmine 14r ☎ 055 292186 🚌 B

FORNACCE POGGI

Located on the southern outskirts of Florence, this is the place for terra-cotta garden pots, oil vats and other things—all made with traditional methods in antique shapes and forms.

➕ Off map ✉ Via Imprunetana 16 ☎ 055 201 1077 🚌 Off the bus routes

MACHIAVELLI

At this tourist store, near the Ponte Vecchio, highlights include fruit bowls made of rings of ceramic geese.

➕ bIV ✉ Via Por Santa Maria 39r ☎ 055 239 8586 🚌 In the pedestrian zone

MASTROCILIEGIA

Playful plates and mugs with huge, brightly colored designs in a variety of styles.

➕ L2 ✉ Piazza Mino 3, Fiesole ☎ 055 598962 🚌 7

PAMPALONI

As well as ceramics, this *oggettistica* (high-quality gift shop at the wedding present market) has a good range of silverware and porcelain.

➕ aIV ✉ Borgo Santi Apostoli 47r ☎ 055 289094 🚌 4

RICHARD GINORI

Florence's own porcelain designer. Also does dinner services to order with your family crest, a picture of your home or whatever else you want.

➕ aIII ✉ Via Rondinelli 17r ☎ 055 210041 🚌 6, 11, 17

SGIBOLI TERRACOTTE

Pots here are designed, painted, and fired in Florence by the family owners and are bought by Florentines as well as tourists. The delightful designs for house and garden come in majolica and unglazed terra-cotta—and at very good prices.

➕ cIII ✉ Via Sant'Egidio 4r ☎ 055 247 9713 🄲 Closed Mon morning 🚌 14, 23

Pottery facts

Traditional Italian ceramics are majolica (pronounced *maiolica*), terracotta covered with a brilliant tin-based glaze. Arabic ceramics (which came to Italy via Spain), inspired pots made for the Medici court at Montelupo, near Florence, sold in a ceramics museum (➤ 21) there. Deruta in Umbria makes flowery designs in blue on white or yellow and turquoise on white are also much in evidence, as are rustic styles from Puglia. Tuscan peasant wares, white or yellow, splashed with green or blue spots are increasingly popular. Among the best-known classic designs is Gran Faenza, with green, red, and blue floral designs on a pale gray-blue background. All stores on this page offer shipping.

STATIONERY, CARDS & CALENDARS

Marbled paper

The skill of marbling paper was brought to Florence from Venice, where it had been learned from the East in the 12th century. Today's Florentine paper goods range greatly in price and quality, but even the cheap goods are very attractive—and easily transported.

GIULIO GIANNINI E FIGLIO

The best-known of Florence's stationery shops, established in 1856, sells tasteful greeting cards and books bound in leather, as well as beautifully finished desktop paraphernalia, letter racks, and pen holders, all covered with marbled paper.

🔲 aIV 🖂 Piazza Pitti 37r ☎ 055 212621 🔲 B, C

MERCATO SAN LORENZO

There is a great variety of cheap stationery in the markets of Florence, especially the Mercato San Lorenzo. Look especially for calendars, with themes such as architecture or botanical prints, all remarkably inexpensive.

🔲 bII 🖂 Piazza San Lorenzo 🔲 In the pedestrian zone

IL PAPIRO

These stores in the center of Florence sell excellent marbled paper goods in particularly pretty colors. These include little chests of drawers and tiny jewelry boxes.

🔲 bII 🖂 Via Cavour 55r; Piazza del Duomo 24r; Lungarno Acciaiuoli 42r ☎ 055 215262; 🔲 aIV/bIII 🖂 Via dei Tavolini 13r ☎ 055 213823

PINEIDER

Chic, expensive stationery and book bindings. One of the characteristic papers covering diaries and address books is decorated with great artists' signatures.

🔲 bIII 🖂 Piazza della Signoria 13r ☎ 055 284655

🔲 aIII 🖂 Via de' Tornabuoni 76r ☎ 055 211605 🔲 In the pedestrian zone

SCRIPTORIUM

This store draws on two great Florentine crafts—leather working and papermaking—to create objects of great beauty and refined taste that are almost too beautiful to be used. The plain paper books are notable, bound with exquisitely soft leather in subdued natural shades.

🔲 aIV 🖂 Piazza Pitti 6 🔲 bIII 🖂 Via dei Servi 5r ☎ 055 238 2272 🔲 In the pedestrian zone

SORBI

A kiosk in the middle of Piazza della Signoria now in its third generation of ownership, this is the very best place in Florence to buy postcards. Save yourself many a frustrating hour and come here first to look for postcards, particularly those of the great art in Florence's museums and churches.

🔲 bIII 🖂 Piazza della Signoria ☎ 055 294554 🔲 In the pedestrian zone

IL TORCHIO

As you walk into this store, you are instantly aware that this is a place where things are made, not just a showroom. You can buy sheets of marbled paper or have it made up to suit your requirements. There are also ready-made marbled paper goods available.

🔲 bIV 🖂 Via dei Bardi 17 ☎ 055 234 2862 🔲 B, C

ANTIQUES & PRINTS

ANTIK

If you're looking for something particularly unusual, this is the place to come.

✚ G7 ✉ Via dei Serragli 146 ☎ 055 220687 🚍 6, 11, 36, 37, 68

ART NOUVEAU

Period jewelry in all sorts of styles (mainly 20th century) with a range of prices that should suit most pockets.

✚ aIII ✉ Via della Scala 43a ☎ 055 284539 🚍 17, 22, 29, 30, 64, 65

BOTTEGA DELLE STAMPE

Framed and unframed antique or art nouveau prints (known in Italian as "Liberty"). Elegant.

✚ aIV ✉ Borgo San Jacopo 56r ☎ 055 295396 🚍 C

CASTORINA

Carved and decorated wood, including friezes, tables, chairs, and other items, both painted and lacquered furniture.

✚ aIV ✉ Via Santo Spirito 15r ☎ 055 212885 🚍 11, C

HALL INTERNATIONAL

The building that houses this store is a treat in itself: an art nouveau townhouse. You'll find very expensive antiques.

✚ H6 ✉ Borgo Ognissanti 26 ☎ 055 283502 🚍 9, C

LEONARDO SARUBBI

A delightfully shabby cavern of a shop near the Palazzo Pitti selling reasonably priced reproductions of antique prints including many 17th- and 18th-century views of Florence and botanical prints. Relaxed and casual.

✚ aIV ✉ Sdrucciolo de' Pitti 11r ☎ 055 238 1850 🚍 B, C

MERCATO DELLE PULCI

Bric-a-brac and junk stands in Piazza dei Ciompi sell all manner of bits and pieces. On the last Sunday in every month you'll find a full-scale flea market. A great place to browse, with the odd bargain to be had among a lot of very pricey garbage.

✚ cIII ✉ Piazza dei Ciompi 🚍 B

STUDIO PUCK

Great selection of historic prints, water-colored by hand, to buy framed or unframed.

✚ aIV ✉ Via dello Sprone ☎ 055 280954 🚍 3, 13, 32

VANDA NENCIONI

Good selection of pretty gilded frames as well as period and modern prints.

✚ bIII ✉ Via della Condotta 36r ☎ 055 215345 🚍 In the pedestrian zone

What is an antique?

Under Italian law an "antique" need not be old, but need only be made of old materials. For this reason, what would be called "reproduction" elsewhere is labeled as an "antique" in Italy. Hundreds of stores all over Florence sell antiques, from the glamorous international emporia on Borgo Ognissanti to the flea market in Piazza dei Ciompi—there are whole streets of them. The most important include Borgo Ognissanti (✚ aIII) and Via Maggio (✚ aIV), for very expensive antiques gorgeously displayed; and streets such as Via dei Serragli (✚ H7) in the Oltrarno area, where considerably less grand stores are here and there among the artisans' workshops.

BARS BY NIGHT

Time out

Going out in Italy doesn't have to mean actually going anywhere. In summer, a particularly enjoyable and popular way of spending time after dinner is to stroll through the streets of the historic center, stopping off for an ice cream or a drink at a bar. You'll see plenty of groups of Italians of all ages doing the same thing.

CABIRIA

A trendy, bohemian bar in Piazza Santo Spirito with outdoor seating. This is Florence's answer to a Left-Bank Paris café. Uncharacteristically for Italy, people linger over their coffees, snacks, and beer. Food is served at all times of the day and night and there are paintings on the walls inside for sale.
✚ alV ✉ Piazza Santo Spirito ☎ 055 215732 ⏰ Closed Tue 🚌 B

CAFFÈ NOTTE

Pleasantly low-key bar situated close to Piazza Santo Spirito; much frequented by the artists and artisans who live and work in the Oltrarno area. Stays open until 2AM.
✚ H7 ✉ Via delle Caldaie 28r ☎ 055 223067 ⏰ Closed Mon 🚌 B

HARRY'S BAR

This trendy bar is the only example of a true American-style bar in Florence, and the best place for elegant cocktails. The food is international and very good; you can also get a first-class hamburger. The service is speedy and exemplary. On the banks of the River Arno.
✚ alll ✉ Lungarno Vespucci 22r ☎ 055 239 6700 ⏰ Closed Sun 🚌 C

MONTECARLA CLUB

Outrageous leopard-skin sofas and chairs, and plastic snakes set the tone for a wacky night out. The music is soft; the entertainment includes table and board games, and there is a selection of weird and wonderfully strong cocktails.
✚ blV ✉ Via dei Bardi 2 ☎ 055 234 0259 🚌 B, C

PICCOLO CAFÉ

A lively gay bar which is located in the Santa Croce area.
✚ clV ✉ Borgo Santa Croce 27 ☎ 055 241704 🚌 23, 71

REX CAFFÈ

A heavy-drinking and billiards-playing kind of place. Very sociable and frequented by the 25–35 age group, with Florentines and foreigners mixing freely in a convivial atmosphere. Open until 1AM.
✚ clll ✉ Via Fiesolana 23r ☎ 055 248 0331 🚌 14, 23, 71

SATANASSA BAR

A popular and centrally located gay bar which shares the same address as the Tabasco 2 disco. Air-conditioned—a real bonus in summer.
✚ clll ✉ Via dei Pandolfini 26; 1st floor ☎ 055 243356 🚌 14

ZOE

A sleek, brightly colored design sets the atmosphere. There is a daily happy "hour" from 6 to 9PM.
✚ J7 ✉ Via dei Renai 13r ☎ 055 243111 ⏰ 8AM–1AM 🚌 C, 23, 71

Clubs & Discos

LA DOLCE VITA

The chosen haunt of the beautiful people. In summer the lively action often spills out into the piazza, so you can enjoy the spectacle as a passerby.

H7 ✉ Piazza del Carmine ☎ 055 284595 🕔 Closed Sun 🚌 B

MARACANA

A Brazilian club in an old theater, with shows and live music. Go early for a full dinner; later on, try the tropically flavored pizza.

all ✉ Via Faenza 4 ☎ 055 210298 🚌 Close to the railroad station

MARAMAO

A Mercato Sant'Ambrogio bar and restaurant that never sleeps, with breakfast, lunch, and dinner at good prices and interesting and varied live music. Very popular with the Florentines—always a good sign. In summer the action moves outside to the piazza.

cIII ✉ Via dei Macci 79r ☎ 055 244341 🚌 14

MECCANÒ

A chic club where you can dance into the small hours.

F5 ✉ Via degli Olmi 1 ☎ 055 331371 🚌 1, 2, 9, 12, 26, 27

SPACE ELECTRONIC

Upstairs you'll find a vast dance floor, where a huge variety of music is played, from up-to-the-minute hits to 50s and 60s classics. Downstairs there is karaoke and room to chat. At Easter and in June and July, this clubs caters extensively to groups of young Americans, who have a tendency to leave, Cinderella fashion, at midnight.

alII ✉ Via Palazzuolo 37 ☎ 055 293082 🚌 5 minutes' walk from the station

STONEHENGE ROCK CLUB

An atmosphere-hunter's paradise, where heavy metal, blues, and rock are played in a small, smoky room.

all ✉ Via dell'Amorino 16r ☎ 055 282180 🕔 Closed Mon 🚌 7, 10, 12, 25, 31

TABASCO 1

A very popular gay disco, not far from the Piazza della Signoria.

bIII ✉ Piazzetta Santa Cecilia 3r 🕔 Closed Mon ☎ 055 213000 🚌 In the pedestrian zone

TENAX

Trendy and up-to-date music and a huge dance floor; very popular with both Florentines and foreigners.

D3 ✉ Via Pratese 47 ☎ 055 308160 🕔 Closed Mon and Wed 🚌 Towards the airport

TONIGHT CLUB

Comfortable and intimate with low lighting, cane furniture, and live music and other entertainment every night.

bIV ✉ Via dei Benci 19r ☎ 055 234 0239 🕔 10PM–4AM 🚌 23, 71

Late start

Florentine clubs start and end late. The first trickle of action is usually about 10:30PM or 11PM. Closing time is between 3AM and 5AM. The entrance fee is generally around L25,000 and includes one drink.

OPERA & CLASSICAL MUSIC

Opera's rebirth

Florence is one of the birthplaces of opera. At the end of the 16th century, a group of dilettanti attempted to re-create the musical glories of ancient Greek theater. The first performance, Jacopo Peri's *Euridice*, was held in the amphitheater of the Giardino di Boboli (➤ 27).

FESTIVALS

ESTATE FIESOLANA

A season of music, opera, and ballet from late June to August known as the Sunset Concerts, runs primarily in the open-air Roman Theater in Fiesole (➤ 20). Performances are by Tuscan and Italian groups with the occasional visitor from abroad. The main attraction is chamber and symphonic music, hosted by The Badia Fiesolana. Other events are staged in Santa Croce or the courtyard of the Palazzo Pitti. Concerts in all these venues are an unbeatable experience.

Fondazione Toscana Spettacolo ✚ H6 ✉ Via Luigi Alamanni 41 ☎ 055 21985 **Roman Theater** ✚ Off map ✉ Via Marini 🚌 7 **Box office** ✚ all ✉ Via Faenza 139 ☎ 055 210804

MAGGIO MUSICALE FIORENTINO

This major musical festival held between May and early July includes opera and ballet as well as orchestral concerts and chamber music. It has its own orchestra, chorus, and ballet troupe. The main venue is the Teatro Comunale; the Teatro della Pergola and the Teatro Verdi are used for more intimate recitals. The main box office is the Teatro Comunale (below).

VENUES

PALAZZO DEI CONGRESSI

The main venue from October to June for the classical music company, *Musicus Concertus*.

✚ al ✉ Viale Filippo Strozzi ☎ 055 26025 (Musicus Concertus ☎ 055 287347)

SANTA MARIA DEI RICCI

Many organ recitals are held in this church.

✚ bIII ✉ Via del Corso 🚌 In the pedestrian zone

TEATRO COMUNALE

The largest of Florence's concert halls—the main venue of the Maggio Musicale and the festival's box office—also has its own classical season from mid-September to December. The opera season then begins, finishing mid-January and from then through April, symphony concerts are held. The Ridotto or Piccolo is the Teatro Comunale's smaller auditorium.

✚ G6 ✉ Corso Italia 16 ☎ 055 27791/055 211158 🚌 C

TEATRO DELLA PERGOLA

An important venue for classical music in Florence, with some Maggio Musicale and Estate Fiesolana concerts held here. From October to April the Amici della Musica organize Saturday afternoon concerts here.

✚ cIII ✉ Via della Pergola 12 ☎ 055 247 9651 🚌 23, 71

TEATRO VERDI

This theater puts on drama, ballet, and opera from January to April.

✚ dIV ✉ Via Ghibellina 101 ☎ 055 239 6242 🚌 14

LIVE MUSIC

AUDITORIUM FLOG

This is probably the best known of Florence's live music venues, where music of all kinds is performed; regular themed disco evenings music spot is featured.
✚ H4 ✉ Via Mercati 24b
☎ 055 487145 🚌 4

BAR STAZIONE SANTA MARIA NOVELLA

On summer Tuesdays at noon the station bar presents free live jazz that's well worth missing a train for.
✚ all ✉ Stazione Santa Maria Novella 🚌 In the main station

IL BARRETTO

A small, intimate and fashionable bar, frequented by professionals, serving excellent drinks in congenial surroundings with civilized live piano music in the background.
✚ alll ✉ Via del Parione 50r
☎ 055 294122 🚌 C

BE BOP

This club in an old cellar serves up strictly live jazz. Wednesday is the big night—go early to get a seat.
✚ bll ✉ Via dei Servi 28r

CHIODSO FISSO CLUB

Popular, well-established wine bar run by a dedicated folk music enthusiast. You will find Italian folk music at its best in this atmospheric candlelit setting. Very centrally located.
✚ blll ✉ Via Dante Alighieri 16r ☎ 055 238 1290 🚌 In the pedestrian zone

CITTÀ DI FIRENZE

An elegant riverside restaurant with an American-style bar, where you can eat and drink to the accompaniment of live piano music.
✚ alll ✉ Lungarno Corsini 4
☎ 055 217706 🚌 C

DU MONDE

A wonderfully civilized venue for light jazz music in the Oltrarno. Come here to enjoy a candlelit dinner with piano music. Later, settle down for some wonderful jazz. Very popular, so reserve ahead.
✚ J7 ✉ Via di San Niccolò 103r ☎ 055 234 4953
🕐 Closed Mon 🚌 13, 23, 71

JAZZ CAFE

Another very popular venue among real jazz aficionados. Although technically a private club, it is very easy to become a member (see panel, right).
✚ clll ✉ Via Nuova dei Caccini 3 ☎ 055 247 9700
🕐 Closed Mon 🚌 14, 23, 71

STONEHENGE ROCK CLUB

Regular live rock music in an unpretentious bar venue that stays open till late as a nightclub (▶ 79). Not for the faint-hearted or ingénue.
✚ all ✉ Via dell'Amorino 16r
☎ 055 282180 🕐 Closed Mon
🚌 7, 10, 12, 25, 31

Clubbing Italian style

Many clubs and music venues (and even a few bars and restaurants) are officially private clubs or *associazione culturale*. This doesn't mean that visitors are unwelcome but rather that it's easier for them to get a license as a club than as a public *locale*. It's easy to become a member; you may be charged a few thousand lire over and above the official entry price, but it's still worth doing so even if you're only going to use your membership once. Many clubs actually have free membership. All you need to do is fill in your name, address, date of birth and sometimes occupation on a form and you'll be presented with a membership card.

SPORTS

Soccer is all

Many Florentines take much more immediate pride in their soccer team than in their artistic heritage. "I Viola" (The Purples) is the familiar way of referring to *La Fiorentina*, a team in the top division of the Serie A soccer league, whose most famous 1990s players included Roberto Baggio, soccer genius, Buddhist, and national hero until his untimely failure to score a penalty in the final of the 1994 World Cup, which Italy then lost.

SPECTATOR SPORTS

POLO
A polo tournament is held annually in Florence in June. On other occasions polo is played in the Piazza Santa Croce; however, the usual location is the racecourse —the Ippodromo delle Muline—in the park of Le Cascine (► 56).
🔲 G6 ✉ Ippodromo delle Muline, Le Cascine ☎ 055 422 6076

SOCCER
The magnificent Stadio Franchi, also known as Stadio Comunale or the Palazzo dello Sport, is where I Viola play soccer.
🔲 L5 🚌 17

PARTICIPATORY SPORTS

BOWLING
BOWLING PALASPORT
Near the railroad station.
🔲 all ✉ Via Faenza 71
☎ 055 238 1380

CANOEING
SOCIETA CANOTTIERI COMUNALI
Rent a canoe and paddle your way along the Arno.
🔲 K7 ✉ Lungarno Ferrucci 6
☎ 055 681 2649

EXERCISE
GYMNASIUM
Fairly good weights, but not the latest technology.
🔲 alll ✉ Via Palazzuolo 49r
☎ 055 293308

SQUASH
CENTRO SQUASH
🔲 D6 ✉ Via Empoli 16
☎ 055 732 3055

SWIMMING
PISCINA COMUNALE BELLARIVA
An outdoor Olympic swimming pool with a smaller one for children in pleasant shady gardens east of the city.
🔲 L7 ✉ Lungarno Colombo 6
☎ 6055 677521 🕐 Jun–Sep
🚌 14

PISCINA LE PAVONIERE
Most popular (used by Florentines but also visitors) outdoor pool in Florence, in Le Cascine (► 56).
🔲 G6 ✉ Le Cascine ☎ 055 333979 🕐 Jun to Sep 🚌 17 to Piazza Vittorio Veneto and then D

ZODIAC
A huge complex with four swimming pools (two indoor), pleasant gardens and a bar. Take the N2 to La Certosa and follow the signs for Tavernuzze, just outside Florence.
🔲 Off map to south ✉ Via Grandi 2 ☎ 055 202 2888
🚌 37

TENNIS
CIRCOLO CARRAIA
On the hill leading up to San Miniato. The floodlit outdoor courts get busy during lunchtimes and early evenings but are quieter in summer and during weekdays. Bring a racket.
🔲 J7 ✉ Via Monti alle Croci
☎ 055 234 6353

ZODIAC
See above.
🔲 Off map to south ✉ Via Grandi 2, Tavernuzze ☎ 055 202 2850

PAGEANTS IN TUSCANY

AREZZO

GIOSTRA DEL SARACINO

This jousting tournament in Crusade-era costume takes place in the town's central square of Arezzo, the Piazza Grande. Two knights, representing the town's four *contrade* (districts) charge toward a wooden model of a Saracen, which they aim to hit while avoiding the attached cat of three tails that swings back and can unseat them. The other side do everything they legitimately can to unnerve the knight, including making a deafening noise. The winner gets a golden lance.
➕ Off map ✉ Piazza Grande, Arezzo 🚆 40 minutes' train journey from Florence 🕐 Last Sun in Aug and 1st Sun in Sep 🛈 Piazza della Repubblica 22 ☎ 0575 377678

FLORENCE

CALCIO IN COSTUME

A soccer game between four teams of men who wear their district's medieval colors. The games, played in Piazza Santa Croce according to somewhat archaic rules, are preceded by a long procession accompanied by drums and trumpets. The winning team is presented with a live cow.
➕ clV ✉ Piazza Santa Croce 🕐 Late Jun

PISA

GIOCO DEL PONTE

A grand tug-of-war between the inhabitants of the north and the south of Pisa on the Ponte di Mezzo, which divides the city. Participants wear Renaissance costume, and some have period armor; everyone carries shields decorated with their district emblems. The aim is to push a hefty carriage over the bridge into the river.
➕ Off map ✉ Ponte di Mezzo 🕐 Last Sun in Jun 🚆 1 hour's train journey from Florence

REGATA DI SAN RANIERI

Colorful boat races on the River Arno are preceded by pageantry and processions. At night the buildings along the river are illuminated by flaming torches.
➕ Off map ✉ River Arno, Pisa ☎ 050 42291 🕐 Jun 17 🛈 Piazza della Stazione 11

SIENA

CORSO DEL PALIO

The most famous pageant of all, Siena's Palio is a breakneck horse race in the Piazza del Campo, a tradition since 1283. The horses are blessed in the churches of the 17 *contrade*; the jockeys ride bareback, wearing their district colors. The winner takes the *palio* or banner.
➕ Off map ✉ Piazza del Campo ☎ 0577 280551 🕐 Jul 2, Aug 16 🛈 Piazza del Campo 56

Medieval mayhem

All towns of Tuscany go in for pageantry. Participants dress up in the medieval or Renaissance costumes of their particular district or town and parade through the streets, then join in an aggressive, often violent competition—soccer, jousting or horse racing—with tremendous gusto. Visitors watch—as much as they can as it's crowded and there's a lot of jostling. Everyone has a wonderful time and a great deal to eat afterwards.

LUXURY HOTELS

Prices

Approximate prices for a double room per night:

Budget   up to L200,000
Moderate   up to L350,000
Luxury   over L350,000

Reservations

Peak season in Florence runs from February to October, but the city's hotels are almost invariably busy. Telephone, write or fax well in advance for a room (virtually all receptionists speak some English, French or German). Leave a credit card number or send an international money order for the first night's stay to be certain of the reservation.

BRUNELLESCHI

A modern hotel housed in a medieval tower in a peaceful location just behind the Via Calzaiuoli.
🏨 bIII ✉ Piazza Santa Elisabetta 3 ☎ 055 562068, fax 055 219653 🚍 In the pedestrian zone

DELLA SIGNORIA

A modern luxury hotel with views of the Ponte Vecchio from the upper floors.
🏨 aIII ✉ Via delle Terme 1 ☎ 055 214530, fax 055 216101 🚍 In the pedestrian zone

EXCELSIOR

The grandest hotel in Florence, plush and immensely comfortable, but located in a not-so-grand piazza. Some rooms have a view of the River Arno, and there is a roof terrace.
🏨 H6 ✉ Piazza Ognissanti 3 ☎ 055 264201, fax 055 210278 🚍 9, C

HELVETIA E BRISTOL

An 18th-century hotel in a superb location near the Duomo. Each room is decorated differently and though all have rich furnishings, many have antiques, too.
🏨 aIII ✉ Via dei Pescioni 2 ☎ 055 287814, fax 055 288353 🚍 6, 11, 36, 37

HOTEL J & J

Close to touristy Santa Croce, a quiet hotel in a 16th-century monastery, with a glamorous international clientele. 🍴
🏨 cIII ✉ Via di Mezzo 20 ☎ 055 234 5005, fax 055 240282 🚍 B

KRAFT

There are both traditional and modern rooms in this quiet and comfortable hotel, which also has a small roof-top swimming pool and some terrific views.
🏨 G6 ✉ Via Solferino 2 ☎ 055 284273, fax 055 239 8267 🚍 C

MONNA LISA

In a 15th-century palace with courtyards and a garden. Beautiful public spaces, but some rooms are cramped and noisy.
🏨 cII ✉ Borgo Pinti 27 ☎ 055 247 9751, fax 055 247 9755 🚍 6, 31, 32

PRINCIPE

A small, elegant hotel with an old-world feel and air-conditioned, sound proof rooms, many with terraces overlooking the Arno.
🏨 aIII ✉ Lungarno Vespucci 34 ☎ 055 284848, fax 055 283458 🚍 C

TORRE DI BELLOSGUARDO

There are stupendous views of Florence from this fabulous hotel in a 16th-century villa and a huge 14th-century tower. Spacious rooms are elegantly decorated with antiques. Swimming pool.
🏨 Off map to southwest ✉ Via Roti Michelozzi 2 ☎ 055 229 8145, fax 055 229008

VILLA CORA

A beautifully decorated villa with its own grounds outside the city (there is a free shuttle).
🏨 H8 ✉ Viale Machiavelli 18 ☎ 055 298451, fax 055 229086 🚍 12, 13, 38

MID-RANGE HOTELS

ANNALENA
In a Medici palazzo opposite the Boboli Gardens, this hotel once favored by artists and writers has pretty rooms with rather old-fashioned decor, some with terraces and views.

✚ H7 ⊠ Via Romana 34 ☎ 055 222402, fax 055 222403 🚌 36, 37

APRILE
Rooms in this former Medici home come in different styles, sizes, and prices.

✚ alll ⊠ Via della Scala 6 ☎ 055 216237, fax 055 280947 🚌 2, 17, 22

BALESTRI
Close to the River Arno between the Uffizi and Santa Croce, with spacious and comfortable rooms.

✚ bIV ⊠ Piazza Mentana 7 ☎ 055 214743, fax 055 239 8042 🚌 23, 71

BEACCI TORNABUONI
Recently refurbished rooms of varying quality with air-conditioning and mini-bars on the top three floors of a 14th-century *palazzo*.

✚ alll ⊠ Via de' Tornabuoni 3 ☎ 055 212645, fax 055 283594 🚌 6, 11, 36, 37

LE DUE FONTANELLE
Modern hotel in the delightful Piazza della Santissima Annunziata.

✚ cII ⊠ Piazza della Santissima Annunziata 14 ☎ 055 280086, fax 055 294461 🚌 6, 31, 32

IL GUELFO BIANCO
A hotel well adapted for business travelers. The spacious, comfortable rooms are decorated in fresh, clear colors.

✚ bII ⊠ Via Cavour 57r ☎ 055 288330, fax 055 295203 🚌 1, 7, 33

HERMITAGE
A well-known hotel overlooking the Ponte Vecchio.

✚ bIV ⊠ Vicolo Marzio 1, Piazza del Pesce ☎ 055 287216, fax 055 212208 🚌 In the pedestrian zone

PORTA ROSSA
Good enough for Byron and Stendhal, this elegant, spacious hotel is in a 14th-century building close to the Ponte Vecchio.

✚ alll ⊠ Via Porta Rossa 19 ☎ 055 287551, fax 055 282179 🚌 In the pedestrian zone

RESIDENZA
Traditional comfort hotel on the top four floors of a 17th-century *palazzo* on the super-elegant Via de' Tornabuoni.

✚ alll ⊠ Via de' Tornabuoni 8 ☎ 055 218684, fax 055 284197 🚌 6, 11, 36, 37

VILLA AURORA
This hotel in Fiesole with a panorama of Florence offers exceptional value. Some rooms have saunas and Jacuzzis, many have terraces and all have air-conditioning. Central Florence is only a 20 minute bus ride away.

✚ L2 ⊠ Piazza Mino 39, Fiesole ☎ 055 59100, fax 055 59587 🚌 7

Which room?
The room with a view is a much sought-after thing. However, it can often come with street noise. Most Florentine hotels are in *palazzi* built around courtyards, so that the rooms with views face onto the street, while the ones looking over the courtyards are pleasantly quiet. You might like to forego the romance to ensure a good night's sleep.

BUDGET HOTELS

Last-minute reservations

If you arrive without a reservation, try the ITA (Informazioni Turistiche Alberghiere) office on the railroad station concourse (🕐 Daily 8:30–9 ☎ 055 282893). You'll pay a fee of L3,000–L10,000 for finding a room depending on the category of hotel.

ABACO

Small, friendly family-run hotel very close to the station and the Duomo. Clean, neat rooms and facilities for washing clothes and cooking.

✚ all ✉ Via dei Banchi 1 ☎ (and fax) 055 2381919 🚇 5 minutes' walk from the station

AZZI

Small, cheap, clean and in a quiet location close to the station.

✚ all ✉ Via Faenza 56 ☎ (and fax) 055 213806 🚇 5 minutes' walk from the station

BRETAGNA

Affordable rooms with views overlooking the River Arno.

✚ allI ✉ Lungarno Corsini 6 ☎ 055 289618, fax 055 289619 🚇 C

CRISTINA

A small, clean hotel in a medieval palace off a quiet street in the heart of Florence.

✚ bIII ✉ Via della Condotta 4 ☎ 055 214484 🚇 In the pedestrian zone

FIRENZE

A large, modern hotel in a very quiet courtyard in the center of Florence.

✚ bIII ✉ Piazza dei Donati 4 ☎ 055 214203, fax 055 212073 🚇 In the pedestrian zone

LOCANDA ORCHIDEA

Family-run hotel close to the Duomo on the third floor of a 12th-century *palazzo*.

✚ bIII ✉ Borgo degli Albizi 11 ☎ (and fax) 055 248 0346 🚇 In the pedestrian zone

NUOVA ITALIA

Modern, clean hotel located very close to the station, with friendly, English-speaking staff.

✚ all ✉ Via Faenza 26 ☎ 055 268430, fax 055 210941 🚇 5 minutes' walk from the station

IL PERSEO

Clean and friendly, with modern rooms. Close to the railroad station and the Duomo.

✚ bIII ✉ Via Cerretani 1 ☎ 055 212504, fax 055 288377 🚇 5 minutes' walk from the station.

POR SANTA MARIA

Small, clean hotel right by the Mercato Nuovo with great views of the Ponte Vecchio and Piazza della Signoria. Managed with loving pride and care. Take elevator to the 4th floor to find the reception desk. No breakfast.

✚ bIII ✉ Via Calimaruzza 3 ☎ (and fax) 055 216370 🚇 In the pedestrian zone

SORELLE BANDINI

Perfect for the more bohemian traveler, this *pensione* is on the top story of a 1505 *palazzo* and has a fabulous loggia, ideal for picnics, and huge rooms with frescoed, slightly crumbling ceilings. The breakfast room looks over a panorama of terra-cotta-tile roofs to the Palazzo Pitti. The owners keep cats.

✚ aIV ✉ Piazza Santo Spirito 9 ☎ 055 215308, fax 055 282761 🚇 B, 36, 37

FLORENCE
travel facts

ARRIVING & DEPARTING

Before you go
- Visas are not required.
- Anyone entering Italy must have a valid passport (or official identity card for E.U. nationals).
- There are no vaccination requirements.

When to go
- Florence can be extremely hot and humid in the summer, sometimes uncomfortably so.
- Peak season runs from February to October—although many consider it virtually uninterrupted. In June and July the city is particularly overrun with tour groups.
- If you like heat, go in August. Although many Florentines will be on vacation and some restaurants will be shut, it's a good time because everything is quieter than normal.

Arriving by train
- The main train station is Santa Maria Novella.
- Almost all buses depart from the forecourt and there are usually taxis waiting.
- Give yourself plenty of time to buy your ticket (the lines are long) and remember to validate it before you get on the train. Do this by inserting the corner into the orange box at the head of each platform.

Arriving by air
- Flights arrive both at Florence's airport and Pisa's Galileo Galilei airport.
- Florence's Amerigo Vespucci airport, known as La Peretola, is about 4 miles west of Florence, connected by a bus service from the station. Until recently very small, it handles flights from an increasing number of destinations ☎ 055 306 1700/055 373498.
- Pisa airport has long been a gateway to Florence. There are direct train connections from the airport to Florence's Santa Maria Novella station (Pisa Tourist Information Office ☎ 050 500707).

Customs regulations
- E.U. nationals do not have to declare goods imported for their personal use.
- The limits for U.S. citizens and other non-E.U. visitors are 200 cigarettes or 100 small cigars or 250g of tobacco; 1 liter of alcohol (over 22 percent alcohol) or 2 liters of fortified wine; 50g of perfume.

ESSENTIAL FACTS

Electricity
- Voltage is 220 volts and sockets take two round pins.

Etiquette
- Make the effort to speak some Italian: however bad, it will be appreciated.
- Shake hands on introduction and on leaving; once you know people better you can replace this with a kiss (*bacio*) on each cheek.
- Use the polite form, *lei*, unless the other person uses *tu*.
- Always say *buon giorno* (hello) and *arrivederci* (goodbye) in stores.
- Italians do not get drunk in public.
- Smoking is common everywhere.

Insurance
- Travel insurance with an option that covers loss or theft of cash is indispensable; pickpockets are rife and skilled.
- Make a statement (*denuncia*) at a

police station within 24 hours of any event for which you wish to make a claim.

Money and credit cards

- The euro has been the official currency of Italy since January 1, 1999. However, the lira remains a denomination of the euro and lire bills and coins will continue to be legal tender until euro bills are introduced on January 1, 2002.
- American Express office ✉ Via Dante Alighieri 22r ☎ 055 50981
- Credit cards are widely accepted.
- Cash machines are increasingly common. Debit or credit cards can also be used to draw cash and are a convenient way to deal with currency exchange.

National holidays

- Jan 1: New Year's Day;
- Jan 6: Epiphany;
- Easter Sunday;
- Easter Monday;
- Apr 25: Liberation Day;
- May 1: Labor Day;
- Aug 15: Assumption;
- Nov 1: All Saints' Day;
- Dec 8: Immaculate Conception;
- Dec 25: Christmas Day;
- Dec 26: St. Stephen's Day.

Opening times

- Banks: 8:30–1:20; in some instances also 2:45–4 Mon–Fri.
- Post offices: Mon–Fri 8:15–1:30; Sat 8:15–12:30.
- Stores: normally 8:30–1 and from 3 or 4 through 7 or 8; or 10–7.
- Museums: see individual entries.
- Churches: 7 or 8–12:30 and then from between 3 and 4 until 7:30. Main tourist attractions often stay open longer. No two are the same.

Places of worship

- Anglican: St. Mark's ✉ Via Maggio 16 ☎ 055 294764

- American Episcopal Church: St. James' ✉ Via Rucellai 9 ☎ 055 294417
- Lutheran ✉ Lungarno Torrigiani 11 ☎ 055 234 2775
- Synagogue ✉ Via Farini 4 ☎ 055 245252/3
- Russian Orthodox ✉ Via Leone X 8 ☎ 055 490148
- Greek Orthodox ✉ Viale Mattioli 76
- Mosque ✉ Piazza Scarlatti (off Via dei Geppi)

Restrooms

- Italian restrooms are improving but you can have some nasty shocks in the most unsuspected places.
- Expect to pay about L500 for restrooms. Those away from the main tourist areas are usually free.
- There are virtually no public toilets in Florence.
- Carry your own toilet paper or at least a packet of tissues.
- Most bars and cafés have restrooms, which usually allow anybody to use them (although it's polite to have at least a drink).

Street numbers

- One building can have two totally different numbers in Florence. The red lettering system is for stores, restaurants and businesses, while the blue system is for hotels or residences. Red numbers have an "r" after them.

Student travelers

- Bring an ISIC card to get reductions on museum entry fees.
- If you intend to stay at youth hostels (► 86) get a youth hostel card before leaving for Italy.

Time differences

- Italy is 6 hours ahead of Eastern Standard Time and 9 hours ahead of Pacific Standard Time. Clocks change on the last Saturday in October and March.

Tourist information office

- Principal tourist office ✉ Via Cavour 1r ☎ 055 290832/3, fax 055 276 0381

Visitors with disabilities

- Facilities for visitors with disabilities are generally poor, although museums are being improved.

Women travelers

- Women are generally safe traveling alone or together in Florence.
- After dark avoid the Cascine, Santa Maria Novella, and the railroad station.

PUBLIC TRANSPORTATION

Local buses

- Just about everything is within walking distance, but it can be tiring to see it all on foot. The bus system is run by the city *comune*. Routes are numbered and many (but not all) start and end at the train station at regular intervals, although traffic soon messes this up. Recently, zippy little electric buses identified by letters rather than numbers have been introduced, linking all kinds of hitherto inaccessible places.
- Bus tickets cannot be bought on board the bus and should be bought beforehand at a bar or tobacco store. Your ticket is not valid unless you stamp it—to do this, insert it into the small orange box on the bus and it will be stamped with the time. The ticket is then valid for 60 minutes on any bus. Failure to validate your ticket can result in a hefty fine.
- Bus maps are not easily obtained. Try the tourist information office by the railroad station.

Taxis

- Official Florentine taxis are comfortable, clean, and white. You can hail them from central places such as the railroad station or Piazza del Duomo. Otherwise, telephone one of the official cab companies: Radio Taxi SO.CO.TA. ☎ 055 4798/4242; Radio Taxi CO.TA.FI. ☎ 055 4390
- The meter starts running the moment the call is made.
- Supplements are charged for baggage and for journeys made between 10PM and 7AM.

Walking

- The historic center of Florence is sufficiently small for walking to be the best way of getting around. Much of the center is pedestrian-only, and it would take longer to get to many locations in this book by bus than to walk there. But you can overdo it, and it pays to take a bus occasionally to avoid blisters and save your tendons.

Long-distance buses

- There are three main companies in Florence.
- Lazzi links Florence with major European cities and the region to the north and the west of Florence, and runs express services to Rome ✉ Piazza della Stazione 47 ☎ 055 351061 (national and international services).
- SITA serves the south and east region ✉ Via Santa Caterina da Siena 15r ☎ 055 483651 (Tuscany); 055 214721 (national)
- CAP serves the region to the northeast of Florence, the Mugello ✉ Via Nazionale 13 ☎ 055 214637

DRIVING

Bicycles

- Bicycles can be rented from Ciao e Basta ✉ Lungarno Pecori Giraldi 1 ☎ 055 2342726

Cars

- The brochure *Florence Concierge* is available in hotels and tourist information offices.
- Car rental companies are all located in Borgo Ognissanti or Via Maso Finiguerra.
- Avis ✉ Borgo Ognissanti 128r ☎ 055 213629
- Program ✉ Borgo Ognissanti 135r ☎ 055 282916
- Tolls are payable on highways (*autostrade*).
- Most gas stations in the country now take credit cards, but not all.
- Breakdown service: ACI ✉ Viale G Amendola 36, Florence ☎ 116/055 24861

Motorcycles

- Mopeds and motorcycles can be rented from Motorent ✉ Via San Zanobi 9r ☎ 055 490113

MEDIA & COMMUNICATIONS

Mail

- Main post office ✉ Via Pellicceria 8 ☎ 055 216122/160 🕐 Mon–Sat 8:15–7
- There is another big post office at ✉ Via Pietrapiana 53–55 ☎ 055 27741 (same hours)
- Stamps (*francobolli*) can be bought either from post offices or from tobacco stores displaying a white T sign on a black or blue background.
- Mail boxes are small and red and marked *Poste* or *Lettere*. The slot on the left is for all addresses within the city and the slot on the right is for all other destinations.

Telephones

- Public phones are bright orange and can be found all over Florence. There are also a few telephone centers in the city (there is one at Via Cavour 21r 🕐 Daily 8AM–10PM). The telephone company is Telecom Italia.
- Few public telephones take coins. Telephone cards (*carta* or *scheda* or *tessera telefonica*) cost L5,000, L10,000 or L15,000; this is by far the most practical way to use a public telephone.
- Information ☎ 12
- International information ☎ 176
- International operator (Europe) ☎ 170; you can place collect international calls by dialing 17200 followed by your country code (which will give you the operator).
- International operator (rest of the world) ☎ 170
- Cheap rate is all day Sunday and 10PM–8AM (international); 8:30PM–8AM (national) on other days.
- To call Italy from the U.S., dial 011 followed by 39 (the code for Italy) then the number, including the relevant city code. For example, to call the tourist office in Florence: 011 39 055 290832.
- Florence's area code, 055, must be dialed before all numbers whether or not you are calling from within Florence.

Press

- The Florentines preferred newspaper is *La Nazione*, a national paper produced in Florence.
- You can buy foreign newspapers and magazines at the station and at Sorbi, in Piazza della Signoria.

Television

- State-run television channels RAI1, RAI2 and RAI3 offer fewer game shows and advertisements than do the Mediaset-owned Italia 1, Italia 4 and Canale 5.
- Telemontecarlo is another privately run station available throughout Italy.

EMERGENCIES

Telephone numbers
- Police, fire, and ambulance ☎ 113
- Police headquarters (for thefts, passport problems, etc.) ☎ 055 49771

Embassies and consulates
- British Consulate ✉ Lungarno Corsini 2 ☎ 055 284133
- U.S. Consulate ✉ Lungarno Amerigo Vespucci 38 ☎ 055 239 8276

Lost property
- Lost property office ✉ Via Circondaria 17 ☎ 055 328 3942 🕐 9–noon. Closed Sun
- Report losses of passports to the local police station and other items to the Questura at Via Zara 2 ☎ 055 49771.

Medicines and medical treatment
- Medical emergencies ☎ 118
- First aid: Misericordia ambulance service ☎ 055 212222
- Tourist medical service: has English-speaking doctors on 24-hour call ✉ Via Lorenzo il Magnifico 59 ☎ 055 475 4111
- Hospital: Santa Maria Nuova ✉ Piazza Santa Maria Nuova 1 ☎ 055 27581 Interpreters can be arranged free through Associazione Volontari Ospedalieri ☎ 055 403126.
- Pharmacies are indicated by a large green or red cross.
- All-night pharmacies: Comunale 13 della Stazione ✉ At the train station ☎ 055 289435; All'insegna del Moro-Taverna ✉ Piazza San Giovanni 20r ☎ 055 211343; Molteni ✉ Via dei Calzaiuoli 7r ☎ 055 289490; Paglicci ✉ Via della Scala 61 ☎ 055 215612. Rota system ☎ 167 420707 (freephone) for details.

Precautions
- Take care of all wallets and hand-bags at all times as pickpockets tend to target tourists.
- Keep the receipts and numbers of your traveler's checks separate from the traveler's checks themselves.
- Take a copy of the front page of your passport and keep it separately.
- List the numbers and expiry dates of your credit cards and keep the list separately.

LANGUAGE

- However bad your Italian, try a few words in Italian. Even if you are not understood, the effort will be appreciated as a sign of respect and politeness.
- Italian pronunciation is totally consistent. *C*s and *g*s are hard when they are followed by an *a*, *o*, or *u* (as in "cat" and "got"), and soft if followed by an *e* or an *i* (as in "child" or "geranium").
- The Tuscans often pronounce their *c*s and *ch*s as *h*s.
- Unless you know someone very well, it is best to stick to the polite form (*lei*).

Useful words and phrases

good morning	buon giorno
good afternoon/ evening	buona sera
good night	buona notte
hello/goodbye (informal)	ciao
hello (answering the telephone)	pronto
goodbye (informal)	arrivederci
goodbye (formal)	arrivederla
please	per favore
thank you	grazie
thank you very much	grazie mille
you're welcome	prego
how are you?	come sta/stai?
I'm fine	sto bene
I'm sorry	mi dispiace

excuse me/			polizia
I beg your pardon	scusi/scusa	call a doctor/an	
excuse me		ambulance	chiamate un
(in a crowd)	permesso		medico/
			un'ambulanza
Basic vocabulary		first aid	pronto soccorso
yes	sì	where is the nearest	
no	no	hospital?	dov'è l'ospedale
I do not understand	non ho capito		più vicino?
left	sinistra		
right	destra		
entrance	entrata	**Numbers**	
exit	uscita		
open	aperto	1	uno
closed	chiuso	(first	primo)
good	buono	2	due
bad	cattivo	(second	secondo)
big	grande	3	tre
small	piccolo	(third	terzo)
with	con	4	quattro
without	senza	(fourth	quarto)
more	più	5	cinque
less	meno	(fifth	quinto)
near	vicino	6	sei
far	lontano	7	sette
hot	caldo	8	otto
cold	freddo	9	nove
early	presto	10	dieci
late	inritardo	11	undici
here	qui/qua	12	dodici
there	là/li	13	tredici
now	adesso	14	quattordici
later	più tardi	15	quindici
today	oggi	16	sedici
tomorrow	domani	17	diciassette
yesterday	ieri	18	diciotto
how much is it?	quant'è?	19	diciannove
when?	quando?	20	venti
do you have...?	avete...?	21	ventuno
		30	trenta
Emergencies		40	quaranta
help!	aiuto!	50	cinquanta
where is the nearest		60	sessanta
telephone?	dov'è il	70	settanta
	telefono più	80	ottanta
	vicino?	90	novanta
there has been an		100	cento
accident	c'è stato un	1,000	mille
	incidente	1,000,000	milione
call the police	chiamate la		

INDEX

Citypack
Florence

Important note

Time inevitably brings changes, so always confirm prices, travel facts, and other perishable information when it matters. Although Fodor's cannot accept responsibility for errors, you can use this guide in the confidence that we have taken every care to ensure its accuracy.

Copyright   © 1997, 1999 by The Automobile Association
Maps copyright   © 1997, 1999 by The Automobile Association
Fold-out map: © RV Reise- und Verkehrsverlag Munich · Stuttgart
    © Cartography: GeoData

Published in the United States by Fodor's Travel Publications, Inc.
Published in the United Kingdom by AA Publishing
Fodor's is a registered trademark of Random House, Inc.

ISBN 0–679–00444–0
Second Edition

FODOR'S CITYPACK FLORENCE

AUTHOR *Susannah Perry* SECOND EDITION UPDATED BY *Jane Shaw*
CARTOGRAPHY *The Automobile Association, RV Reise- und Verkehrsverlag*
COVER DESIGN *Fabrizio La Rocca, Tigist Getachew*
ORIGINAL COPY EDITORS *Beth Ingpen, Nia Williams*
INDEXER *Marie Lorimer*

Acknowledgments

The author would like to thank Jenny Hardwick for her support and companionship. The Automobile Association would like to thank the following photographers, libraries and associations for their assistance in the preparation of this book.
Basilica di Santa Croce 46b; The Bridgeman Art Library Ltd 24a *The Tribute Money, c*1427 (fresco) by Masaccio, Tommaso (1401–28), Brancacci Chapel, Santa Maria del Carmine, Florence, 24b *Adam & Eve banished from Paradise* by Masaccio, Tommaso (1401–28) Brancacci Chapel, Santa Maria del Carmine, Florence, 26b *The Madonna of the Chair* by Raphael, Sanzio of Urbino (1482–1520) Palazzo Pitti, Florence, 38 *The Birth of Venus, c*1485 (tempera on canvas) by Botticelli, Sandro (1444/5–1510) Galleria degli Uffizi, Florence, 44a & 44b *The Annunciation* by Angelico, Fra (Guido di Pietro) (*c*1387–1455) Museo di San Marco dell'Angelico, Florence; Mary Evans Picture Library 39b; Istituto e Museo di Storia della Scienza 39a; Museo dell'Opera del Duomo 36b; Spectrum Colour Library 46a; Tony Stone Images 59.
All remaining pictures are held in the Association's own library (AA PHOTO LIBRARY) and were taken by Clive Sawyer with the exception of the following pages: J. Edmunson 30b, 35b, 36a, 37b, 41a, 42a, 43a, 47b, 51a, 53a; K. Paterson 16b, 17b, 21, 34b, 54, 55, 57, 58; T. Souter 60.

Special sales

Color separation by Daylight Colour Art Pte Ltd, Singapore
Manufactured by Dai Nippon Printing Co. (Hong Kong) Ltd
10 9 8 7 6 5 4 3 2 1

Titles in the Citypack series

- Amsterdam • Atlanta • Beijing • Berlin • Boston • Chicago • Dublin • Florence •
- Hong Kong • London • Los Angeles • Miami • Montreal • New York • Paris •
- Prague • Rome • San Francisco • Seattle • Shanghai • Sydney • Tokyo •
- Toronto • Venice • Washington, D.C. •

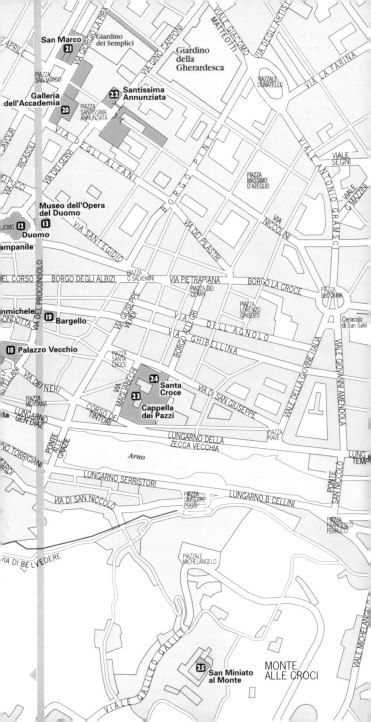

CITYPACK
Florence

The Citypack map covers the city in detail, while the Citypack guide gives you just the information you need to experience the best of Florence:

- Top attractions and their must-see sights
- The best pageants, opera, and classical music
- Great walks and strolls
- The best museums and landmarks, parks and green spaces, views, children's activities, and freebies

- Restaurants, hotels, shopping, nightlife— an unabashedly opinionated selection, with pithy descriptions of each recommendation
- Offbeat sights even locals don't know
- Tips on getting the most from your visit

The author: London resident Susannah Perry spent six years as a tour guide in Florence.